W9-CTN-629

Frommer's®

P O R T A B L E

The Big Island of Hawaii

1st Edition

by Jeanette Foster & Jocelyn Fujii

Macmillan • USA

ABOUT THE AUTHORS

A resident of the Big Island, **Jeanette Foster** has skied the slopes of Mauna Kea—during a Fourth of July ski meet, no less—and scuba dived with manta rays off the Kona Coast. A prolific writer widely published in travel, sports, and adventure magazines, she's also a contributing editor to *Hawaii* magazine.

Kauai-born **Jocelyn Fujii**, a resident of Honolulu, is one of Hawaii's leading journalists. She has authored *Under the Hula Moon: Living in Hawaii* and *The Best of Hawaii*, as well as articles for *The New York Times, National Geographic Traveler, Islands, Condé Nast Traveller, Travel Holiday,* and other national and international publications.

In addition to this guide, Jeanette and Jocelyn also co-author *Frommer's Hawaii, Frommer's Hawaii from $60 a Day,* and *Frommer's Honolulu, Waikiki & Oahu.*

MACMILLAN TRAVEL USA

Macmillan General Reference USA, Inc.
1633 Broadway
New York, NY 10019

Find us online at **www.frommers.com**

Copyright © 2000 by Macmillan General Reference USA, Inc.
Maps copyright © by Macmillan General Reference USA, Inc.

ISBN 0-02-863091-2
ISSN 1524-430X

Editor: Kathy Iwasaki
Production Editor: Robyn Burnett
Photo Editor: Richard Fox
Design by Michele Laseau
Staff Cartographers: John Decamillis and Roberta Stockwell
Page Creation: Natalie Hollifield and John Bitter

SPECIAL SALES

Bulk purchases (10+ copies) of Frommer's and selected Macmillan travel guides are available to corporations, organizations, mail-order catalogs, institutions, and charities at special discounts, and can be customized to suit individual needs. For more information write to Special Sales, Macmillan General Reference, 1633 Broadway, New York, NY 10019.

Manufactured in the United States of America
5 4 3 2 1

Contents

List of Maps

AN INVITATION TO THE READER

In researching this book, we discovered many wonderful places—hotels, restaurants, shops, and more. We're sure you'll find others. Please tell us about them, so we can share the information with your fellow travelers in upcoming editions. If you were disappointed with a recommendation, we'd love to know that, too. Please write to:

Frommer's Portable The Big Island of Hawaii, First Edition
Macmillan Travel
1633 Broadway
New York, NY 10019

AN ADDITIONAL NOTE

Please be advised that travel information is subject to change at any time—and this is especially true of prices. We therefore suggest that you write or call ahead for confirmation when making your travel plans. The authors, editors, and publisher cannot be held responsible for the experiences of readers while traveling. Your safety is important to us, however, so we encourage you to stay alert and be aware of your surroundings. Keep a close eye on cameras, purses, and wallets, all favorite targets of thieves and pickpockets.

WHAT THE SYMBOLS MEAN
✪ Frommer's Favorites

Our favorite places and experiences—outstanding for quality, value, or both.

The following abbreviations are used for credit cards:

AE	American Express	EU	Eurocard
CB	Carte Blanche	JCB	Japan Credit Bank
DC	Diners Club	MC	MasterCard
DISC	Discover	V	Visa
ER	enRoute		

FIND FROMMER'S ONLINE

Arthur Frommer's Budget Travel Online (**www.frommers.com**) offers more than 6,000 pages of up-to-the-minute travel information—including the latest bargains and candid, personal articles updated daily by Arthur Frommer himself. No other Web site offers such comprehensive and timely coverage of the world of travel.

Planning a Trip to the Big Island

by Jeanette Foster

*T*he Big Island of Hawaii—the island that lends its good name to the entire 1,500-mile-long Hawaiian archipelago—is where Mother Nature pulled out all stops. Simply put, it's spectacular.

The Big Island has it all: fiery volcanoes and sparkling waterfalls, black-lava deserts and snowcapped mountain peaks, tropical rain forests and alpine meadows, a glacial lake, and miles of beaches filled with a rainbow of black, green, and golden sands. The Big Island has an unmatched diversity of terrain and climate. A 50-mile drive will take you from snowy winter to sultry summer, passing through spring or fall along the way. The island looks like the inside of a barbecue pit on one side, and a lush jungle on the other.

The Big Island is the largest island in the Pacific (4,038 sq. miles—about the size of Connecticut), the youngest (800,000 years), and the least populated (with 30 people per sq. mile). It has the nation's wettest city, the southernmost point in the United States, the world's biggest telescope, the ocean's biggest trophy marlin, and America's greatest collection of tropical luxury resorts. It also has the highest peaks in the Pacific, the most volcanoes of any Hawaiian island, and the newest land on earth.

Five volcanoes—one still erupting—have created this continental island, which is growing bigger daily. At its heart is snowcapped Mauna Kea (or "White Mountain"), the world's tallest sea mountain, complete with its own glacial lake. Mauna Kea's nearest neighbor is Mauna Loa (or "Long Mountain"), creator of one-sixth of the island; it's the largest volcano on earth, rising 30,000 feet out of the ocean floor (of course, you can only see the 13,796 feet that are above sea level). Erupting Kilauea makes the Big Island bigger every day—and, if you're lucky and your timing is good, you can stand just a few feet away and watch it do its work.

Steeped in tradition and shrouded in the primal mist of creation, the Big Island called to the Polynesians across 2,000 miles of open ocean. In fact, ancient Hawaiian chants talk about a great burning

The Big Island

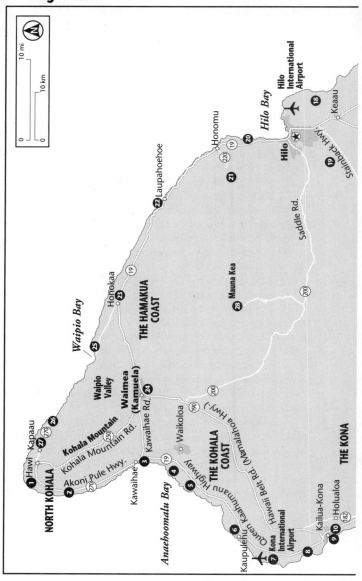

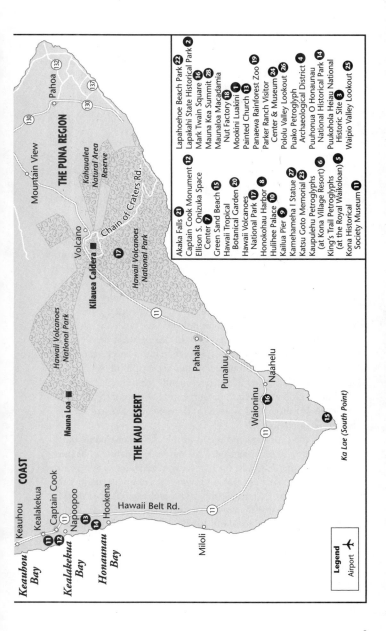

COAST

Keauhou
Kealakekua
Captain Cook
Napoopoo
Hookena
Miloli

Keauhou Bay
Kealakekua Bay
Honaunau Bay

Hawaii Belt Rd.

Keauhou Bay
Kealakekua Bay
Honaunau Bay

THE KAU DESERT

Pahala
Punaluu
Naalehu
Waioninu

Ka Lae (South Point)

Mauna Loa
Hawaii Volcanoes National Park

Kilauea Caldera
Hawaii Volcanoes National Park

Chain of Craters Rd.
Volcano

Mountain View

THE PUNA REGION

Pahoa

Kahaualea Natural Area Reserve

Legend
✈ Airport

Akaka Falls ㉑
Captain Cook Monument ⑫
Ellison S. Onizuka Space Center ⑦
Green Sand Beach ⑮
Hawaii Tropical Botanical Garden ⑳
Hawaii Volcanoes National Park ⑰
Honokohau Harbor ⑧
Hulihee Palace ⑩
Kailua Pier ⑨
Kamehameha I Statue ㉗
Katsu Goto Memorial ㉓
Kaupulehu Petroglyphs (at Kona Village Resort) ⑥
King's Trail Petroglyphs (at the Royal Waikoloan) ⑤
Kona Historical Society Museum ⑪

Lapahoehoe Beach Park ㉒
Lapakahi State Historical Park ②
Mark Twain Square ⑯
Mauna Kea Summit ㉘
Maunaloa Macadamia Nut Factory ⑱
Mookini Luakini ①
Painted Church ⑬
Panaewa Rainforest Zoo ⑲
Parker Ranch Visitor Center & Museum ㉔
Pololu Valley Lookout ㉖
Puako Petroglyph Archaeological District ④
Puuhonua O Honaunau National Historical Park ⑭
Puukohola Heiau National Historic Site ③
Waipio Valley Lookout ㉕

3

in the night skies which guided the sojourners to the land of volcanoes. The Big Island radiates what the Hawaiians call "mana," a sense of spirituality that's still apparent through the acres of petroglyphs etched in the black lava, the numerous *heiaus* (ancient temples), burial caves scattered in the cliffs, sacred shrines both on land and in the sea, and even in the sound the wind makes as it blows across the desolate lava fields.

The Big Island is not for everyone, however. It refuses to fit the stereotype of a tropical island. Some tourists are taken aback at the sight of stark fields of lava or black-sand beaches. You must remember that it's *big* (expect to do lots of driving). And you may have to go out of your way if you're looking for traditional tropical beauty, such as a quintessential white-sand beach.

On the other hand, if you're into watersports, this is paradise. The two tall volcanoes mean 350 days of calm water on the leeward side. The underwater landscape of caves, cliffs, and tunnels attracts a stunning array of colorful marine life just waiting to be visited by divers and snorkelers. The island's West Coast is one of the best destinations in the world for big-game fishing. And its miles of remote coastline are a kayaker's dream of caves, secluded coves, and crescent-shaped beaches reachable only by sea.

On land, hikers, bikers, and horseback riders can head up and down a volcano, across black-sand beaches, into remote valleys, and through rain forests without seeing another soul. Bird watchers are rewarded with sightings of the rare, rapidly dwindling native birds of Hawaii. Golfers can find nirvana on top championship courses, less-crowded municipal courses, and even some unusual off-the-beaten-track choices.

This is the least-explored island in the Hawaiian chain—but if you're looking to get away from it all and back to nature in its most primal state, that might be the best thing of all about it. Where else can you witness fiery creation and swim with dolphins, ponder the stars from the world's tallest mountain and catch a blue marlin, downhill ski, and surf the waves in a single day? You can do all this, and more, on only one island in the world—the Big Island of Hawaii.

In the pages that follow, we've compiled everything you need to know to plan your trip. We think that the process of planning can be part of the excitement of your trip. So, in addition to reading this guide, we suggest that you spend some time either on the Internet (we've included Web site addresses throughout this book) or calling and writing for brochures. We fully believe that searching out the best deals and planning your dream vacation to Hawaii should be half the fun.

1 Visitor Information

For information about traveling in Hawaii, contact the **Hawaii Visitors and Convention Bureau (HVCB),** Suite 801, Waikiki Business Plaza, 2270 Kalakaua Ave., Honolulu, HI 96815 (☎ **800/ GO-HAWAII,** or 808/923-1811; www.gohawaii.com). The bureau publishes the helpful *Accommodations and Car Rental Guide* and supplies free brochures, maps, and the *Islands of Aloha* magazine, the official HVCB magazine. The HVCB also has a mainland office at 180 Montgomery St., Suite 2360, San Francisco, CA 94104 (☎ **800/353-5846**). The **Big Island Visitors Bureau** is at 250 Keawe St., Hilo, HI 96720 (☎ **808/961-5797;** fax 808/961-2126).

PARK INFORMATION

The Big Island has a national park and three national historic sites. For hiking and camping information, contact the following offices: **Hawaii Volcanoes National Park,** P.O. Box 52, Hawaii National Park, HI 96718 (☎ **808/985-6000**; www.nps.gov/havo); **Puuhonua O Honaunau National Historical Park,** P.O. Box 129, Honaunau, HI 96726 (☎ **808/328-2326**; www.nps.gov/puho); **Puukohola Heiau National Historic Site,** P.O. Box 44340, Kawaihae, HI 96743 (☎ **808/882-7218**; www.nps.gov/puhe); and **Kaloko-Honokohau National Historical Park,** 72-4786 Kanalani St., Kailua-Kona, HI 96740 (☎ **808/329-6881**; www.nps.gov/ kaho).

SITE SEEING: HAWAII ON THE NET

Here are some useful sites:

- **Hawaii Visitors & Convention Bureau:** www.gohawaii.com
- **Hawaii State Vacation Planner:** www.hshawaii.com
- **Planet Hawaii:** www.planet-hawaii.com/travel
- The Big Island's **Kona-Kohala Resort Association:** www.kkra.org
- **Big Island Visitors Bureau:** www.bigisland.org
- **Hawaii Yellow Pages:** www.surfhi.com
- **Weather information:** http://lumahai.soest.hawaii.edu/ index.html or www.weather.com/weather/us/states/Hawaii.html or www.cnn.com/WEATHER/cities/us.hawaii.html

2 When to Go

Most visitors don't come to Hawaii when the weather's best in the islands; rather, they come when it's at its worst everywhere else. Thus, the **high season**—when prices are up and resorts are often booked to capacity—is generally from mid-December through March or mid-April. The last 2 weeks of December in particular is the prime time for travel to Hawaii; if you're planning a holiday trip, make your reservations as early as possible, expect to travel with holiday crowds, and expect to pay top dollar for accommodations, car rentals, and airfare.

The **off-season,** when the best bargain rates are available and the islands are less crowded, are spring (from mid-April to mid-June) and fall (from September to mid-December)—a paradox, since these are the best seasons to be in Hawaii, in terms of reliably great weather. If you're looking to save money, or if you just want to avoid the crowds, this is the time to visit. Hotel rates and airfares tend to be significantly lower—and good packages and special deals are often available.

Note: If you plan to come to Hawaii between the last week in April and mid-May, be sure you book your accommodations, inter-island air reservations, and car rentals in advance. In Japan, the last week of April is called **Golden Week,** because three Japanese holidays take place one after the other. Waikiki is especially busy with Japanese tourists during this time, but the neighbor islands also see dramatic increases.

Due to the large number of families traveling in **summer** (June through August), you won't get the fantastic bargains of spring and fall. However, you'll still do much better on packages, airfare, and accommodations than you will in the winter months.

CLIMATE

Since Hawaii lies at the edge of the tropical zone, it technically has only two seasons, both of them warm. There's a dry season that corresponds to **summer,** and a rainy season in **winter** from November to March. It rains every day somewhere in the islands any time of the year, but the rainy season sometimes brings gray weather that can spoil your tanning opportunities. Fortunately, it seldom rains in one spot for more than 3 days straight.

The **year-round temperature** usually varies no more than 15°F. At the beach, the average daytime high in summer is 85°F (29.4°C), while the average daytime high in winter is 78°F (25.6°C);

Packing Tip

One last thing: **It really can get cold in Hawaii.** If you plan to venture into the Big Island's Hawaii Volcanoes National Park, bring a warm jacket; 40°F upcountry temperatures, even in summer when it's 80°F at the beach, are not uncommon. It's always a good idea to bring at least a windbreaker, a sweater, or a light jacket. And be sure to toss some **rain gear** into your suitcase if you'll be in Hawaii from November to March.

nighttime lows are usually about 10° cooler. But how warm it is on any given day really depends on *where* you are on the island.

Hawaii is full of **microclimates,** thanks to its interior valleys, coastal plains, and mountain peaks. On the Big Island, Hilo is the wettest city in the nation, with 180 inches of rainfall a year, while at Puako, only 60 miles away, it rains less than 6 inches a year. If you travel into the mountains, the climate can change from summer to winter in a matter of hours, since it's cooler the higher you go. So if the weather doesn't suit you, just go to the other side of the island—or head into the hills.

HOLIDAYS

When Hawaii observes holidays, especially those over a long weekend, travel between the islands increases, interisland airline seats are fully booked, rental cars are at a premium, and hotels and restaurants are busier.

Federal, state, and county government offices are closed on all federal holidays: January 1 (New Year's Day), the third Monday in January (Martin Luther King, Jr. Day), the third Monday in February (Presidents' Day, Washington's Birthday), the last Monday in May (Memorial Day), July 4 (Independence Day), the first Monday in September (Labor Day), the second Monday in October (Columbus Day), November 11 (Veteran's Day), the fourth Thursday in November (Thanksgiving Day), and December 25 (Christmas).

State and county offices also are closed on local holidays, including Prince Kuhio Day (March 26), honoring the birthday of Hawaii's first delegate to the U.S. Congress; King Kamehameha Day (June 11), a statewide holiday commemorating Kamehameha the Great, who united the islands and ruled from 1795 to 1819; and Admissions Day (the third Friday in August), which honors the admittance of Hawaii as the 50th state on August 21, 1959.

Other special days celebrated in Hawaii by many people but which involve no closing of federal, state, and county offices are the Chinese New Year (February 5 in 2000), Girls' Day (March 3), Buddha's Birthday (April 8), Father Damien's Day (April 15), Boys' Day (May 5), Samoan Flag Day (in August), Aloha Festivals (in September and October), and Pearl Harbor Day (December 7).

THE BIG ISLAND CALENDAR OF EVENTS

Please note that, as with any schedule of upcoming events, the following information is subject to change; always confirm the details before you plan your schedule around an event. For a complete and up-to-date list of events throughout the islands, check out www.calendar.gohawaii.com or www.hawaiian.net/~mahalo/calendar/current.html

January
- **Senior Skins Tournament,** Mauna Lani Resort, Kohala. Longtime golfing greats participate in this four-man tournament for $500,000 in prize money. Call ☎ **808/885-6655.**
- **MasterCard Championship,** Jack Nicklaus Signature Course, Four Seasons Resort Hualalai, Kona. Formerly known as the Tournament of Champions, this is the season-opening competition for golfers who have won a Senior PGA Tour event. Call ☎ **808/325-8000.**

March
- **Kona Brewer's Festival,** King Kamehameha's Kona Beach Hotel Luau Grounds, Kailua-Kona. This annual event features microbreweries from around the world, with beer-tasting, food, and entertainment. Second Saturday in March. Call ☎ **808/936-2009.**
- **Prince Kuhio Celebrations,** on all islands. Various festivals throughout the state celebrate the birth of Jonah Kuhio Kalanianaole, born March 26, 1871, who was elected to Congress in 1902.

April
✪ **Merrie Monarch Hula Festival,** Hilo. Hawaii's biggest hula festival features three nights of modern (*auana*) and ancient (*kahiko*) dance competition in honor of King David Kalakaua, the "Merrie Monarch" who revived the dance. April 23 to 29. Tickets sell out by January 30, so reserve early. Call ☎ **808/935-9168.**

- **Bankoh Ki-ho'alu Kona-Style Hawaiian Slack Key Guitar Festival,** King Kamehameha Kona Beach Hotel, Kona. The best of Hawaii's folk music—slack key guitar—performed by the best musicians in Hawaii. It's five hours long and absolutely free. Call ☎ **808/239-4336** or e-mail: kahokuproductions@yahoo.com

May

- ✪ **Annual Lei Day Celebrations,** various locations on all islands. May Day is Lei Day in Hawaii, celebrated with lei-making contests, pageantry, arts, and crafts. May 1. Call ☎ **808/322-3441,** ext. 218, for Big Island events.
- **Outrigger Canoe Season,** all islands. From May to September, nearly every weekend, canoe paddlers across the state participate in outrigger canoe races. Call ☎ **808/261-6615** for this year's schedule of events.

June

- ✪ **King Kamehameha Celebration,** statewide. It's a state holiday with a massive floral parade, *hoolaulea* (party), and much more. First weekend in June. Call ☎ **808/329-1603** for Big Island events.
- **Waikii Music and Cultural Festival**, Waikii. Two days of Hawaiian music and culture on Father's Day weekend in the rolling hills of Waikii Ranch, on the Saddle Road between Waikoloa and Hilo. Call ☎ **808/965-8444.**

July

- ✪ **Turtle Independence Day,** Mauna Lani Resort and Bungalows, Kohala Coast. Scores of endangered green sea turtles, which have been raised in captivity, race down to the sea each year when they're released from the historic fishponds at Mauna Lani. July 4. Call ☎ **808/885-6677.**
- **Parker Ranch Rodeo,** Waimea. Hot rodeo competition in the heart of cowboy country. Call ☎ **808/885-7311**.
- **Crater Rim Run and Marathon,** Hawaii Volcanoes National Park. Some 1,000 runners from around the globe line up to compete in races over uneven lava terrain, up the walls of volcanic craters, and through lush rain forests for these 5-, 10- and 26.2-mile races. Late July. Call ☎ **808/967-8222.**
- **Cuisines of the Sun,** Mauna Lani Bay Hotel and Bungalows, Kohala Coast. Chefs from the world's sunny places prepare a host of dishes during this 5-day eating and drinking extravaganza. Call

☎ **800/367-2323** or 808/885-6622, or see www.maunalani.com for this year's schedule.

August

- **Annual Hawaiian International Billfish Tournament,** Kailua-Kona. One of the world's most prestigious billfish tournaments, the HIBT attracts teams from around the globe. Based on the new moon. Call ☎ **808/329-6155.**

- **Admissions Day,** all islands. Hawaii became the 50th state on August 21, 1959, so the state takes a holiday (all state-related facilities are closed) on the third Friday in August.

September

○ **Aloha Festivals,** various locations statewide. Parades and other events celebrate Hawaiian culture and friendliness throughout the state. Call ☎ **800/852-7690,** 808/545-1771, or 808/885-8086 for a schedule of events.

○ **Long Distance Outrigger Canoe Races,** Kailua Pier to Honaunau and back. Some 2,500 paddlers from all over Hawaii, the U.S. mainland, Canada, and the Pacific vie in the world's longest canoe event. Labor Day weekend. Call ☎ **808/329-0833.**

○ **Sam Choy Poke Recipe Contest,** Hapuna Beach Prince Hotel and Mauna Kea Beach Resort, Kohala Coast. Top chefs from across Hawaii and the U.S. mainland as well as local amateurs compete in making this Hawaiian delicacy, *poke* (pronounced po-KAY): chopped raw fish mixed with seaweed and spices. Here's your chance to sample poke at its best. Call ☎ **808/885-8086.**

October

○ **Ironman Triathlon World Championship,** Kailua-Kona. Some 1,500-plus world-class athletes run a full marathon, swim 2.4 miles, and bike 112 miles on the Kona–Kohala Coast of the Big Island. Spectators can watch the action along the route for free. The best place to see the 7am start is along the seawall on Alii Drive, facing Kailua Bay; get there before 5:30am to get a seat. The best place to see the bike-and-run portion is along Alii Drive (which will be closed to traffic; park on a side street and walk down). To watch the finishers come in, line up along Alii Drive from Holualoa Street to the finish at Palani Road/Alii Drive; the first finisher can come as early as 2:30pm, and the course closes at midnight. Call ☎ **808/329-0063** for more information.

November

- **Hawaii International Film Festival,** various locations throughout the state. A cinema festival with a cross-cultural spin featuring filmmakers from Asia, the Pacific Islands, and the U.S. mainland. First two weeks in November. Call ☎ **808/528-FILM,** or look up **www.hiff.org**.
- ✪ **Annual Kona Coffee Cultural Festival,** Kailua-Kona. Celebrates the coffee harvest with a bean-picking contest, lei contests, songs and dance, and the Miss Kona Coffee pageant. Call ☎ **808/326-7820** for this year's schedule.
- **Winter Wine Escape,** Hapuna Beach Prince Hotel, Mauna Kea Resort, Kohala Coast. Wine tasting and food samplings during this weekend culinary event. Call ☎ **808/880-1111**.

December

- ✪ **First Night,** Kailua-Kona. Hawaii's largest festival of arts and entertainment takes place on three different islands, including a large celebration on the Big Island. For 12 hours, musicians, dancers, actors, jugglers, magicians, and mimes perform. Afterwards, fireworks bring in the New Year. Alcohol-free. December 31. Call ☎ **808/326-7820**.

3 Getting Married on the Big Island

Whatever your budget, Hawaii is a great place for a wedding. Not only does it exude romance and natural beauty, but after the ceremony, you're already on your honeymoon. And the members of your wedding party will most likely be delighted, since you've given them the perfect excuse for their own island vacation. Many couples who were married long ago come to Hawaii to renew their vows and enjoy a second honeymoon.

More than 20,000 marriages are performed annually on the islands, mostly on Oahu; nearly half are for couples from somewhere else. The booming wedding business has spawned more than 70 companies that can help you organize a long-distance event and stage an unforgettable wedding, Hawaiian style or your style. However, you can also plan your own island wedding, even from afar, and not spend a fortune doing it.

THE PAPERWORK

The state of Hawaii has some very minimal procedures for obtaining a marriage license. The first thing you should do is contact the **Honolulu Marriage License Office,** State Department of Health

Building, 1250 Punchbowl St., Honolulu, HI 96813 (☎ **808/ 586-4545;** www.hawaii.gov), which is open Monday through Friday from 8am to 4pm. They'll mail you their brochure, *Getting Married,* and direct you to the marriage-licensing agent closest to where you'll be staying in Hawaii.

When you get to Hawaii, the prospective bride and groom must go together to the marriage-licensing agent to get a license. A license costs $25 and is good for 30 days. Both parties must be 15 years of age or older (couples 15 to 17 years old must have proof of age, written consent of both parents, and written approval of the judge of the family court) and not be more closely related than first cousins. That's it.

Contrary to some reports from the media, gay couples cannot marry in Hawaii. Although the state courts ruled a few years ago that the state of Hawaii had to show a compelling reason why the state won't issue a marriage license to gay couples, the issue is still being decided in the courts, with lots of discussion in the state legislature. Until the issue is decided, the state will not issue marriage licenses to same-sex couples.

PLANNING THE WEDDING

DOING IT YOURSELF   The marriage-licensing agents, who range from employees of the governor's satellite office in Kona to private individuals, are usually friendly, helpful people who can steer you to a nondenominational minister or marriage performer who's licensed by the state of Hawaii. These marriage performers are great sources of information for budget weddings. They usually know wonderful places to have the ceremony for free or for a nominal fee.

If you don't want to use a wedding planner (see below), but you do want to make arrangements before you arrive in Hawaii, our best advice is to get a copy of the daily newspapers on the island where you want to have the wedding. People willing and qualified to conduct weddings advertise in the classifieds. They're great sources of information, as they know the best places to have the ceremony and can recommend caterers, florists, and everything else you'll need. If you want to have your wedding on the Kona/Waimea side of the Big Island, get **West Hawaii Today,** P.O. Box 789, Kailua-Kona, HI 96745 (☎ **808/329-9311**); for the Hilo/Puna side, try the **Hawaii Tribune Herald,** P.O. Box 767, Hilo, HI 96720 (☎ **808/ 935-6621**).

USING A WEDDING PLANNER   Wedding planners—many of whom are marriage-licensing agents as well—can arrange everything for you, from a small, private, outdoor affair to a full-blown formal ceremony in a tropical setting. They charge anywhere from $225 to a small fortune—it all depends on what you want. On the Big Island, contact **Paradise Weddings Hawaii,** P.O. Box 383433, Waikoloa, HI 96738 (☎ **800/428-5844;** or 808/883-9067; **www.planet-hawaii.com/weddings/**). The Hawaii Visitors and Convention Bureau (see "Visitor Information") can provide contact information for other wedding coordinators.

4   Tips for Travelers with Special Needs

FOR TRAVELERS WITH DISABILITIES

Travelers with disabilities are made to feel very welcome in Hawaii. The **Hawaii Center for Independent Living,** 414 Kauwili St., Suite 102, Honolulu, HI 96817 (☎ **808/522-5400;** fax 808/586-8129; www.hawaii.gov/health/cpd_indx.htm; e-mail: cpdppp@aloha.net), can provide information and send you a copy of the *Aloha Guide to Accessibility* ($15).

Travel services for the disabled include: **Enable Travel Services,** New Frontiers, 7545 S. University Blvd., Littleton, CO 80122, which plans trips for travelers with disabilities; the **Society for the Advancement of Travel for the Handicapped,** 347 Fifth Ave., Suite 610, NY, NY 10016 (☎ **212/447-7284;** e-mail: sathtravel@aol.com), a nonprofit educational organization that serves as a central clearinghouse for the exchange of information on travel facilities for the disabled; and **Travelin' Talk Network,** P.O. Box 3534, Clarksville, TN 37043-6670 (☎ **615-552-6670**), which has a directory of members willing to share their knowledge of certain areas with disabled travelers.

Publications for disabled travelers include **Annual Directory of Travel Agencies for the Disabled,** Twin Peaks Press, P.O. Box 129, Vancouver, WA 98666-0129 (☎ **360/694-2462**); **Travel Resources for Deaf and Heard of Hearing People,** c/o Gallaudet University, 800 Florida Ave., NE, Washington DC 20002-3695 (☎ **202/651-5051** or TTY 202/651-5052, www.gallaudet.edu/~nicd); and **The Wheelchair Traveler,** 123 Ball Hill Road, Milford, NE 03055 (☎ **603/673-4539**), which has information on hotels, restaurants, and sightseeing for wheelchair users.

Resources on the Internet include: **Access-Able Travel Source,** www.access-able.com, which provides information; and **Accessible Vans of America,** www.accessiblevans.com, which has details on renting a van in Hawaii.

Travel Tip

Discounts for seniors are available at almost all of Hawaii's major attractions, and occasionally at hotels and restaurants. The Outrigger hotel chain, for instance, offers travelers age 50 and older a 20% discount off regular published rates—and an additional 5% off for members of AARP. When making reservations or buying tickets, always ask. And always carry identification with proof of your age—it can really pay off.

For travelers with disabilities who wish to do their own driving, hand-controlled cars can be rented from **Avis** (☎ 800/331-1212) and **Hertz** (☎ 800/654-3131). The number of hand-controlled cars in Hawaii is limited, so be sure to book well in advance—at least a week. For wheelchair-accessible vans, contact **Accessible Vans of Hawaii,** 186 Mehani Circle, Kihei, HI 96753 (☎ 800/303-3750 or 808/879-5521; fax 808/879-0640), which has vans on the Big Island. Hawaii recognizes other states' windshield placards indicating that the driver of the car is disabled, so be sure to bring yours with you.

Vision-impaired travelers who use a guide dog can now come to Hawaii without the hassle of quarantine. A recent court decision ruled that visitors with guide dogs only need to present documentation that the dog is a trained guide dog and has had rabies shots. For more information, contact the **Animal Quarantine Facility** (☎ 808/483-7171; www.hawaii.gov).

FOR GAYS & LESBIANS

Hawaii is known for its acceptance of all groups. The number of gay- or lesbian-specific accommodations on the islands is limited, but most accommodations greet gay and lesbian visitors like any other travelers—with aloha. The best guide for gay and lesbian travelers is the **Rainbow Handbook Hawaii.** The book is available for $14.95 by writing P.O. Box 100, Honaunau, HI 96726 (☎ 800/ 260-5528; www.rainbowhandbook.com/).

On the Big Island, pick up a copy of **Outspoken: Queer Publication from East Hawaii,** P.O. Box 1746, Pahoa, HI 96778 (☎ 808/965-4004; www.aesweb.com/out/). For the latest information on the gay-marriage issue in Hawaii, contact the **Hawaii Marriage Project** (☎ 808/532-9000).

Pacific Ocean Holidays (☎ 800/735-6600 or 808/923-2400; gayhawaii.com) offers vacation packages that feature gay-owned and gay-friendly lodgings. The company also publishes the *Pocket Guide to Hawaii: A Guide for Gay Visitors & Kamaaina.* Send $5 for a copy (mail order only), or access the online version on their Web site.

FOR FAMILIES

The larger hotels and resorts have supervised programs for children and can refer you to qualified baby-sitters. By state law, hotels can only accept children ages 5 to 12 in supervised activities programs, but they often accommodate younger children by simply hiring baby-sitters to watch over them. You can also contact **People Attentive to Children (PATCH),** which can refer you to baby-sitters who have taken a training course on child care. On the Big Island, call ☎ **808/322-7101** on the Kona side of the island, ☎ **808/934-0831** in Hilo.

Baby's Away (ares.csd.net/~babyaway) rents cribs, strollers, highchairs, playpens, infant seats, and the like; call ☎ **800/931-9030** or 808/329-7475. The staff will deliver whatever you need to wherever you're staying and pick it up when you're done.

5   Getting There & Getting Around

ARRIVING IN THE ISLANDS

All major American and many international carriers fly to Honolulu International Airport. Some also fly direct to Kailua-Kona.

United Airlines (☎ 800/225-5825; www.ual.com) offers the most frequent service from the U.S. mainland, but **American Airlines** (☎ 800/433-7300; www.americanair.com), **Continental Airlines** (☎ 800/231-0856; www.continental.com), **Delta Airlines** (☎ 800/221-1212; www.delta-air.com), **Hawaiian Airlines** (☎ 800/367-5320; www.hawaiianair.com), **Northwest Airlines** (☎ 800/225-2525; www.nwa.com), and **TWA** (☎ 800/221-2000; www2.twa.com) all have regular flights. In addition to flying to Honolulu, United and Hawaiian both fly nonstop from Los Angeles and San Francisco to the Big Island. Continental offers the only daily nonstops to Honolulu from the New York area (Newark). For information on airlines serving Hawaii from places other than the U.S. mainland, see chapter 2.

The Big Island has two major airports for jet traffic between the islands: **Kona International Airport** and **Hilo International Airport.** The Kona Airport receives direct overseas flights from Japan (Japan Airlines) and Canada (Canada 3000), as well as direct mainland flights from Los Angeles and San Francisco on United and

Hawaiian. Otherwise, you'll have to pick up an interisland flight in Honolulu (see below).

AGRICULTURAL SCREENING AT THE AIRPORTS   At Honolulu International and the neighbor-island airports, baggage and passengers bound for the mainland must be screened by agricultural officials before boarding. The process is usually quick and easy. Officials will confiscate fresh avocados, bananas, mangoes, and many other kinds of local produce in the name of fruit-fly control. Pineapples, coconuts, and papayas inspected and certified for export, boxed flowers, leis without seeds, and processed foods (macadamia nuts, coffee, jams, dried fruit, and the like) will pass. Call federal or state agricultural officials before leaving for the airport if you're not sure about your trophy.

INTERISLAND FLIGHTS

If your initial flight lands in Honolulu, it's easy to move on to the Big Island. Don't expect to jump a ferry; everyone island-hops by plane. In fact, almost every 20 minutes of every day from just before sunrise to well after sunset (usually around 8pm), a plane takes off or lands at Honolulu International Airport on the interisland shuttle service. If you miss a flight, don't worry; they're like buses—another one will be along real soon.

Aloha Airlines (☎ **800/367-5250** or 808/484-1111; www.alohaair.com) is the state's largest provider of interisland air transport service. It offers more than 175 regularly scheduled daily jet flights throughout Hawaii, using an all-jet fleet of Boeing 737 aircraft. Aloha is the only interisland carrier (and perhaps the only airline in the world) to guarantee that if you're not satisfied with your flight, you can get your money back.

Hawaiian Airlines (☎ **800/367-5320** or 808/835-3700; www.hawaiianair.com), Hawaii's first interisland airline (which also files daily to Hawaii from the West Coast, see above), has carried more than 100 million passengers to and around the state. It's one of the world's safest airlines.

MULTI-ISLAND PASSES   At press time, the standard interisland fare on both interisland carriers was $98. However, both airlines offer multiple-flight deals.

Aloha Airlines offers the **Seven-Day Island Pass**, which allows visitors unlimited travel on Aloha and Island Air flights for 7 consecutive days. The price is $321. Aloha also offers a 1-month version for $999. And for $315, you can buy a **Coupon Book,** which contains six blank tickets that you can use—for yourself or any other traveler—any time within 1 year of purchase. If you and a companion are island-hopping two or three times during your stay, this is an excellent deal.

Hawaiian Airlines offers the **Hawaiian Island Pass,** which gives you unlimited interisland flights for $299 per person for 5 consecutive days, $349 for 7 days, $369 for 10 days, and $409 for 2 weeks. Because Hawaiian Airlines also flies to and from the mainland U.S., you may also be able to apply your transpacific flight toward discounts on your interisland travel; be sure to inquire when booking.

CAR RENTALS

Hawaii has some of the lowest car-rental rates in the country. To rent a car in Hawaii, you must be at least 25 years of age and have a valid driver's license and a credit card.

At the airports, you'll find most major rental-car agencies, including **Alamo** (☎ 800/327-9633; www.goalamo.com), **Avis** (☎ 800/321-3712; www.avis.com), **Budget** (☎ 800/935-6878; www.budgetrentacar.com), **Dollar** (☎ 800/800-4000; www. dollarcar.com), **Enterprise** (☎ 800/325-8007; www. pickenterprise.com), **Hertz** (☎ 800/654-3011; www.hertz.com), **National** (☎ 800/227-7368; www.nationalcar.com), and **Thrifty** (☎ 800/367-2277; www.thrifty.com). It's almost always cheaper to rent a car through your hotel (unless there's one already included in your package deal).

MULTI-ISLAND DEALS   If you're going to visit multiple islands, it's usually easiest—and cheapest—to book with one rental-car company and carry your contract through on each island for your entire stay; you just drop off your car on the island you're leaving, and there will be one waiting for you on the next island with the same company. By booking your cars this way, as one interisland rental, you can usually take advantage of weekly rates that you'd be excluded from if you treated each rental separately. Both **Avis** (☎ 800/321-3712; www.avis.com) and **Hertz** (☎ 800/654-3011; www.hertz.com) have interisland rental arrangements.

INSURANCE   Hawaii is a no-fault state, which means that if you don't have collision-damage insurance, you are required to pay for all damages before you leave the state, whether or not the accident was your fault. Your personal car insurance may provide rental-car coverage; read your policy or call your insurer before you leave home. Bring your insurance identification card if you decline the optional insurance, which usually costs from $12 to $20 a day. Obtain the name of your company's local claim representative before you go. Some credit-card companies also provide

A Tip on Road Maps

The best and most detailed road maps are published by *This Week Magazine,* a free visitor publication that you'll find in most hotels and lots of other places around the island.

collision-damage insurance for their customers; check with yours before you rent.

DRIVING LAWS   Hawaiian state law mandates that all passengers in a car must wear a **seat belt,** and all infants must be strapped into car seats. The fine is enforced with vigilance, so buckle up—you'll pay a $50 fine if you don't. **Pedestrians** always have the right of way, even if they're not in the crosswalk. You can turn **right on red** from the right lane after a full and complete stop, unless there's a sign forbidding you to do so.

TRAVEL DEALS FOR NET SURFERS

It's possible to get some great deals on airfare, hotels, and car rentals via the Internet. The Web sites we've highlighted below are worth checking out, especially since all services are free.

E-SAVERS PROGRAMS   Several major airlines, most of which service the Hawaiian islands, offer a free e-mail service known as **E-Savers,** through which they'll send you their best bargain airfares on a weekly basis. Here's how it works: Once a week (usually Wednesday), subscribers receive a list of discounted flights to and from various destinations, both international and domestic. Now here's the catch: These fares are available only if you leave the next Saturday (or sometimes Friday night) and return the following Monday or Tuesday. It's really a service for the spontaneously inclined and travelers looking for a quick getaway (for Hawaii, that usually means travelers from the West Coast). But the fares are cheap, so it's worth taking a look. Another caveat: You get frequent-flier miles if you purchase one of these fares, but you can't use miles to buy the ticket.

The following airlines have Web sites, where you not only can get on the e-mail lists but also can book flights directly: **American Airlines** (www.americanair.com), **Continental Airlines** (www.flycontinental.com), **Northwest Airlines** (www.nwa.com), **TWA** (www.twa.com), **US Airways:** (www.usairways.com). **Epicurious Travel (travel.epicurious.com),** is a good travel site that allows you to sign up for all these airline e-mail lists at once.

LOW AIRFARE WEB SITES   Several sites can search for low air-fares using systems similar to those of travel agents. **Internet Air Fare** (www.air-fare.com) tracks all the major carriers to Hawaii and lists not only the lowest airfare, but also the lowest fares for seven other categories, including last-minute airfare and even the lowest first class fare. **Airlines of the Web** (www.itn.net/airlines) has a unique feature—ITN's Low Fare Ticker, which allows you to monitor fares around the clock—particularly useful during fare wars. Its Fare Mail service will notify you via e-mail when a flight you're interested in dips below your personal price threshold. **AirSaver.com** (www.airsaver.com) specializes in consolidated tickets, which sometimes can save you big bucks off the cheapest airfares. If the fares aren't low enough, you can choose to go on the e-mail list if airfares drop.

COMPLETE TRAVEL WEB SITES   For a multiservice travel site, check out **Arthur Frommer's Budget Travel** (www.frommers.com), home of the Encyclopedia of Travel and *Arthur Frommer's Budget Travel* magazine and daily newsletter. This site not only has lots of info on Hawaii but also has the latest (updated daily) deals on airfare, hotels, car reservations and package deals. Microsoft's **Expedia** (www.expedia.com) features a Fare Tracker that allows you to search for the cheapest flight to a certain destination, and even to subscribe to an e-mail service that gives you updated information on the cheapest flight every week. The site's Travel Agent will also steer you to bargains on hotels and car rentals. You can book everything, including flights, right online. **Travelocity** (www.travelocity.com) offers a similar service.

Other great sites include **The Hottest Airfares on Earth** (www.etn.nl/hotfares.htm), a clearinghouse of information from low-cost ticket suppliers, tour operators, and travel agents, with low airline fares, packages and hotel deals. **Travel Shop** (www.aonestoptravel.com) not only has discounts on airfare, accommodations, rental cars, etc., but also has access to consolidated rates on every aspect of travel to Hawaii. It even promises to meet or beat any quote you get from a travel agent or airline.

Also, check out **Pleasant Hawaiian Holidays** (www.pleasantholidays.com), the site of one of Hawaii's largest travel companies, which offers low-cost package deals. Don't miss the Surround Video tours, 360° views of hotels and destinations.

Travelzoo (www.travelzoo.com) also often has package deals to Hawaii (at press time it was offering 7 nights on Maui with condo, car, and airfare from Los Angeles for $595).

AN UNUSUAL SITE At **Priceline** (www.priceline.com), you name your price for a flight or a room, and the site searches for an airline or hotel to accommodate you. Within an hour, you'll find out whether you have a taker at the price you stated. The service is free.

6 Tips on Accommodations

Hawaii offers all kinds of accommodations, from simple rooms in restored plantation homes and quaint cottages on the beach to luxurious ocean-view condo units and opulent suites in beachfront resorts. Each type has its pluses and minuses—so before you book, make sure you know what you are getting into.

TYPES OF ACCOMMODATIONS

RESORTS In Hawaii, a resort offers everything a hotel does—and more. You can expect such amenities as direct beach access, with beach cabanas and chairs; pools (often more than one) and a Jacuzzi; a spa and fitness center; restaurants, bars, and lounges; a 24-hour front desk; concierge, valet, and bell services; room service (often around the clock); an activities desk; tennis and golf (some of the world's best courses are at Hawaii resorts); ocean activities; a business center; kids' programs; and more.

The advantages of a resort are that you have everything you could possibly want in the way of services and things to do; the disadvantage is that the price generally reflects this. Don't be misled by a name—just because a place is called "ABC Resort" doesn't mean it actually *is* a resort. Make sure you're getting what you pay for.

HOTELS In Hawaii, "hotel" can indicate a wide range of options, from few or no on-site amenities to enough extras to call it a miniresort. Generally, a hotel offers daily maid service and has a restaurant, on-site laundry facilities, a swimming pool, and a sundries/convenience-type shop (rather than the shopping arcades that most resorts have these days). Top hotels also have activities desks, concierge and valet service, room service (though it may be limited), business centers, an airport shuttle, a bar or lounge, and maybe a few more shops. The advantage of staying in a hotel is privacy and convenience; the disadvantage generally is noise: either thin walls between rooms or loud music from a lobby lounge late into the night. Hotels are often a short walk from the beach rather than on the beachfront (although there are exceptions). Since they come with fewer amenities than full-fledged resorts, hotels tend to be cheaper.

CONDOS   The roominess and convenience of a condo—which is usually a fully equipped, multiple-bedroom apartment—makes this a great choice for families. Condominium properties in Hawaii are generally several apartments set in either a single high-rise or a cluster of low-rise units. Condos generally have amenities such as some maid service (ranging from daily to weekly; it may or may not be included in your rate, so be sure to ask), a swimming pool, laundry facilities (either in your unit or in a central location), and an on-site front desk or a live-in property manager. The advantages of a condo are privacy, space, and conveniences—which usually include full kitchen facilities, a washer and dryer, a private phone, and more. The downsides are the standard lack of an on-site restaurant and the density of the units (versus the privacy of a single-unit vacation rental).

Condos vary in price according to size, location, and amenities. Many of them are on or near the beach, and they tend to be clustered in resort areas. While there are some very high-end condos, most tend to be quite affordable, especially if you're traveling in a group that's large enough to require more than one bedroom.

BED-AND-BREAKFASTS   Hawaii has a wide range of places that call themselves B&Bs: Everything from a traditional B&B—several bedrooms (which may or may not share a bathroom) in a home, with breakfast served in the morning—to what is essentially a vacation rental on an owner's property that comes with fixings for you to make your own breakfast. Make sure that the B&B you're booking matches your own mental picture. Would you prefer conversation around a big dining-room table as you eat a hearty breakfast, or just a muffin and juice to enjoy in your own private place? Laundry facilities and a private phone are not always available at B&Bs. We've reviewed lots of wonderful B&Bs in the island chapters that follow. If you have to share a bathroom, we've spelled it out in the listings; otherwise, you can assume that you will have your own.

The advantages of a traditional B&B are its individual style and congenial atmosphere. B&Bs are great places to meet other visitors to Hawaii, and the host is generally very happy to act as your own private concierge, giving you tips on where to go and what to do. In addition, they're usually an affordable way to go (though fancier ones can run $150 or more a night). The disadvantages are lack of privacy, usually a set time for breakfast, few amenities, generally no maid service, and the fact that you'll have to share the quarters beyond your bedroom with others. Also, B&B owners usually require a minimum stay of 2 or 3 nights, and it's often a drive to the beach.

VACATION RENTALS   This is another great choice for families and for long-term stays. "Vacation rental" usually means that there will be no one on the property where you're staying. The actual accommodation can range from an apartment in a condominium building to a two-room cottage on the beach to an entire fully equipped house. Generally, vacation rentals allow you to settle in and make yourself at home for a while. They have kitchen facilities (which can be either a complete kitchen or a just a kitchenette with microwave, refrigerator, burners, and coffeemaker), on-site laundry facilities, and phone; some also come outfitted with such extras as TV, VCR, and stereo. The advantages of a vacation rental are complete privacy, your own kitchen (which can save you money on meals), and lots of conveniences. The disadvantages are a lack of an on-site property manager and generally no maid service; and often, a minimum stay is required (sometimes as much as a week). If you book a vacation rental, be sure that you have a 24-hour contact so that when the toilet won't flush or you can't figure out how to turn on the air conditioning, you have someone to call.

BARGAINING ON PRICES

Accommodation rates can often be bargained down, but it depends on the place. In general, each type of accommodation allows a different amount of latitude in bargaining on their published rates (called rack rates).

The best bargaining can be had at **hotels** and **resorts.** Both regularly pay travel agents a commission of as much as 30%; if business is slow, some places may give you the benefit of at least part of this commission if you book directly instead of going through an agent. Most hotels and resorts also have *kamaaina* (local) rates for islanders, which they may extend to visitors during slow periods. There's also a host of special rates available for the military, seniors, members of the travel industry, families, corporate travelers, and long-term stays. It's always a good idea to ask for a discounted or local rate. Also ask about **package deals,** where for the same price as a room, you can get a car rental or free breakfast. Hotels and resorts have packages for everyone: golfers, tennis players, families, honeymooners, and more (for more on these, see "Money-Saving Package Deals," below). We've found that it's worth the extra few cents to make a local call to the hotel; sometimes the local reservations person knows about package deals that the 800 operators are unaware of. If all else fails, try to get the hotel or resort to upgrade you to a better room for the same price as a budget room, or waive the extra fees for children or the parking fee. Persistence and asking politely can pay off.

Bed-and-breakfasts are the hardest to bargain with on price. Sometimes you can successfully negotiate down the minimum stay, or you may be able to get a discount if you're staying a week or longer. But generally, a B&B owner has only a few rooms and has already priced the property at a competitive rate; expect to pay what's asked. **Vacation rentals** and **condos** offer somewhat more leeway. In addition to asking for a discount on a multinight stay, ask whether they can throw in a rental car to sweeten the deal; believe it or not, they often will.

USING A BOOKING AGENCY VS. DOING IT YOURSELF

If you don't have the time to call several places yourself to bargain for prices, then you might consider a booking agency. The time an agency spends on your behalf may well be worth any fees you'll have to pay. The top reservations service in the state is ✪ **Hawaii's Best Bed & Breakfasts,** P.O. Box 563, Kamuela, HI 96743 (☎ **800/ 262-9912** or 808/885-4550; fax 808/885-0559; www. bestbnb.com). It will charge you $15 to book the first two locations, and $5 for each additional location. Barbara and Susan Campbell personally select traditional homestays, cottages, and inns, based on each one's hospitality, distinctive charm, and attention to detail. They also book vacation rentals, hotels and resorts. Other great statewide booking agents are **Bed & Breakfast Hawaii,** P.O. Box 449, Kapaa, HI 96746 (☎ **800/733-1632** or 808/822-7771; fax 808/ 822-2723; www.bandb-hawaii.com), offering a range of accommodations from vacation homes to B&Bs, starting at $65 a night; and **Ann and Bob Babson,** 3371 Keha Dr., Kihei, HI 96753 (☎ **800/ 824-6409** or 808/874-1166; fax 808/879-7906; www.maui.net/ ~babson), who can steer you in the right direction for both accommodations and car rentals. For vacation rentals, contact **Hawaii Beachfront Vacation Homes** (☎ **808/247-3637** or 808/ 235-2644; www.hotspots.hawaii.com/beachrent1.html). **Hawaii Condo Exchange** (☎ **800/442-0404**; wwte.com/condos) acts as a consolidator for condo and vacation-rental properties.

7 Money-Saving Package Deals

More often than not, the most cost-effective way to travel to Hawaii is to book an all-inclusive travel package that includes some combination of airfare, accommodation, rental car, meals, airport and baggage transfers, and sight-seeing. The best place to start looking for a package deal is in the travel section of your local Sunday newspaper. Also check the ads in the back of such national travel magazines as *Travel & Leisure, National Geographic Traveler,* and *Condé Nast Traveler.* For instance, **Liberty Travel** (☎ **888/271-1584** to be connected with the agent closest to you; www.libertytravel.com), one of the biggest packagers in the Northeast, usually boasts a full-page ad in Sunday papers. You won't get much in the way of service, but you will get a good deal. At press time, Liberty was offering a 7-day/ 6-night package to Hawaii with accommodations at the Sheraton Moana Surfrider on Waikiki Beach for $1,029 per person, double occupancy, including round-trip airfare from New York City, all airport transfers, a double room (hotel tax included), a flower-lei greeting, and some sight-seeing—not a bad deal, considering that the Moana's cheapest room officially goes for $265 a night, and round-trip airfare is at least $650 or $700 each, and often much more. Of course, package prices are always in flux, but this should give you an idea of how well you can do. **American Express Travel** (☎ **800/ AXP-6898;** www. americanexpress.com/travel) can also book you a well-priced Hawaiian vacation.

Some packagers book Hawaiian vacations exclusively. **Pleasant Hawaiian Holidays** (☎ **800/2-HAWAII** or 800/242-9244; www.pleasantholidays.com or www.2hawaii.com) is, by far, the biggest and most comprehensive packager to Hawaii; it offers an extensive, high-quality collection of 50 condos and hotels in every price range. **Sunscapes** (☎ **800/229-8376** or 425/643-1620; www.sunscapes.com) sells only Hawaii vacations, concentrating on budget and moderately priced hotels and condos.

Other reliable packagers include the airlines themselves, which often package their flights together with accommodations. **United Vacations** (☎ **800/328-6877;** www.unitedvacations.com) is the most comprehensive airline packager to Hawaii, offering great air-inclusive and land-only deals on a surprisingly wide selection of accommodations throughout the islands. Other airlines offering good-value packages to the islands are **American Airlines Vacations** (☎ **800/321-2121;** www.2travel.com/americanair/hawaii.html), **Continental Airlines Vacations** (☎ **800/634-5555** or 800/301-3800; www.coolvacations.com), **Delta Dream Vacations** (☎ **800/ 872-7786;** www.deltavacations.com), and **TWA Getaway Vacations** (☎ **800/GETAWAY** or 800/438-2929; www.twa.com). If you're traveling to the islands from Canada, ask your travel agent

Package-Buying Tip

For one-stop shopping on the Web, go to **www.vacationpackager. com,** a Web-search engine that can link you up with many different package-tour operations; be sure to look under both "Hawaii" and "Hawaiian Islands." Or point your browser to **www.2travel.com/ 2where/hawaii/index.html** which takes you directly to a page with links to all the big-name packagers offering package tours to Hawaii.

about package deals through **Air Canada Vacations** (☎ **800/ 776-3000;** www.aircanada.ca).

GREAT PACKAGE DEALS AT HAWAII'S TOP HOTEL CHAINS

With some 28 properties in Hawaii, **Outrigger** (☎ **800/ OUTRIGGER;** fax 800/622-4852, www.outrigger.com) offers excellent affordable accommodations, all with consistently dependable, clean, and well-appointed rooms. The chain's price structure is based entirely on location, room size, and amenities. You'll be comfortable at any of the chain's outposts: The small rooms at the budget Outriggers are just as tastefully decorated as the larger, more expensive Outrigger rooms right on the beach. Outrigger's empire also includes good-value condominiums and resorts on the neighbor islands. Package deals include discounted rates for spring and fall stays, a car package, discounts for multinight stays, family plans, cut rates for seniors, and even packages for scuba divers (2 days of two-tank boat dives and a 3-night stay starts at $311 per person, double occupancy).

The **Aston** chain (☎ **800/92-ASTON;** fax 808/922-8785; www.aston-hotels.com), which celebrated 50 years in Hawaii in 1998, has some 20 hotels, condominiums, and resort properties scattered throughout the islands. They range dramatically in price and style, from the luxurious Aston Kauai Beach Villas to beachside condominiums at Kona-by-the-Sea on the Big Island. Aston offers package deals galore, including family packages; discounted senior rates; car, golf, and shopping packages; and multinight stay deals, including a wonderful Island Hopper deal, where you can travel from island to island and get 25% off on 7 nights or more at Aston properties.

Marc Resorts Hawaii (☎ **800/535-0085;** fax 800/633-5085; www.marcresorts.com) has 25 properties on every island but Lanai. It offers packages for seniors, multinight stays, honeymooners, and golfers, as well as corporate discounts and car-rental deals.

2

For Foreign Visitors

by Jeanette Foster

T he pervasiveness of American culture around the world may make you feel that you know the USA pretty well, but leaving your own country for the States—especially the unique island state of Hawaii—still requires some additional planning.

1 Preparing for Your Trip

ENTRY REQUIREMENTS

Immigration laws are a hot political issue these days; the following requirements may have changed somewhat by the time you plan your trip. Check at any U.S. embassy or consulate for current information and requirements. You can also plug into the U.S. State Department's Internet site at http://state.gov.

DOCUMENT REGULATIONS   Canadian citizens may enter the United States without visas; they need only proof of residence.

The U.S. State Department has a **Visa Waiver Pilot Program** allowing citizens of certain countries to enter the United States without a visa for stays of up to 90 days. At press time, these countries included Andorra, Argentina, Australia, Austria, Belgium, Brunei, Denmark, Finland, France, Germany, Iceland, Ireland, Italy, Japan, Liechtenstein, Luxembourg, Monaco, the Netherlands, New Zealand, Norway, San Marino, Slovenia, Spain, Sweden, Switzerland, and the United Kingdom. Citizens of these countries need only a valid passport and a round-trip air or cruise ticket in their possession upon arrival. If they first enter the United States, they may then visit Mexico, Canada, Bermuda, and the Caribbean islands and return to the United States without needing a visa. Further information is available from any U.S. embassy or consulate.

Citizens of all other countries must have (1) a valid **passport** with an expiration date at least 6 months later than the scheduled end of their visit to the United States, and (2) a **tourist visa,** which may be obtained without charge from the nearest U.S. consulate.

To obtain a visa, you must submit a completed application form (either in person or by mail) with a $1^1/_2$-inch-square photo, and you must demonstrate binding ties to a residence abroad. Usually, you can obtain a visa at once or within 24 hours, but it may take longer during the summer rush from June to August. If you cannot go in person, contact the nearest U.S. embassy or consulate for directions on applying by mail. Your travel agent or airline office may also be able to provide you with visa applications and instructions. The U.S. consulate or embassy that issues your visa will determine whether you will be issued a multiple- or-single-entry visa and any restrictions regarding the length of your stay.

U.K. citizens can obtain up-to-date passport and visa information by calling the **U.S. Embassy Visa Information Line** at ☎ **0891/200-290** or the **London Passport Office** at ☎ **0990/210-410** (for recorded information).

Foreign driver's licenses are recognized in Hawaii, although you may want to get an international driver's license if your home license is not written in English.

MEDICAL REQUIREMENTS   Inoculations are not needed to enter the United States unless you are coming from or have stopped over in areas known to be suffering from epidemics, particularly cholera or yellow fever. If you have a disease requiring treatment with medications that contain narcotics or require a syringe, carry a valid signed prescription from your physician to allay suspicions that you are smuggling drugs.

CUSTOMS REQUIREMENTS   Every adult visitor may bring in the following, free of duty: 1 liter of wine or hard liquor, 200 cigarettes or 100 cigars (but no cigars from Cuba) or 3 pounds of smoking tobacco, and $100 worth of gifts. These exemptions are offered to travelers who spend at least 72 hours in the United States and who have not claimed exemptions within the preceding 6 months. It is forbidden to bring into the country foodstuffs (particularly cheese, fruit, cooked meats, and canned goods) and plants (vegetables, seeds, tropical plants, and so on). Foreign tourists may bring in or take out up to $10,000 in U.S. or foreign currency with no formalities; larger sums must be declared to customs on entering or leaving, which involves filing form CM 4790. For more information, call the U.S. Customs office at ☎ **202/927-1770,** or check out www.customs.ustreas.gov.

In addition, you cannot bring fresh fruits and vegetables into Hawaii, even if you're coming from the U.S. mainland and have no need to clear customs. Every passenger is asked shortly before landing to sign a certificate declaring that he or she does not have fresh fruits and vegetables in his or her possession.

INSURANCE The U.S. has no nationwide health system, and the cost of medical care in Hawaii is extremely high. We strongly advise you to secure health-insurance coverage before setting out. You may even want to take out a comprehensive travel policy that covers (for a relatively low premium) sickness or injury costs (medical, surgical, and hospital); loss or theft of your baggage; trip-cancellation costs; guarantee of bail in case you're arrested; and costs of accident, repatriation, or death. Such packages (for example, "Europ Assistance" in Europe) are sold by automobile clubs at attractive rates, as well as by insurance companies and travel agencies. U.K. travelers might call the **Association of British Insurers** (☎ **0171/600-3333**), which gives advice by phone and publishes the free *Holiday Insurance,* a guide to policy provisions and prices.

MONEY

CURRENCY The American monetary system has a decimal base: 1 U.S. **dollar** ($1) = 100 **cents** (100¢). Dollar bills commonly come in $1 ("a buck"), $5, $10, $20, $50, and $100 denominations (the last two are not welcome when as payment for small purchases and often are not accepted in taxis or movie theaters). There are six denominations of coins: 1¢ (one cent, or a "penny"), 5¢ (five cents, or a "nickel"), 10¢ (10 cents, or a "dime"), 25¢ (25 cents, or a "quarter"), 50¢ (50 cents, or a "half-dollar"), and the rare $1 piece.

EXCHANGING CURRENCY Exchanging foreign currency for U.S. dollars is usually painless in Oahu. Generally, the best rates of exchange are available through major banks, most of which exchange foreign currency. There also are currency services at **Honolulu International Airport.** Most of the major hotels also offer currency-exchange services, but generally the rate of exchange is not as good as what you'll get at a bank.

On the other islands, it's not so easy. None of the other airports have currency-exchange facilities. You have to either go to a bank (call first to see whether currency exchange is available) or use your hotel.

TRAVELER'S CHECKS It's actually cheaper and faster to get cash at an **automatic teller machine** (ATM) than to fuss with traveler's checks. Traveler's checks are, however, readily accepted at most hotels, restaurants, and large stores. But do not bring traveler's checks denominated in any currency other than U.S. dollars.

CREDIT CARDS Credit cards are widely used in Hawaii. You can save yourself trouble by using "plastic money" rather than cash or traveler's checks in most hotels, restaurants, and retail stores (a growing number of food and liquor stores now accept credit cards, too). You must have a credit card to rent a car in Hawaii.

SAFETY

GENERAL   While tourist areas are generally safe, visitors should always stay alert, even in laid-back Hawaii. It's wise to ask the island tourist office if you're in doubt about which neighborhoods are safe. Avoid deserted areas, especially at night. Generally speaking, you can feel safe in areas where there are many people and open establishments.

Avoid carrying valuables with you on the street, and don't display expensive cameras or electronic equipment. Hold onto your pocketbook, and place your billfold in an inside pocket. In theaters, restaurants, and other public places, keep your possessions in sight.

Remember also that hotels are open to the public and that, in a large hotel, security may not be able to screen everyone who enters. Always lock your room door—don't assume that once inside your hotel, you're automatically safe.

DRIVING   Safety while driving is particularly important. Ask your rental agency about personal safety, or ask for a brochure of traveler safety tips when you pick up your car. From the agency get written directions or a map with the route marked in red showing you how to get to your destination.

Recently, more crime has involved burglary of tourist rental cars in hotel-parking structures and at beach parking lots. Park in well-lighted and well-traveled areas whenever possible. Never leave any packages or valuables in sight in the car. If someone attempts to rob you or steal your car, do not try to resist the thief or carjacker—report the incident to the police department immediately.

2 Getting to & Around the United States

Airlines serving Hawaii from places other than the U.S. mainland include **Air Canada** (☎ 800/776-3000; www.aircanada.ca); **Canadian Airlines** (☎ 800/426-7000; www.cdnair.ca); **Canada 3000** (☎ 888/CAN-3000; www.canada3000.com); **Air New Zealand** (☎ 0800/737-000 in Auckland, 643/379-5200 in Christchurch, 800/926-7255 in the U.S.), which runs 40 flights per week between Auckland and Hawaii; **Qantas** (☎ 008/177-767 in Australia, 800/ 227-4500 in the U.S.), which flies between Sydney and Honolulu

Money-Saving Tip

The **ETN (European Travel Network)** operates a Web site offering discounts on international airfares to the United States, as well as on accommodations, car rentals, and tours; point your Internet browser to **www.discount-tickets.com**.

daily (plus additional flights 4 days a week); **Japan Air Lines** (☎ 03/5489-1111 in Tokyo, 800/525-3663 in the U.S.); **All Nippon Airways (ANA;** ☎ 03/5489-1212 in Tokyo, 800/235-9262 in the U.S.); **China Airlines** (☎ 02/715-1212 in Taipei, 800/227-5118 in the U.S.); **Garuda Indonesian** (☎ 251-2235 in Jakarta, 800/342-7832 in the U.S.); **Korean Airlines** (☎ 02/656-2000 in Seoul, 800/223-1155 on the East Coast, 800/421-8200 on the West Coast, 800/438-5000 from Hawaii); and **Philippine Airlines** (☎ 631/816-6691 in Manila, 800/435-9725 in the U.S.).

Travelers coming from Europe can take advantage of the **APEX (Advance Purchase Excursion)** fares offered by all major U.S. and European carriers. Aside from these, attractive values are offered by **Icelandair** (☎ 354/5050-100 in Reykjavik, 0171/388-5599 in London, 800/223-5500 in the U.S.; www.icelandair.is) on flights from Luxembourg to New York and by **Virgin Atlantic Airways** (☎ 0293/747-747 in Britain, 800/862-8621 in the U.S.; www.fly.virgin.com) from London to New York/Newark. You can then catch a connecting domestic flight to Honolulu.

Some large American airlines—such as **TWA, American Airlines, Northwest, United,** and **Delta**—offer travelers on transatlantic or transpacific flights special discount tickets under the name **Visit USA,** allowing travel between any U.S. destinations at reduced rates. These tickets must be purchased before you leave your foreign point of departure. This system is the best, easiest, and fastest way to see the United States at a low cost. You should obtain information well in advance from your travel agent or the office of the airline concerned, since the conditions attached to these discount tickets can change without advance notice.

The visitor arriving by air should cultivate patience and resignation before setting foot on U.S. soil. Getting through immigration control may take as long as 2 hours on some days, especially summer weekends. Add the time it takes to clear customs, and you'll see that you should make a very generous allowance for delay in

planning connections between international and domestic flights—
an average of 2 to 3 hours at least.

For further information about travel to Hawaii, see "Getting
There & Getting Around" in chapter 1.

FAST FACTS: For the Foreign Traveler

Automobile Organizations   Auto clubs will supply maps, suggested routes, guidebooks, accident and bail-bond insurance, and
emergency road service. The major auto club in the United States,
with 955 offices nationwide, is the **American Automobile Association** (AAA; often called "triple A"). Members of some foreign
auto clubs have reciprocal arrangements with the AAA and enjoy
its services at no charge. If you belong to an auto club, inquire about
AAA reciprocity before you leave. The AAA can provide you with
an **International Driving Permit** validating your foreign license.
You may be able to join the AAA even if you are not a member of
a reciprocal club. To inquire, call ☎ **800/736-2886.**

Some car-rental agencies now provide automobile club–type services, so you should inquire about their availability when you rent
your car.

Climate   See "When to Go" in chapter 1.

Electricity   Hawaii, like the U.S. mainland and Canada, uses
110–120 volts, 60 cycles, compared to the 220–240 volts, 50 cycles
used in most of Europe and in other areas of the world, including
Australia and New Zealand. Small appliances of non-American
manufacture, such as hair dryers or shavers, will require a plug
adapter with two flat, parallel pins; larger ones will require a 100-
volt transformer.

Embassies & Consulates   All embassies are located in Washington, D.C. Some consulates are located in major cities, and most
nations have a mission to the United Nations in New York City.
Listed here are the embassies and some consulates of the major
English-speaking countries. Travelers from other countries can
obtain telephone numbers for their embassies and consulates by
calling directory information for Washington, D.C. (☎ **202/
555-1212**).

The embassy of **Australia** is at 1601 Massachusetts Ave. NW,
Washington, DC 20036 (☎ **202/797-3000;** www.austemb.org).
There is also an Australian consulate in Hawaii at 1000 Bishop
St., Penthouse Suite, Honolulu, HI 96813 (☎ 808/524-5050).

The embassy of **Canada** is at 501 Pennsylvania Ave. NW, Washington, DC 20001 (☎ **202/682-1740;** www. cdnemb-washdc.org). Canadian consulates are also at 1251 Avenue of the Americas, New York, NY 10020 (☎ **212/768-2400**), and at 550 South Hope St., 9th floor, Los Angeles, CA 90071 (☎ **213/346-2700**).

The embassy of **Japan** is at 2520 Massachusetts Ave. NW, Washington, DC 20008 (☎ **202/939-6700;** www. embjapan.org). The consulate general of Japan is located at 1742 Nuuanu Ave., Honolulu, HI 96817 (☎ **808/536-2226**). There are several other consulates, including one in New York at 299 Park Ave., New York, NY 10171 (☎ **212/371-8222**).

The embassy of **New Zealand** is at 37 Observatory Circle NW, Washington, DC 20008 (☎ **202/328-4800;** www.emb.com/ nzemb). The only New Zealand consulate in the United States is at 12400 Wilshire Blvd., Los Angeles, CA 90025 (☎ **310/ 207-1605**).

The embassy of the **Republic of Ireland** is at 2234 Massachusetts Ave. NW, Washington, DC 20008 (☎ **202/462-3939**). There's a consulate office in San Francisco at 44 Montgomery St., Suite 3830, San Francisco, CA 94104 (☎ **415/392-4214**).

The embassy of the **United Kingdom** is at 3100 Massachusetts Ave. NW, Washington, DC 20008 (☎ **202/462-1340**). British consulates are at 845 Third Ave., New York, NY 10022 (☎ **212/ 745-0200**), and 11766 Wilshire Blvd., Suite 400, Los Angeles, CA 90025 (☎ **310/477-3322**).

Emergencies   Call ☎ **911** to report a fire, call the police, or get an ambulance.

Gasoline (Petrol)   One U.S. gallon equals 3.8 liters, while 1.2 U.S. gallons equals 1 Imperial gallon. You'll notice that several grades (and price levels) of gasoline are available at most gas stations. And you'll notice also that their names change from company to company. The ones with the highest octane are the most expensive, but most rental cars take the least expensive "regular" gas, with an octane rating of 87.

Holidays   See "When to Go" in chapter 1.

Languages   English is the language of Hawaii. Major Hawaii hotels may have multilingual employees, and some major resorts have multilingual staffs who speak English, Japanese, Korean, and several dialects of the Philippines.

Legal Aid   The ordinary tourist will probably never become involved with the American legal system. If you're pulled over for a minor infraction (for example, driving faster than the speed limit), never attempt to pay the fine directly to a police officer; you may wind up arrested on the much more serious charge of attempted bribery. Pay fines by mail or directly into the hands of the clerk of the court. If accused of a more serious offense, it's wise to say and do nothing before consulting a lawyer (under the U.S. Constitution, you have a right to both remain silent and to consult an attorney). Under U.S. law, an arrested person is allowed one telephone call to a party of his or her choice; call your embassy or consulate.

Mail   Mailboxes generally are found at intersections, are blue with a blue-and-white eagle logo, and carry the inscription "U.S. Postal Service." If your mail is addressed to a U.S. destination, don't forget to add the five-digit postal code, or zip code, after the two-letter abbreviation of the state to which the mail is addressed. The abbreviation for Hawaii is HI.

International airmail rates are 60¢ for half-ounce letters (40¢ for letters going to Mexico and 46¢ for letters to Canada) and 50¢ for postcards (35¢ to Mexico and 40¢ to Canada). All domestic first-class mail goes from Hawaii to the U.S. mainland by air.

Taxes   The United States has no VAT (value-added tax) or other indirect taxes at a national level. Every state, and every city in it, has the right to levy its own local tax on all purchases, including hotel and restaurant checks, airline tickets, and so on. In Hawaii, sales tax is 4%; there's also a 7.25% hotel-room tax and a small excise tax, so the total tax on your hotel bill will be 11.42%.

Telephone & Fax   The telephone system in the United States is run by private corporations, so rates, particularly for long-distance service and operator-assisted calls, can vary widely—especially on calls made from public telephones. Local calls—that is, calls to other locations on the island you're on—made from public phones in Hawaii cost 35¢. The international-country code for Hawaii is 1, just as it is for the rest of the United States and Canada.

Generally, hotel surcharges on long-distance and local calls are astronomical. You are usually better off using a **public pay telephone,** which you will find clearly marked in most public buildings and private establishments as well as on the street.

Most **long-distance and international calls** can be dialed directly from any phone. For calls to Canada and other parts of the United States, dial 1, followed by the area code and the seven-digit number. For international calls, dial 011, followed by the country code, city code, and telephone number of the person you wish to call.

In Hawaii, interisland phone calls are considered long-distance and are often as costly as calling the U.S. mainland.

For **reversed-charge or collect calls,** and for **person-to-person calls,** dial 0 (zero, not the letter "O"), followed by the area code and number you want; an operator will then come on the line, and you should specify that you are calling collect, person-to-person, or both. If your operator-assisted call is international, ask for the overseas operator.

Note that all phone numbers with the area code 800 or 888 are toll-free.

For **local directory assistance** ("information"), dial 411; for **long-distance information,** dial 1, then the appropriate area code and 555-1212.

Fax facilities are widely available and can be found in most hotels and many other establishments. Try **Mail Boxes, Etc.** (check the local Yellow Pages) or any photocopying shop.

Telephone Directories   There are two kinds of telephone directory in the United States. The general directory, the *White Pages,* lists private and business subscribers in alphabetical order. The inside front cover lists emergency numbers, and you'll also find a guide to long-distance and international calling, complete with country codes and area codes. The second directory, printed on yellow paper (hence its name, *Yellow Pages*), lists all local services, businesses, and industries by type of activity, with an index at the front—everything from automobile repair to places of worship by religious denomination.

Time   See "Fast Facts: The Big Island" in chapter 3.

Tipping   It's part of the American way of life to tip. Many service employees receive little direct salary and must depend on tips for their income. The following are some general rules:

In **hotels,** tip bellhops at least $1 per piece of luggage ($2 to $3 if you have a lot of luggage), and tip the housekeeping staff $1 per person, per day. Tip the doorman or concierge only if he or she has provided you with some specific service (for example, calling a cab for you or obtaining difficult-to-get theater tickets). Tip the valet-parking attendant $1 every time you get your car.

In **restaurants, bars, and nightclubs,** tip service staff 15 to 20% of the check, tip bartenders 10 to 15%, and tip valet-parking attendants $1 per vehicle. Tip the doorman only if you were provided with some specific service (such as his calling a cab for you). Tipping is not expected in cafeterias and fast-food restaurants.

Tip **cab drivers** 15% of the fare.

As for **other service personnel,** tip skycaps at airports at least $1 per piece ($2 to $3 if you have a lot of luggage), and tip hairdressers and barbers 15 to 20%. Tipping ushers at movies and theaters and gas-station attendants is not expected.

Toilets   Foreign visitors often complain that public toilets are hard to find in most U.S. cities. True, there are none on the streets, but visitors can usually find one in a bar, fast-food outlet, restaurant, hotel, museum, department store—and it will probably be clean. (The cleanliness of toilets at service stations, parks, and beaches is more open to question.) Note, however, a growing practice in some restaurants and bars of displaying a notice that "toilets are for the use of patrons only." You can ignore this sign, or better yet, avoid arguments by paying for a cup of coffee or a soft drink, which will qualify you as a patron.

3

Getting to Know the Big Island

by Jeanette Foster

*M*ost people arrive on the Big Island at Kona International Airport, on the island's West Coast, and discover there are only two ways to go: clockwise or counterclockwise. Nobody knows why, but most Americans go clockwise, and Europeans go counterclockwise. Whichever way you go, all you need to know is that from Keahole, Kilauea volcano is counterclockwise, and the ritzy Kohala Coast is clockwise. (If you land in Hilo, of course, the volcano is clockwise, and Kohala is counterclockwise.)

If you think you can "do" the Big Island in a day, forget it. You need about 3 days just to do Hawaii Volcanoes National Park justice. It's best to spend at least a week here.

1 Orientation

VISITOR INFORMATION

The **Big Island Visitors Bureau** has two offices on the Big Island: one at 250 Keawe St., Hilo, HI 96720 (☎ **808/961-5797;** fax 808/ 961-2126); and on the other side of the island at 75-5719 W. Alii Dr., Kailua-Kona, HI 96740 (☎ **808/329-7787;** fax 808/ 326-7563; www.bigisland.org). **Hawaii's Big Island Driving Tour** is available here. This step-by-step guide takes you on the Big Island's Circle Island tour, pointing out all the wonders along the way, with legends, facts, and bits of trivia thrown in for fun; stop in and pick one up, or call, and the Bureau will send it to you.

On the west side of the island, there are two additional places to contact for information: the **Kona–Kohala Resort Association,** 69-275 Waikoloa Beach Dr., Kamuela (Waimea) HI 96743 (☎ **800/318-3637** or 808/886-4915; fax 808/886-1044; www.kkra.org); and **Destination Kona,** P.O. Box 2850, Kailua-Kona, HI 96745 (☎ **808/322-6809;** fax 808/322-8899). On the east side, you can contact **Destination Hilo,** P.O. Box 1391, Hilo, HI 96721 (☎ **808/935-5294;** fax 808/969-1984).

The Big Island's best free tourist publications are *This Week,* the *Beach and Activity Guide,* and *101 Things to Do on Hawaii The Big Island.* All three offer lots of useful information, as well as discount coupons on a variety of island adventures. Copies are easy to find all around the island.

The *Beach and Activity Guide* is affiliated with the **Activity Connection,** King Kamehameha Mall, Kuakini Hwy. (behind the King Kamehameha Hotel), Kailua-Kona (☎ **800/459-7156** or 808/ 329-1038; fax 808/327-9411; e-mail farnham@aloha.net), a discount activity desk offering real discounts (no fees, no timeshares) of up to 15% on activities, including island tours, snorkeling and dive trips, submarine and horseback rides, luaus, and more. Stop by the office; it's open daily from 7:30am to 5:30pm.

THE REGIONS IN BRIEF

Refer back to the two-page map on pp. 2-3 in chapter 1 as you read about the island's geography below.

THE KONA COAST

One Hawaiian word everyone seems to know is Kona, probably because it's synonymous with great coffee and big fish—both of which are found in abundance along this 70-mile-long stretch of black lava–covered coast.

A collection of tiny communities devoted to farming and fishing along the sunbaked leeward side of the island, the Kona Coast has an amazingly diverse geography and climate for such a compact area. The oceanfront town of **Kailua-Kona,** a quaint fishing village that now caters more to tourists than boat captains, is its commercial center; sooner or later, everyone meets on Kailua-Kona's Alii Drive, a 2-mile retail strip of shops and restaurants that's fun to cruise on foot or by car, especially on Saturday night. The lands of Kona range from stark, black, dry, coastal desert to cool, cloudy upcountry so fertile that it seems anything could grow here—glossy green coffee, macadamia nuts, tropical fruit, and a riotous profusion of flowers cover the jagged steep slopes. Among the coffee fields, you'll find the funky, artsy village of **Holualoa.** Higher yet in elevation are native forests of giant trees filled with tiny, colorful birds, some perilously close to extinction. About 7 miles south of Kailua-Kona, boarding the ocean, is the resort area of **Keauhou,** a suburban-like series of upscale condominiums, several hotels, a shopping center, and homes in the seven-figure range.

Kona means "leeward side" in Hawaiian—and that means full-on summer sun every day of the year. This is an affordable vacation spot. An ample selection of midpriced condo units, peppered with a few older hotels and B&Bs, line the shoreline, which is mostly rocky lava reef, interrupted by an occasional pocket beach. Here, too, stand two world-class resorts: Kona Village, the site of one of the best luaus in the islands, and Hawaii's newest luxury retreat, the Four Seasons at Hualalai.

SOUTH KONA   Away from the bright lights of the town of Kailua lies the rural South Kona Coast, home to coffee farmers, macadamia nut growers, and people escaping to the country. The serrated South Kona Coast is indented with numerous bays, starting with **Kealakekua,** a marine-life preserve that's the island's best diving spot and the place where Capt. James Cook met his demise; down to **Honaunau,** where a national historic park recalls the days of old Hawaii. Accommodations in this area are mainly inexpensive B&Bs, everything from the very frugal Japanese Manago Hotel to the very classy McCandless Ranch B&B. This coast is a great place to stay if you want to get away from crowds and experience peaceful country living. You'll be within driving distance of beaches and the sites of Kailua.

THE KOHALA COAST

Fringes of palms and flowers, brilliant blankets of emerald green, and an occasional flash of white building are your only clues from the road that this black-lava coast north of Kona is more than bleak and barren. But, oh, is it! Down by the sea, pleasure domes rise like palaces no Hawaiian king ever imagined. This is where the Lear-jet set escapes to play in world-class beachfront hotels set like jewels in the golden sand. But you don't have to be a billionaire to visit the Waikoloa, Mauna Lani, and Mauna Kea resorts: The fabulous beaches and abundant historic sites are open to the public, with parking and other facilities provided by the resorts, including restaurants, golf courses, and shopping.

NORTH KOHALA

Seven sugar mills once shipped enough sugar to sweeten all the coffee in San Francisco from three harbors on this knob of land at the northernmost reaches of the island. **Hawi,** the region's hub and home to the Kohala Sugar Co., was a flourishing town. It even had its own railroad, a narrow-gauge train that hauled cane down to Mahukona, on North Kohala's lee coast.

Today, Hawi's quaint, three-block-long strip of sun-faded, false-front buildings and 1920s vintage shops lives on as a minor tourist stop in one of Hawaii's most scenic rural regions. The small cosmopolitan community of diverse ethnic groups, including Chinese, Japanese, Puerto Rican, Korean, and Filipino laborers, is slowly shrinking as the old-timers die out.

This region is most famous as the birthplace of King Kamehameha the Great; a statue commemorates the royal site. It's also home to the islands' most sacred site, the 1,500-year-old **Mookini Heiau**.

WAIMEA (KAMUELA)

This old upcountry cow town on the northern road between the coasts is set in lovely country: rolling green pastures, big, wide-open spaces dotted by *puu* (hills), and real Marlboro-smoking cowpokes who ride mammoth **Parker Ranch,** Hawaii's largest working ranch. The town is also headquarters for the **Keck Telescope,** the largest and most powerful in the world, bringing world-class, starry-eyed astronomers to town. The nightlife here is far out, in the galactic sense; bring your own telescope. Waimea is home to several affordable B&Bs, and Merriman's Restaurant is a popular foodie outpost at Opelo Plaza.

THE HAMAKUA COAST

This emerald coast, a 52-mile stretch from Honokaa to Hilo on the island's windward northeast side, was once planted with sugarcane; it now blooms with flowers, macadamia nuts, papayas, and marijuana, also known as *pakalolo* (still Hawaii's number one cash crop). Resort-free and virtually without beaches, the Hamakua Coast still has a few major destinations, such as spectacular **Waipio Valley,** a picture-perfect valley with impossibly steep sides, taro patches, a green riot of wild plants, and a winding stream leading to a broad, black-sand beach; and the historic plantation town of **Honokaa** (making a comeback as the B&B capital on the coastal trail). Akaka Falls and Laupahoehoe Beach Park are also worth seeking out.

Elsewhere along the coast, communities are reeling in the wake of the sugar-plantation shutdown, and the cane in the fields is going to seed. Valleys draining Mauna Kea's slopes meet the sea every few miles; they're so choked with foliage that they look like Indonesian jungles.

HILO

When the sun shines in Hilo, it's one of the most beautiful tropical cities in the Pacific. Being here is an entirely different kind of island experience: Hawaii's largest metropolis after Honolulu is a quaint, misty, flower-filled city of Victorian houses overlooking a half-moon bay, with a restored historic downtown and a clear view of Mauna Loa's often snowcapped peak. Hilo catches everyone's eye until it rains—and when it rains in Hilo, it pours.

Hilo is America's wettest town, with 128 inches of rain annually. It's ideal for growing ferns, orchids, and anthuriums, but not for catching a few rays. Yet there's lots to see and do in Hilo, so grab your umbrella. The rain is warm (the temperature seldom dips below 70°F), and there's usually a rainbow afterward.

Hilo's oversized airport and hotels are remnants of a dream: The city wanted to be Hawaii's major port of entry. That didn't happen, but the facilities here are excellent. Hilo is Hawaii's best bargain for budget travelers. It has plenty of hotel rooms—most of the year, that is. Hilo's magic moment comes in spring, the week after Easter, when hula *halau* (schools) arrive for the annual Merrie Monarch Hula Festival competition (see "The Big Island Calendar of Events" in chapter 1 for details). This is a full-on Hawaiian spectacle and a wonderful cultural event. Plan ahead if you want to go: Tickets are sold out the first week in January for the post-Easter event, and the hotels within 30 miles are usually booked solid.

Hilo is also the gateway to Hawaii Volcanoes National Park; it's just an hour's drive up-slope.

THE PUNA REGION

Lava, and lots of it, characterizes the Puna Region on the Big Island's remote eastern shore. Black lava covers almost everything, both ancient sites and latter-day villages, with alacrity: In 1963, lava ran down to Cape Kumukahi and oozed around the lighthouse, which still looks startled; it destroyed the village of Kalapana in 1990. Since it overran Chain of Craters Road in 1988, there's only one way in and out of Puna: Highway 130. Land not buried by lava is planted in red and green anthuriums, golden sunrise papayas, and marijuana. The illegal leaf growers add an edgy element to this remote region. The main town in Puna is **Pahoa,** a town that time forgot, where you might spot residents still dressed like the flower children of the

1960s, complete with peace symbols, dreadlocks, and multicolored VW vans.

HAWAII VOLCANOES NATIONAL PARK & VOLCANO VILLAGE

The sleepy village of Volcano sits in a rain forest on the edge of America's most exciting national park, where a live volcano called Kilauea erupts daily. (If you're lucky, it will be a spectacular sight. At other times, you may not be able to see the molten lava at all— but there's still a lot to see and learn.) Ideally, you should plan to spend 3 days at the park, exploring the trails, watching the volcano, visiting the rain forest, and just enjoying this most unusual, spectacular place. But even if you have only a day, get here—it's worth the trip. Bring your sweats or jacket (honest!); it's cooler up here, especially at night.

If you plan to dally in the park—and you should—Volcano has some great places to stay. Several terrifically cozy B&Bs, some with fireplaces, hide under tree ferns in this cool, misty hamlet. The tiny highland (at 4,000 ft.) community, first settled by Japanese immigrants, is now inhabited by artists, soul-searchers, and others who like the crisp air of Hawaii's high country. It has just enough civilization to sustain a good life: a few stores, a gas station, and a golf course.

KA LAE: SOUTH POINT

This is the Plymouth Rock of Hawaii, where the first Polynesians arrived in seagoing canoes, probably from the Marquesas Islands or Tahiti, around A.D. 500. You'll feel like you're at the end of the world on this lonely, windswept place, the southernmost point of the United States (a geographic claim that belonged to Key West, Florida, until 1959, when Hawaii became the 50th state). Hawaii ends in a sharp black-lava point. Bold 500-foot cliffs stand against the blue sea to the west and shelter the old fishing village of Waiahukini, which was born in A.D. 750 and lasted until the 1860s. Ancient canoe moorings, shelter caves, and *heiau* (temples) poke through windblown pili grass. The East Coast curves inland to reveal a lonely, green-sand beach, a world-famous anomaly that's accessible only by foot or four-wheel drive. For most, the only reason to venture down to the southern tip is to say you did, or to experience the empty vista of land's end.

Everything in the two wide spots in the road called **Naalehu** and **Waiohinu** that pass for towns at South Point claims to be the southernmost this or that. Except for a monkeypod tree planted by Mark

Twain in 1866, there's not much to crow about. There are, thankfully, a gas station, a couple of places to eat and a fruit stand, a picture-postcard 19th-century church, and a couple of B&Bs. These end-of-the-world towns are just about as far removed from the real world as you can get.

2 Getting Around

BY CAR

You'll need a rental car on the Big Island; not having one will really limit what you'll be able to see and do. All the major car-rental firms have agencies at both the airports and at the Kohala Coast resorts; for a complete list, as well as tips on insurance and driving rules, see "Car Rentals" under "Getting There & Getting Around" in chapter 1.

There are more than 480 miles of paved road on the Big Island. The highway that circles the island is called the **Hawaii Belt Road.** On the Kona side of the island, you have two choices: the scenic "upper" road, **Mamalahoa Highway** (Hwy. 190), or the speedier "lower" road, Queen **Kaahumanu Highway** (Hwy. 19). The road that links east to west is called the **Saddle Road** (Hwy. 200), because it crosses the "saddle" between Mauna Kea and Mauna Loa. Saddle Road is the one rental-car agencies ask you to avoid, because it's rough and narrow and the weather conditions can be a handful for motorists.

BY TAXI

Taxis are readily available at both Keahole and Hilo airports. In Hilo, call **Ace-1** (☎ 808/935-8303). In Kailua-Kona, call **Kona Airport Taxi** (☎ 808/329-7779). Taxis will take you wherever you want to go on the Big Island, but it's prohibitively expensive to use them for long distances.

BY BUS

There is an islandwide bus system, but all it does is take passengers from Kona to Hilo and back. It's the **Hele-On Bus** (☎ 808/ 961-8744), and it leaves Kailua-Kona from the Lanihau Shopping Center, at Palani Road and Queen Kaahumanu Highway, every morning at 6:45am, getting into Hilo at 9:30am. The afternoon return trip leaves the bus terminal on Kamehameha Avenue at Mamo Street in Hilo at 1:30pm, arriving back in Kailua-Kona at 4:30pm. The fare is $5.25 each way.

FAST FACTS: The Big Island

American Express   There's an office on the Kohala Coast at the Hilton Waikoloa Village (☎ **808/886-7958**). To report lost or stolen traveler's checks, call ☎ **800/221-7282.**

Area Code   All the Hawaiian Islands are in the **808** area code. Note that if you're calling one island from another, you'll have to dial 1-808 first, and you'll be billed at long-distance rates (which can be more expensive than calling the mainland).

Dentists   In an emergency, contact **Dr. Craig C. Kimura** at Kamuela Office Center (☎ **808/885-5947**); in Kona, call **Dr. Frank Sayre,** Frame 10 Center, behind Lanihau Shopping Center on Palani Rd. (☎ **808/329-8067**); in Hilo, call **Hawaii Smile Center,** Hilo Lagoon Center, 101 Aupuni St. (☎ **808/961-9181**).

Doctors   **Hilo Medical Center** is at 1190 Waianuenue Ave., Hilo (☎ **808/974-4700;** on the Kona side, call **Hualalai Urgent Care,** 75-1028 Henry St. (across the street from Safeway), ☎ **808/ 327-HELP.**

Emergencies   For ambulance, fire, and rescue services, dial ☎ **911** or call ☎ **808/961-6022.** The **Poison Control Center** hotline is ☎ **800/362-3585.**

Hospitals   **Hilo Medical Center,** 1190 Waianuenue Ave., Hilo (☎ **808/974-4700**); **North Hawaii Community Hospital,** Waimea (☎ **808/885-4444**); and **Kona Community Hospital,** on the Kona Coast in Kealakekua (☎ **808/322-9311**) all have 24-hour urgent-care facilities.

Liquor Laws   The legal drinking age in Hawaii is 21. Bars are allowed to stay open daily until 2am; places with cabaret licenses are able to keep the booze flowing until 4am. Grocery and convenience stores are allowed to sell beer, wine, and liquor 7 days a week.

Police   Dial ☎ **911** or call the **Hawaii Police Department** at ☎ **808/326-4646** in Kona, ☎ **808/961-2213** in Hilo.

Safety   Although Hawaii is generally a safe tourist destination, visitors have been crime victims, so stay alert. The most common crime against tourists is rental car break-ins. Never leave any valuables in your car, not even in the trunk. Thieves can be in and out of your trunk faster than you can open it with your own keys. Be especially leery of high-risk areas, such as beaches and resorts. Stay in well-lighted areas after dark.

Smoking It's against the law to smoke in public buildings, including airports, grocery stores, retail shops, movie theaters, banks, and all government buildings and facilities. Hotels have nonsmoking rooms available, restaurants have nonsmoking sections, and car-rental agencies have nonsmoking cars. Most bed-and-breakfasts prohibit smoking inside their buildings.

Taxes Hawaii's sales tax is 4%. The hotel-occupancy tax is 7.25%, and hoteliers are allowed by the state to tack on an additional 0.1666% excise tax. Thus, expect taxes of about 11.42% to be added to every hotel bill.

Time Hawaii is 2 hours behind Pacific Standard Time and 5 hours behind Eastern Standard Time. In other words, when it's noon in Hawaii, it's 2pm in California and 5pm in New York during Standard Time on the mainland. There's no daylight saving time here, so when daylight saving time is in effect on the mainland, Hawaii is 3 hours behind the West Coast and 6 hours behind the East Coast—therefore, in the summer, when it's noon in Hawaii, it's 3pm in California and 6pm in New York.

Hawaii is east of the International Date Line, putting it in the same day as the U.S. mainland and Canada and a day behind Australia, New Zealand, and Asia.

Weather For conditions in and around Hilo, call ☎ **808/935-8555;** for the rest of the Big Island, call ☎ **808/961-5582.** For marine forecasts, call ☎ **808/935-9883.**

4

Accommodations

by Jeanette Foster

*B*efore you reach for the phone to book your vacation dream house, refer to chapter 1 to read up on the types of accommodations available to make sure you book the kind of place you want. Also, remember that the Big Island is really big; see "The Regions in Brief" in chapter 3 to make sure that you choose the best area in which to base yourself.

In the listings below, all rooms have a full private bath (with tub and shower) and free parking unless otherwise noted. Remember to add Hawaii's 11.42% in taxes to your final bill.

1 The Kona Coast

IN & AROUND KAILUA-KONA
VERY EXPENSIVE

✪ **Four Seasons Resort Hualalai at Historic Kaupulehu.** P.O. Box 1119, Kailua-Kona, HI 96745. ☎ **888/340-5662** or 808/325-8000. Fax 808/325-8100. www.fshr.com/locations/Hualalai. 243 units. A/C MINIBAR TV TEL. $450–$625 double, from $750 suite. Extra person $90; children under 18 stay free in parents' room. AE, DC, JCB, MC, V.

This is a great place to relax in the lap of luxury. You're guaranteed to experience Polynesian paralysis after a few days of lying in a hammock and watching the clouds waft across the sky, although plenty of diversions are available. Low-rise clusters of oceanfront villas nestle between the sea and the greens of a new golf course. The Four Seasons has no concrete corridors, no massive central building—it looks like a two-story townhouse project. The rooms are furnished in Pacific tropical style: beige walls, raffia rugs over clay-colored slate, and Madge Tennent etchings over rattan and bamboo settees. The ground-level rooms have bathrooms with private outdoor gardens (surrounded by black-lava rock), so you can shower naked under the tropic sun or nighttime stars.

Dining/Diversions: Pacific Rim cuisine is featured in the main restaurant, Pahu'a, located right at the ocean's edge. More casual fare is served at the poolside ✪ **Beach Tree Bar and Grill.** For reviews of these restaurants, see chapter 5.

Amenities: Sports club and spa, fabulous 18-hole Jack Nicklaus golf course (reserved for guests and residents; call ☎ **808/325-8480** for tee times), Hawaiian history and cultural interpretive center, daily Kids for All Seasons program, five swimming pools (one carved out of black-lava rock), eight tennis courts, complimentary scuba lessons, open lava-rock amphitheater for special events, 24-hour room service, complimentary valet, same-day laundry, 1-hour pressing, twice-daily maid service, multilingual concierge, free shoeshine and sandal repair, early/late arrival facilities.

✪ **Kona Village Resort.** P.O. Box 1299, Kailua-Kona, HI 96745. ☎ **800/ 367-5290** or 808/325-5555. Fax 808/325-5124. www.konavillage.com. 125 bungalows. $440–$735 double. Extra person $180 adult, $130 children 6–12; kids 5 and under stay free. Rates include all meals, tennis, watersports, walking tours, airport transfers, and a Fri-night luau. Packages available. AE, DC, JCB, MC, V.

In all of Hawaii, there's only one Kona Village. For more than 30 years, those seeking the great escape have crossed the black-lava fields to find refuge at this exclusive haven by the sea, with its wonderful dark-sand beach. A blissful languor settles in as you surrender to the gentle staff and peaceful, low-key atmosphere. Maybe it's the spirit of the ancients who once lived here. Maybe it's the deluxe summer-camp setup: thatched-roof island–style bungalows with no air-conditioning and no TVs, a central dining house, and phones only at the office. The resort resembles an eclectic Polynesian village, with proudly tended palms and tropicals, historic sites, and beaches on a secluded cove. Its magic frees children of all ages (except during September, when the resort is reserved for couples only) to relax and play on 82 acres by the sea, behind a lava barrier that keeps the world at bay. The bungalows, renovated in 1998, all have a bedroom, bathroom, and lanai. Standard equipment includes a grind-and-perk coffeemaker, a ceiling fan, and a refrigerator that's replenished daily with free sodas and bottled water. Some units have outdoor hot tubs and an extra anteroom with a single bed.

Dining/Diversions: Breakfast and dinner, served in the communal dining room, feature whatever's fresh in the islands that day. A second restaurant offers more formal dining. Lunch is served on the terrace alfresco: a healthy, tempting buffet of veggies and salads, sashimi, burgers, fish, grilled-to-order steaks, and a help-yourself bin of freshly baked oatmeal cookies. The food is terrific. During holidays and the summer, children can eat at an early kids-only dinner, followed by supervised activities. There's live entertainment most

Kona Coast Accommodations

Affordable Hawaii at Pomaikai (Lucky) Farm Bed & Breakfast **22**
Anne's Three Bears' Bed & Breakfast **2**
Aston Royal Sea Cliff Resort **11**
Dragonfly Ranch: Tropical Fantasy Lodging **23**
Four Seasons Resort Hualalai **1**
Hale E Komo Moi **21**
Hale Maluhia Country Inn **12**
Holualoa Inn **13**
Horizon Guest House **26**
Kailua Plantation House **10**
Kanaloa at Kona **18**
Keauhou Beach Hotel **17**
King Kamehameha's Kona Beach Hotel **4**
Kona Billfisher **7**
Kona Islander Inn **6**
Kona Magic Sands **15**
Kona Seaside Hotel **3**
Kona Sea Spray **16**
Kona Tiki Hotel **9**
Kona Village Resort **1**
Manago Hotel **20**
McCandless Ranch Bed & Breakfast **25**
Merryman's Bed & Breakfast **19**
RBR Farms **24**
Rosy's Rest **14**
Royal Kona Resort **8**
Uncle Billy's Kona Bay Hotel **5**

Legend

Airport ✈

```
0              2 mi
0              2 km
```

47

nights, whether it's dancing to a Hawaiian trio at the Bora Bora Bar, a Paniolo Cookout, or the Friday-night luau (see chapter 7).

Amenities: Watersports, tennis, two pools, petroglyph field, massage, small open-air health club.

MODERATE

Aston Royal Sea Cliff Resort. 75-6040 Alii Dr., Kailua-Kona, HI 96740. ☎ **800/922-7866** or 808/329-8021. Fax 808/326-1887. www.aston-hotels.com. 148 units. A/C TV TEL. $170–$190 studio double, $190–$240 one-bedroom apt. for 4, $220–$280 two-bedroom apt. for 6, $550–$600 villa for 4. AE, CB, DC, DISC, JCB, MC, V.

Families will love these luxuriously appointed apartments and their affordable rates. The architecturally striking five-story white buildings that make up this resort/condo complex, 2 miles from Kailua-Kona, are stepped back from the ocean for maximum views and privacy. (The downside is that there's no ocean swimming here, but the waves are near enough to lull you to sleep.) Atrium gardens and hanging bougainvillea soften the look. For the price of a moderate hotel room, you'll get a spacious unit furnished in tropical rattan with a large, sunny lanai, a full kitchen, and a washer and dryer. Tennis courts, pools, spas, a sauna, and barbecue facilities are available, as well as services such as voice mail, a small store, and an activities desk.

✪ **Kailua Plantation House.** 75-5948 Alii Dr. (near Lunapule St.), Kailua-Kona, HI 96740. ☎ **888/357-4262** or 808/329-3727. Fax 808/326-7323. www.kphbnb.com. 5 units. TV TEL. $160–$235 double. Rates include full breakfast. Extra person 20% more. 2-night minimum. AE, MC, V. No children under 12.

The rates here may be high for a B&B—but if you want to stay on the Kona Coast, an oceanfront room at this incredible house right on the water (the patio steps go right into the Pacific Ocean) is a wonderful splurge. The house is immaculately kept and elegantly decorated in island style, with rattan furniture and tile floors, and the views are fabulous. Ocean breezes keep the rooms cool, the romantic setting keeps couples in the mood, and the generous full breakfast keeps everyone happy. Book a couple of months in advance—everyone wants to stay here. But if you can't get an oceanfront room, stay somewhere else, as the rooms facing Alii Drive are very noisy.

King Kamehameha's Kona Beach Hotel. 75-5660 Palani Rd., Kailua-Kona, HI 96740. ☎ **800/367-6060** or 808/329-2911. Fax 808/922-8061. www.konabeachhotel.com. 462 units. A/C TV TEL. $120–$195 double, from

$300 suite. Package of Aloha (including room, car, and breakfast) starts at $130 (subject to availability). Additional person $25. AE, CB, DC, DISC, JCB, MC, V.

The best deal at this convenient downtown Kailua-Kona hotel is the Package of Aloha, which comes with a double room, a compact car, and breakfast for two, all for just $130—a price that makes the "King Kam" (as locals call it) attractive to travelers on a budget. This place isn't anything fancy—just a standard hotel in need of a little TLC—but it's well located, right in the heart of town, across the street from the pier, where record Pacific blue marlin are weighed in every afternoon. Rooms are ordinary but clean, just like a Holiday Inn, but with views of an ancient banyan tree, the Kona Pier, or sparkling Kailua Bay. There are shops on the premises, as well as a poolside bar and a snack bar. The hotel's own small, gold-sand beach is right out the front door.

Royal Kona Resort. 75-5852 Alii Dr., Kailua-Kona, HI 96740. ☎ **800/ 919-8333** or 808/329-3111. Fax 808/329-9532. www.royalkona.com. 452 units. A/C TV TEL. $140–$250 double. Children 17 and under stay free in parents' room. Extra person $15. AE, CB, DC, DISC, MC, V. Parking $5.

This sprawling hotel was built in 1968, right on the water's edge. The location is excellent, on a rocky promontory within walking distance of all the shops and restaurants in Kailua-Kona. You enter through an open-air lobby, surrounded by the sound of waterfalls and the salt air of the Pacific. The rooms are spread out over three buildings; 70% have an ocean view, and some are just a few feet from the rocky ocean's edge. The design of the building is based on the sloping Hualalai Mountain, so the higher the room, the better the view and the higher the price tag. (Rooms on the lower floors have bigger lanais, but not such spectacular views.) All units have the same layout, with dressing areas, coffeemakers ($3 for coffee), refrigerators, safes ($1.50 a day), two double beds, and a couple of chairs around a small table. All carpeting, bedspreads, and drapes were upgraded in 1997, though we did recently notice some frayed carpets in the hallways and minor maintenance problems.

There's no white-sand beach, so the hotel has created a saltwater lagoon with a man-made sandy beach. In addition, there's a freshwater swimming pool and a children's pool. The Royal Kona Tennis Club is on the property, and two golf courses are just minutes away. There's open-air casual dining right on the ocean's edge at the Tropics Cafe. Monday, Friday, and Saturday nights, there's a luau and Polynesian show. Other perks include room service for breakfast and dinner, an activities desk, four tennis courts (three lit for night play), and a spa.

INEXPENSIVE

✪ **Kona Billfisher**. Alii Dr. (across from the Royal Kona Resort), c/o Hawaii Resort Management, P.O. Box 39, Kailua-Kona, HI 96745. ☎ **800/622-5348** or 808/329-3333. Fax 808/326-4137. www.konahawaii.com. 40 units. A/C TV TEL. High season, $75–$85 one-bedroom condo: low season, $60–$65 one-bedroom condo. 3-night minimum. AE, CB, DC, DISC, JCB, MC, V.

This is our favorite of all the affordable condos on this coast. It's within walking distance of downtown Kailua-Kona, and the big, blue Pacific is just across the street. (Unfortunately, the ocean here is not good for swimming or snorkeling, but there's an on-site swimming pool, and the Kailua Pier, just a mile away, has a good swimming area.) The property is very well maintained (the interiors were renovated in 1998). Each unit comes with a full kitchen and a balcony, and features new furnishings and king-size beds. The one-bedroom units have sliding glass doors that allow you to close off the living room and make it into another private bedroom, so for the price of a one-bedroom unit, you can have a two-bedroom—a real deal. Other on-site facilities include a barbecue area and laundry. Book well in advance.

Kona Islander Inn. 75-5776 Kuakini Hwy. (south of Hualalai Rd.), Kailua-Kona. c/o Hawaii Resort Management, P.O. Box 39, Kailua-Kona, HI 96745. ☎ **800/622-5348** or 808/329-3333. Fax 808/326-4137. www.konahawaii.com. 70 studios. A/C TV TEL. High season: $69–$79 double; low season $35–59 double. AE, MC, V.

This is the most affordable place to stay in Kailua-Kona. These plantation-style, three-story buildings are surrounded by lush, palm-tree–lined gardens with torch-lit pathways that make it hard to believe you're smack-dab in the middle of downtown. The central location—across the street from the historic Kona Inn Shops—is convenient but can be noisy. Built in 1962, the complex is showing some signs of age, but the units were recently outfitted with new appliances, new bedspreads and curtains, and a coat of fresh paint. The studios are small, but extras like lanais and kitchenettes outfitted with microwaves, minifridges, and coffeemakers make up for the lack of space. Facilities include a swimming pool, hot tub, barbecue area, laundry, sundry store, and tour desk.

✪ **Kona Magic Sands**. 77-6452 Alii Dr. (next to Magic Sands Beach Park). Reservations c/o Hawaii Resort Management, P.O. Box 39, Kailua-Kona, HI 9674. ☎ **800/622-5348** or 808/329-3333. Fax 808/326-4137. www. konahawaii.com. 37 units (with shower only). TV. High season, $75–$95 double; low season, $65–$75 double. DISC, JCB, MC, V.

If you want to stay right on the ocean without spending a fortune, this is the place to do it—it's one of the best oceanfront deals you'll find on a Kona condo, and the only one with a beach for swimming and snorkeling right next door. Every unit in this older complex has a lanai that steps out over the ocean, and sunset views you'll dream about long after you return home. These studio units aren't luxurious; they're small (two people max) and cozy, great for people who want to be lulled to sleep by the sound of the waves crashing on the shore. Each studio consists of one long, narrow room with a small kitchen at one end and the lanai at the other, with a living room/ dining room/bedroom combo in between. There are laundry facilities on site, and a good Jameson's By the Sea restaurant just downstairs.

Kona Seaside Hotel. 75-5646 Palani Rd. (at Kuakini Hwy.), Kailua-Kona, HI 96740. ☎ **800/367-7000** or 808/329-2455. Fax 808/922-0052. www.sand-seaside.com. 225 units. A/C TV TEL. $95–$135 double; $145 double with kitchenette. Extra person $15; children under 12 stay free in parents' room. Room/ car packages available from $125. AE, DC, MC, V.

The package deal here is great: For just a few dollars more than the regular room rate, you can have a rental car, too. This budget hotel, located in the heart of Kailua-Kona, stands just steps away from Kailua Bay and Kailua-Kona's shopping, restaurants, and historic sites. The rooms are large and comfy (even if they don't have fancy soaps and extra amenities), but they can be noisy (ask for one away from the road). You may want to splurge on one of the 14 rooms with kitchenettes. There are two pools, laundry facilities, and a restaurant on the premises.

✪ **Kona Tiki Hotel.** 75-5968 Alii Dr. (about a mile from downtown Kailua-Kona), Kailua-Kona, HI 96740. ☎ **808/329-1425.** Fax 808/327-9402. 15 units. $56 double, $62 double with kitchenette. Rates include continental breakfast. Extra person $8; children 2–12 $6. 3-night minimum. No credit cards.

It's hard to believe that places like this still exist. The Kona Tiki, located right on the ocean, away from the hustle and bustle of downtown Kailua-Kona, is one of the best budget deals in Hawaii. All the rooms are tastefully decorated and feature queen beds, ceiling fans, minifridges, and private lanais overlooking the ocean. Although it's called a hotel, this small, family-run operation is more like a large B&B, with lots of aloha and plenty of friendly conversation around the pool at the morning breakfast buffet. The staff is helpful in planning activities. There are no TVs or phones in the rooms, but there's a pay phone in the lobby. If a double with a kitchenette is available, grab it—the extra $6 will save you a bundle in food costs. Book way, way, way in advance.

Uncle Billy's Kona Bay Hotel. 75-5739 Alii Dr., Kailua-Kona, HI 96740. ☎ **800/367-5102** or 808/961-5818. Fax 808/935-7903. www.unclebilly.com. 139 units. A/C TV TEL. High season, $92–$112 double; low season, $84–$104 double. Extra person $10; children 18 and under stay free in parents' room. Room/car packages, seniors discount, and multiday discounts available. AE, DC, DISC, MC, V.

An institution in Kona, Uncle Billy's is where visitors from the other Hawaiian islands stay when they come to this coast. A thatched roof hangs over the hotel lobby area, and a Polynesian long-house restaurant is next door. The rooms are more standard fare, but they're comfortable and come with large lanais; most also have minifridges (request one at booking if you want one), and 16 are condo-style units with kitchens. It can be noisy at night when big groups book in; avoid Labor Day weekend, when all the canoe paddlers in the state want to stay here and rehash the race into the wee morning hours.

UPCOUNTRY KONA: HOLUALOA

✪ **Holualoa Inn.** P.O. Box 222 (76-5932 Mamalahoa Hwy.), Holualoa, HI 96725. ☎ **800/392-1812** or 808/324-1121. Fax 808/322-2472. www.konaweb.com/HINN. 6 units (1 with shower only). $135–$175 double. Rates include full breakfast and sunset pupu platter. Extra person $30. 15% discount for 7 nights or more. AE, MC, V. On Mamalahoa Hwy., just after the Holualoa Post Office, look for Paul's Place General Store; the next driveway is the inn. No children under 13.

The quiet, secluded setting of this B&B—40 pastoral acres just off the main drag of the artsy village of Holualoa, on the slope at 1,350 feet above Kailua-Kona—provides stunning panoramic views of the entire coast. Owned by a *kamaaina* (old-line) family, this contemporary 7,000-square-foot Hawaiian home built of golden woods has six private suites and window-walls that roll back to embrace the gardens and views. Cows graze on the bucolic pastures below the garden Jacuzzi and pool, and the coffee plantation on the property is the source of the morning brew. The inn offers several nice features, such as a gas grill for a romantic dinner next to the pool, a telescope for star gazing, and a billiard table. It's a 15-minute drive down the hill to busy Kailua-Kona, and about 20 minutes to the beach, but the pool has a stunning view of Kailua-Kona and the sparkling Pacific below.

Rosy's Rest. 76-1012 Mamalahoa Hwy. (north of Hualalai Rd.), Holualoa, HI 96725. ☎ **808/322-REST.** Fax 808/322-7378. TV. 2 apts. (with shower only).

$75–$80 double. Rates include continental breakfast. Extra person $10. 2-night minimum. No credit cards.

Looking for a place to kick back and watch the grass grow? Then head upcountry to Rosy's. Rosy Bartsch has a separate two-story building with two apartment units (one upstairs, one downstairs) in a bucolic setting that's guaranteed to relax even the most stressed-out urbanite. The comfortable apartments (a one-bedroom with full kitchen, and a studio with kitchenette) have such features as ohia-framed queen beds and panoramic views of the Kona coastline. A smiling, congenial hostess, Rosy gives her guests as much or as little attention as they want.

KEAUHOU

✪ **Kanaloa at Kona.** 78-261 Manukai St., Kailua-Kona, HI 96740. ☎ **800/688-7444** or 808/322-9625. Fax 808/322-3818. 166 units. TV TEL. $175–$210 one-bedroom apt. (sleeps up to 4); $205–$245 two-bedroom apt. (up to 6); $245–$265 2-bedroom apt. with loft (up to 8). AE, CB, DC, DISC, JCB, MC, V.

These big, comfortable, well-managed, and spacious vacation condos border the rocky coast beside Keauhou Bay, 6 miles south of Kailua-Kona. They're exceptional units, ideal for families, with comforts such as huge bathrooms with spas, dressing rooms, and bidets. In addition, spacious lanais, tropical decor, and lots of appliances make for free-and-easy living. Guests get discounted rates at the two 18-hole golf courses at a nearby country club. Tennis, watersports, pools, and playgrounds are also at hand. And it's easy to stock up on supplies: There's a supermarket at the new mall just up the hill.

Kona Seaspray. 78-6671 Alii Dr. (P.O. Box 390663), Kailua-Kona, HI 96739. ☎ **808/322-2403.** Fax 808/322-2675. 3 units. TV TEL. $90–$100 one-bedroom apt., $125–$150 two-bedroom apt. Extra person $10. 3-night minimum. MC, V.

The Kona Seaspray has three things going for it: a great location, a great price, and the wonderful hospitality of the Millers. It's located just across from the Kahaluu Beach Park, possibly the best snorkeling area in Kona. The prices are a great deal when you consider that the 1-bedroom apartments easily sleep four and the two-bedroom (one-bath) unit can sleep six. This place is not the Ritz (think 1960s decor), but it's spotlessly clean. All the apartments have full kitchens with a microwave and a big refrigerator; you'll also have ceiling fans and cable TV (one unit has a VCR). Not just one but two facilities for laundry are on the property, too. A big swimming pool, surrounded by palm trees, is just outside the front door.

Great Places to Stay with the Kids

In addition to our favorites below, also consider the **Mauna Kea Resort** and **Mauna Lani Bay Hotel and Bungalows** on the Kohala Coast; **Mountain Meadow Ranch Bed & Breakfast** on the Hamakua Coast; and **Hi'iaka House and Log Cabin** in Volcano. *Note:* By state law, hotels can only accept children ages 5 to 12 in supervised activities programs.

Four Seasons Resort Hualalai at Historic Kaupulehu (*see p. 45*)   This is one of Hawaii's most kid-friendly hotels, offering a complimentary "Kids for All Seasons" program. The activities center features everything from sand-sculpting to kite-flying. The Four Seasons also offers such amenities as complimentary milk and cookies for kids on arrival, children's menus in all restaurants, complimentary items for infant needs (cribs, strollers, highchairs, playpens, bottles, toys, and car seats), and child safety features. The hotel also has a game room; a complimentary scuba clinic for ages 12 and older; children's videos; and a host of sailing, snorkeling, and other activities.

Kona Village Resort (*see p. 46*)   Here you'll find a parent's dream: custom-designed programs to entertain your children—from tots to teenagers—from dawn to well after dusk, all at no charge. There's even a dinner seating for children at 5:30pm every day, with a special menu, where children can go unescorted so their parents can enjoy an intimate dinner for two later in the evening. Note that children are not permitted in September, when the resort features a month of romance for couples only.

Kona Billfisher (*see p. 50*)   This condo complex has well-equipped—and very well-priced—one-bedroom units, which sleep four and are great for families. The ocean is just across the street,

SOUTH KONA
EXPENSIVE

✪ **Horizon Guest House.** P.O. Box 268, Honaunau, HI 96726. ☎ **888/ 328-8301** or 808/328-2540. Fax 808/328-8702. www.horizonguesthouse.com. 4 units. $250 double. Rates include full gourmet breakfast. 2-night minimum. MC, V. 30 miles south of Kailua-Kona on Hwy. 11, just before mile marker 100. No children under 14.

Host Clem Classen spent two years researching the elements of a perfect bed and breakfast. The Horizon Guest House is the result.

and there's a great family-style pizza and hamburger joint right next door.

Hale E Homo Mai (*see p. 58*)   Large families—or small families who want a lot of room—will love this rambling Victorian house just down the street from Kealakekua Bay. The interior is open and airy, and the furnishings can take any punishment the kids can dish out. The house sleeps up to 13 (counting the two bedrooms, the pull-out sofa bed, a tiny bed in the alcove, the bed on the lanai, and a couple of beds on the rooftop lanai). Good swimming beaches line the coast, dolphins swim into the bay nearly everyday, and Puuhonua O Honaunau National Historic Park is just a 5-minute drive away.

The Orchid at Mauna Lani (*see p. 61*)   The Keiki Aloha children's program features watersports (from kayaking to snorkeling), Hawaiian cultural activities (storytelling, hula lessons, coconut leaf–weaving, and so on), and just plain fun (face painting, video games, treasure hunts, for example). Fees are $50 for a full day (includes lunch) and $35 for a half day. The resort also offers family packages—you can book a second room at half price.

Guest House at Volcano (*see p. 68*)   If you're bringing the little ones to see the volcano, here's the place to stay. A mother herself, hostess Bonnie Gooddell has childproofed her house ("There's nothing they can ruin," she says), and her guest cottage comes complete with children's toys on the large outside porch and a basketball hoop in the driveway; there's even a swing set. You can take the kids on a hike along the forest trail in the backyard, which cuts through 2 miles of tropical rain forest to the Thurston Lava Tube in Hawaii Volcanoes National Park.

Its 40 acres of pasture land are located at 1,100 feet. You can see 25 miles of coastline from Kealakekua to just about South Point, yet you cannot see another structure or hear any sounds of civilization. The carefully thought out individual rooms (scattered throughout the property to give a feeling of solitude) are filled with some $16,000 worth of Hawaiian furniture and accessories, including hand-quilted Hawaiian bedspreads, a small refrigerator, a coffeemaker, a writing desk, luxurious robes, and a private lanai with coastline views. The property features an "infinite" pool (20 feet by

40 feet), a hot tub that takes advantage of the view, gardens every-where, laundry facilities, outdoor shower, and all the ocean and beach toys you can think of. Clem whips up a gourmet breakfast in the octagonal kitchen in the main house, which also features a media room with library, video collection, TV (which you can take to your room, if you promise to use the headphones so you won't disturb other guests), VCR, and cordless phone. At first glance the price may seem high, but once ensconced on the unique property, you will agree it's worth every penny.

MODERATE

✪ **McCandless Ranch Bed & Breakfast.** P.O. Box 500 (86-4276 Mamalahoa Hwy.), Honaunau, HI 96726. ☎ **808/328-8246.** Fax 808/328-8671. www.alala.com. 2 rooms in house, 1 cottage (with shower only). $115 double; $150 cottage. Rates include continental breakfast. 2-night mini-mum. No credit cards. 30 miles south of Kailua-Kona on Hwy. 11, just past mile marker 101. No children under 15.

Far from the crowds and well off the tourist trail—but definitely worth the drive—the McCandless Ranch is a 17,000-acre working cattle spread owned by a prominent old-time Hawaii family, Cynnie and Ray Salley. It's a real ranch, but it's far from rustic. The quiet, serene atmosphere of the high mountain forest, the fabulous views of the Kona coastline far below, and the impeccable ambiance make this pricey B&B well worth the extra bucks. The two rooms in the main house (each with private entrance) are lavishly furnished in monarchy-era (Victorian) style, with lots of rare koa wood. The cot-tage, next to the 70-foot pool, is a Hawaiian-style residence with kitchen and living room outdoors, under a roof, and a bedroom (inside) featuring an old Hawaiian koa bed frame. The bath, with a huge shower, opens onto a hillside garden.

INEXPENSIVE

Affordable Hawaii at Pomaikai (Lucky) Farm Bed & Breakfast. 83-5465 Mamalahoa Hwy. (south of Kailua-Kona, after mile marker 107), Captain Cook, HI 96704. ☎ **800/325-6427** or 808/328-2112. Fax 808/328-2255. wwte.com/hawaii/pomaikai.htm. 5 units (4 with private bath). $50–$60 double. Rates include continental breakfast. Rates $10 higher for 1-night stays. Extra person $10, $5 children 5 and under. Sixth night free; 10% discount on stays of 7 days or more. DISC, MC, V.

True to its name, Affordable Hawaii offers an inexpensive perch from which to explore the South Kona Coast. Come share ex-Californian Nita Isherwood's century-old 4-acre farm, which is overflowing with macadamia-nut trees, coffee, tropical fruits, avo-cados as big as footballs, and even *jaboticaba*, an exotic fruit that makes a zingy jam and local wine. Two small, inexpensive rooms (one with private bath, one with shared bath) are located at the front of the home, on the highway; the recently built wing called The Greenhouse has two rooms with wooden floors, big windows with screens, full private baths, and private entrances. The most unique room is the old coffee barn, updated into a rustic room for two, with a raised queen bed, a fabulous view of the coastline, a private bathroom (with toilet and sink only), and an outdoor shower. There's a common kitchen for guests' use with a refrigerator, microwave, hot plate, sink, and barbecue grill.

Dragonfly Ranch: Tropical Fantasy Retreat. P.O. Box 675 (19 miles south of Kailua-Kona on Hwy. 160), Honaunau, HI 96726. ☎ **800/487-2159** or 808/328-2159. Fax 808/328-9570. www.dragonflyranch.com. 5 units (3 with private bath; 1 with shower only). $80–$85 double, $150–$200 suite. Rates include continental breakfast. Extra person $20. MC, V. From Hwy. 11, turn onto Hwy. 160 (the road to Puuhonua O Honaunau National Historic Park), between mile markers 103 and 104; after 1^1/2 miles, look for the Dragonfly banner flying in a tree and the TROPICAL FANTASY RETREAT sign above the Dragonfly Ranch mailbox.

Some may find the Dragonfly Ranch too rustic. But if you want to enjoy Hawaii's tropical outdoors and you're thrilled by the island's most unique architecture—structures that bring the outdoors inside—this may be the place for you. The location is ideal, with Puuhounau O Honanunau National Historic Park just down the road, and five bays offering great swimming and diving just minutes away. The place itself, with freestanding cabins tucked away on 2 acres of fruit trees and exotic flowers, truly is a tropical fantasy.

Manago Hotel. P.O. Box 145, Captain Cook, HI 96704. ☎ **808/323-2642.** Fax 808/323-3451. 64 units (some with shared bath). $25 double without bath; $39–$41 double with private bath; $55 double Japanese room with small *furo* tub and private bath. DISC, MC, V.

If you want to experience the history and culture of the 50th state, the Manago Hotel may be the place for you. This living relic is still operated by the third generation of the same Japanese family that opened it in 1917. It offers clean accommodations, tasty home cooking, and generous helpings of aloha, all at budget prices. The older rooms (with community baths) are ultra-Spartan—strictly for desperate budget travelers. The rooms with private baths in the new wing are still pretty spare (freshly painted walls with no decoration and no TV), but they're spotlessly clean and surrounded by Japanese gardens with a koi pond. The room price increases as you go up; the third-floor rooms have the most spectacular views of the Kona coastline. Adventuresome travelers might want to try the Japanese rooms with tatami mats to sleep on and *furo* (deep hot tubs) in each room to soak in. By the end of your stay, you may leave with new friends (the Manago family is very friendly) and an appreciation of Kona's history from all the stories you've heard.

✪ **Merryman's Bed & Breakfast.** P.O. Box 474, Kealakekua, HI 96750. ☎ **800/545-4390** or 808/323-2276. Fax 808/323-3749. www. lavazone2.com/merrymans. 4 units (2 with private bath). $75–$125 double. Rates include full breakfast. Extra person $15. 10% discount for 7 nights or more. DISC, MC, V. From Hwy. 11, make a left at the Goodyear Tire dealer (after mile marker 111) and follow the signs.

Everything about this upcountry B&B is impeccable: the landscaping, the furnishings, the fresh flowers in every room—even breakfast is served with attention to every detail. This charming cedar home, surrounded by immaculate park-like landscaping, sits above the Captain Cook–Kealakekua area, close to beaches, shopping, and restaurants. Guests enjoy watching the sun sink into the ocean from the large lanai or gazing at the starry sky as they soak in the hot tub. Hosts Don and Penny Merryman make a memorable breakfast, which includes Penny's fresh banana pancakes or Don's famous quiche.

RBR Farms. P.O. Box 930, Capt. Cook, HI 96704. ☎ **800/328-9212** or 808/ 328-9212. www.konaweb.com/rbr. 4 rooms (share bathroom), 1 cottage. TV. $75–$85 double, $150 double cottage (sleeps 4). Extra person in cottage $25. Rates include lavish breakfast. 2-night minimum. MC, V. Located 18 miles south of Kailua-Kona off Hwy. 11 past mile marker 106. Turn right at Middle Keei Rd. to intersection of Painted Church Rd., turn right on old coffee road (drive slow, road is rough but passable in rental car). Drive .75 mile on dirt road and look for sign on driveway.

This is a place for vacationers looking for a quiet retreat in the country. Tucked into the hills on a 6.8-acre working coffee and macadamia nut farm is a renovated old plantation home, with a separate cottage, swimming pool, hot tub, and outdoor breezeway where a country-style breakfast is served poolside. The rooms are two to a floor and share a bath; each has a private entrance, color TV, and views of the avocados, mangos, and papayas around the house. The cottage features open beam ceiling, separate bedroom, and fully equipped kitchen. The rooms are all nonsmoking.

FOR LONG-TERM FAMILY STAYS

Hale E Komo Mai. Napoopoo Rd., Kealakekua Bay, Reservations: 1392 Coast Meridian Rd., Port Coquitlam, B.C., Canada V3C 3V4. ☎ **604/462-8315** or 604/462-4148. www.21sthawaii.com/mcconnell. 2 apts. TV TEL. High season, $625 week double (sleeps 4–5); Low season, $580 a week double (sleeps 4–5), entire house, both floors $1,000–$1,100 week double (sleeps up to 13). Additional person $10 a night. No credit cards.

If you have a big family and want to spend time at the beach, this Victorian-style, custom-designed home is your best bet. Shoe-horned onto a small lot just steps from Kealakekua Bay, this three-story house rents out either as two separate units, each on its own floor, or as an entire house (we recommend the entire house, so you can have it all to yourself). The best feature is the third-floor rooftop lanai, which runs the entire length of the house, and has a 360° view (the owners will even stick a couple of beds up here so the kids can camp out). The first floor has a full kitchen and bedroom with queen-sized bed and a queen-sized sofa bed in the living room. The second floor has a bedroom/sitting room, outdoor kitchen, and another bed outside on the lanai. Amenities include laundry facilities, picnic table and barbecue, beach toys, and the manicured lawn. The caretaker of the property lives nearby, and can point you in the right direction for any activities. Good swimming beaches line the coastline, dolphins swim into the bay nearly everyday, and Puuhonua O Honaunau National Historic Park is just a 5-minute drive away.

2 The Kohala Coast

VERY EXPENSIVE

Hapuna Beach Prince Hotel. At Mauna Kea. 62-100 Kaunaoa Dr., Kamuela, HI 96743. ☎ **800/882-6060** or 808/880-1111. Fax 808/880-3112. www.hapunabeachprincehotel.com. 386 units. A/C MINIBAR TV TEL. $325–$495 double, from $925 suite. Extra person $45. AE, DC, JCB, MC, V.

This hotel enjoys one of the best locations on the Kohala Coast, adjacent to the magnificent white sands of Hapuna Beach. The Hapuna Beach Prince is a bit more formal than other hotels on the Kohala Coast. Guests, many from Japan, dress up here, some in the latest Tokyo fashions. You won't feel comfortable parading around the lobby and public areas in your T-shirt and flip-flops. The building is artistically designed and makes use of fine materials, including natural slate and wood.

The rooms are comfortable, all attuned to the fabulous ocean view and the sea breezes, though they're small for a luxury hotel. But the sprawling grounds make up for it. And the service is friendly and caring, with an unassuming confidence that springs from the Japanese ownership's low-key, hands-on managerial approach. Some complain about the long walk from the lobby to their rooms.

Dining/Diversions: The food is uniformly excellent throughout the five restaurants (ranging from Hawaiian regional cuisine to Japanese), including the sushi bar (where there's a wide variety of sakes to sample) and oyster bar. In the evening, there's always a local trio singing Hawaiian songs in the open-air, beachfront Reef Lounge.

Amenities: Health and fitness club, 18-hole championship links-style golf course designed by Arnold Palmer and Ed Seay (reserved for guests and residents), tennis pavilion with four Omni courts, pool, Jacuzzis, specialty boutiques, 24-hour room service, valet, spa treatments.

Mauna Kea Beach Hotel. 62-100 Mauna Kea Beach Dr., Kohala Coast, HI 96743. ☎ **800/882-6060** or 808/882-7222. Fax 808/880-3112. www.maunakeabeachhotel.com. 310 units. A/C TV TEL. $325–$565 double, from $555 suite. Extra person $45. AE, DC, JCB, MC, V.

Laurance S. Rockefeller was sailing around Hawaii ("looking for a place to swim," as he tells it) when he spotted a perfect crescent of gold sand and dropped anchor. In 1965, he built the Mauna Kea on the spot. Over the years, all the new luxury hotels have eclipsed this grande dame in architectural style (its 1960s New Brutalist style is heavy and dated) and amenities (no TVs—although they're available on request, along with a VCR, if you're desperate). Still, the beach out front is divine, and the landscaped grounds have a maturity seen nowhere else on this coast. Also, no other hotel has been able to claim the loyalty of its old-money guests, who keep returning to savor the relaxed clubby ambiance, remote setting, world-class golf course, and old Hawaii ways—the next generation is welcome to find themselves a new and better beach hotel somewhere else.

Dining/Diversions: Jackets are required for dinner at The Provençal-inspired Batik Room. Breakfast and more casual Mediterranean/Italian dinners are served at the open-air Pavilion, and lavish lunch buffets at The Terrace (see chapter 5). All three have live music. Drinks and light fare are served at the beachside Hau Tree Gazebo, which hosts Saturday clambakes. The Tuesday night luau features outstanding Hawaiian music and hula by Nani Lim and her award-winning dancers. There are coffee mugs in your room, so you can trot down to the free coffee-and-pastry bar in the morning. As a sister hotel to the Hapuna Beach Prince Hotel, Mauna Kea Beach Hotel gives guests the right to dine at either resort and charge everything to their room.

Amenities: Two top-ranked, award-winning championship courses: Robert Trent Jones, Sr.'s famous Mauna Kea course and the Arnold Palmer–designed Hapuna course. Pool, spa and fitness center, 13-court oceanside tennis complex, watersports, horseback riding on Parker Ranch, guided art tours, shops, beauty salon, free movies, free children's summer program, concierge, room service, dry cleaning, twice-a-day towel service, turndown treats.

✪ **Mauna Lani Bay Hotel & Bungalows.** 68-1400 Mauna Lani Dr., Kohala Coast, HI 96743. ☎ **800/367-2323** or 808/885-6622. Fax 808/885-4556. www.maunalani.com. 350 units. A/C MINIBAR TV TEL. $325–$575 double, $895 suite, $450–$725 villa (3-day minimum), $3,500–$4,400 bungalow. AE, CB, DC, DISC, JCB, MC, V.

Burnt out? In need of tranquillity and gorgeous surroundings? Look no further. Sandy beaches and lava tide pools are the focus of this serene seaside resort, where gracious hospitality is dispensed in a setting that's exceptional for its historic features. From the lounge chairs on the pristine beach to the turndown service at night, everything here is done impeccably.

Louvered doors open onto the guest rooms, which are done in natural tones with teak accents, each with a lanai. They're arranged to capture maximum ocean views, and they surround interior atrium gardens and pools where endangered baby sea turtles are raised for a Fourth of July "Independence Day" release to the sea. The bungalows are posh, two-bedroom, 4,000-square-foot enclaves with their own private pool and spa. A shoreline trail leads across the whole 3,200-acre resort, giving you an intimate glimpse into the ancient past, when people lived in lava caves and tended the large complex of spring-fed and tidal fishponds.

Dining: The CanoeHouse is one of the most visually appealing beachside restaurants on the coast, but it's astronomically priced and has mediocre food and service (see chapter 5). Instead, try the Gallery, at the Francis I'i Brown Golf Course Clubhouse, where island ingredients are prepared with understated excellence.

Amenities: Two celebrated 18-hole championship golf courses, tennis complex, spa, pool, shops, 24-hour room service, nightly turndown, twice-daily towel service.

✪ **The Orchid at Mauna Lani.** 1 N. Kaniku Dr., Kohala Coast, HI 96743. ☎ **800/845-9905** or 808/885-2000. Fax 808/885-1064. www. orchid-maunalani.com. 539 units. A/C MINIBAR TV TEL. $375–$625 double, $575–$655 Club-level double, from $575 suite. Extra person $50–$80; children 17 and under stay free in parents' room. AE, CB, DC, DISC, JCB, MC, V. Valet parking $5.

Located on 32 acres of oceanfront property, the Orchid is the place for watersports nuts, cultural explorers, families with children, or those who just want to lie back and soak up the sun. This elegant beach resort takes full advantage of the spectacular ocean views and historical sites on its grounds. The result: readers of *Condé Nast Traveler* magazine gave the Orchid the highest approval rating among Big Island resorts in 1997. The sports facilities here are extensive, and there's an excellent Hawaiiana program: The "Beach Boys" demonstrate how to do everything from creating drums from the trunks of coconut trees to paddling a Hawaiian canoe or strumming a ukulele.

We recommend spending a few dollars more to book a room with an ocean view, so you can watch that magnificent aqua blue surf roll into the white-sand beach. The spacious rooms feature big lanais, a sitting area, and marble bathrooms, each with a double vanity and separate shower.

Dining/Diversions: There are three restaurants to choose from: The Grille, the Orchid Court, and Brown's Beach House (see chapter 5), all with a casual, relaxed atmosphere (no need to pack your suit jacket).

Amenities: Two 18-hole championship golf courses, 10 tennis courts (7 lit for night play), swimming pools and whirlpools, a fine swimming cove, a well-equipped fitness center, excellent beach activities and watersports (including 2-hour complimentary use of equipment), historical sites, walking and jogging trails, 24-hour room service, twice-daily towel service, valet, nightly turndown, activity and car desk, business service center, children's program, and free shuttle within the resort.

EXPENSIVE

Hilton Waikoloa Village. 69-425 Waikoloa Beach Dr., Waikoloa, HI 96738. ☎ **800/HILTONS** or 808/886-1234. Fax 808/886-2900. www.hilton.com/hawaii/waikoloa/index.html. 1,240 units. A/C MINIBAR TV TEL. $250–$520 double, from $770 suite. Extra person $35; children 18 and under stay free in parents' room. AE, DC, DISC, JCB, MC, V.

This is a great place to bring the kids. It's not just another beach hotel (it actually has no real beach)—it's a fantasy world all its own, perfect for families, honeymooners, and everyone who loves Vegas and Disneyland. Its high-rise towers are connected by silver-bullet trams, boats, and museum-like walkways lined with Asian/Pacific reproductions. The kids will love it, but Mom and Dad may get a little weary waiting for the tram or boat to take them to breakfast. The 62 acres feature tropical gardens, cascading waterfalls, exotic wildlife, exaggerated architecture, a 175-foot waterslide twisting into a 1-acre pool, hidden grottos, and man-made lagoons. The biggest hit of all (for some) is the dolphin lagoon, where, if you're lucky enough to be selected by lottery, you can pay to swim with real dolphins. There are many other activities.

The recently updated, contemporary rooms are spacious and luxurious, with built-in platform beds, lanais, and loads of amenities, from spacious dressing areas with hair dryers and comfy bathrobes to coffeemakers and extensive minibars.

Dining/Diversions: There are plenty of bars and six restaurants to choose from, including Imari, for Japanese cuisine; the award-winning Donatoni's Italian Restaurant; and the Palm Terrace, for a family buffet. For everyday casual dining, try Hang Ten, the open-air cafe by the dolphin lagoon, or the Kamuela Provision Co., out on a prominent point. There's evening entertainment galore, including a Friday-night luau.

Amenities: 24-hour room service, business center, activities and car-rental desk, in-house doctor, American Express Travel desk, and self-service laundry. 25,000-square-foot spa with cardio machines and weights; three huge swimming pools; eight tennis courts; two championship 18-hole golf courses by Robert Trent Jones, Jr. and Tom Weiskopf; a mini shopping center; a fabulous children's program.

Outrigger Waikoloa Beach Resort. 69-275 Waikoloa Beach Rd., Kamuela, HI 96743. ☎ **800/922-5533** or 808/886-6789. Fax 808/886-7852. www.outrigger.com. 555 units. A/C MINIBAR TV TEL. $175–$227 double; $310 Royal Cabana Club double, $400–$775 suite. Extra person $25; children 17 and under stay free in parents' room. AE, CB, DC, DISC, JCB, MC, V.

In 1999, the Outrigger Resorts purchased this well-established resort and spent $23 million and five months redesigning and rebuilding it. This formerly "nice" beachfront hotel is now among the full-service, premier resorts of the Kohala Coast. It sits on one of the Kohala coast's best ocean sports bays—Anaehoomalu Bay (or A-Bay, as the locals call it). The gentle sloping beach has everything: swimming, snorkeling, diving, kayaking, windsurfing, and even old royal fishponds. Golfers will enjoy the adjacent Waikoloa Beach Course, designed by Robert Trent Jones, Jr., and the nearby Tom Weiskopf-designed Kings course.

3 Waimea

Belle Vue. Off Opelo Rd., P.O. Box 1295, Kamuela, HI 96743 ☎ and fax **808/885-7732.** www.hawaiinow.com/bellevue. 2 units. TV TEL. $85–$135 double. Extra person $20. AE, MC, V.

This two-story vacation rental truly has a beautiful view. Sitting in the hills overlooking Waimea and surrounded by manicured gardens, the Belle Vue is a charming home, just 15 minutes from the Kohala Coast beaches. Each unit has a separate entrance on each floor. The penthouse is a large cathedral-ceiling studio apartment with small kitchen, huge bedroom, luxurious bathroom, and a view of Mauna Loa and Mauna Kea mountains down to the Pacific Ocean. The one-bedroom apartment has a full kitchen, fireplace, and pull-out sofa bed.

Jenny's Country Cottage. Off Mamalahoa Hwy., 2 miles east of Waimea town center. Reservations c/o Hawaii's Best Bed and Breakfasts, P.O. Box 563, Kamuela, HI, 96743 ☎ **800/262-9912** or 808/885-4550. Fax 808/885-0559. www.bestbnb.com. 1 cottage. TV TEL. $95 double. Rate includes continental breakfast. Extra person $15. 2-night minimum. DISC.

This nearly century-old restored cottage, on a 4-acre farm with goats and a taro patch, has cheerful country appeal with hardwood floors and lace curtains, as well as a four-poster bed (a family heirloom) and other furniture made of rare koa wood; there's also a full kitchen. The host family lives on the property, as it has for generations.

Kamuela's Mauna Kea View Bed & Breakfast. P.O. Box 6375, Kamuela, HI 96743. ☎ **808/885-8425.** Fax 808/885-6514. wwww.hawaii-inns.com/bigisle/kohala/maunakea. 1 suite, 1 cottage (with shower only). TV TEL. $65 cottage double, $75 suite double. Rates include continental breakfast. Extra person $15. 2-night minimum. AE, MC, V. From junction of Hwy. 19 and Hwy. 190, continue east on Hwy. 19 for 3 miles; turn right on Kalake St.; it's the last house on the right.

This B&B has a great location. Retired Parker Ranch manager Richard Mitchell must've used his ranch connections to get this fabulous property, which borders Parker Ranch's 225,000 acres and looks straight up at 14,000-foot Mauna Kea. The 1,000-square-foot suite features two bedrooms, a full kitchen, a dining area, a living room with a fireplace (handy on chilly winter nights), a covered deck, and a Jacuzzi. The 440-square-foot cottage is a chalet-style studio with a separate, second sleeping area, kitchenette, and deck.

✪ **Waimea Garden Cottages.** Reservations c/o Hawaii's Best Bed and Breakfast, P.O. Box 563 (off Mamalahoa Hwy., 2 miles west of Waimea town center), Kamuela, HI 96743. ☎ **800/262-9912** or 808/885-0559. Fax 808/885-0559. www.bestbnb.com. 2 cottages. TV TEL. $135–$150 double. Rates include continental breakfast. Extra person $15. 3-night minimum. DISC.

Imagine rolling hills on pastoral ranch land. Then add a babbling stream. Now set two cozy Hawaiian cottages in the scene, and complete the picture with mountain views—and you have Waimea Garden Cottages. One cottage has the feel of an old English country cottage, with oak floors, a fireplace, and French doors opening onto a spacious brick patio. The other is a remodeled century-old Hawaiian wash house, filled with antiques, eucalyptus wood floors, and a full kitchen. Extra touches keep guests returning again and again, like the plush English robes, the sandalwood soaps in the bath, the mints next to the bed, and the fresh flower arrangements throughout. Hosts Barbara and Charlie Campbell live on the 1¹/₂-acre property; Barbara also runs Hawaii's premier B&B booking service, Hawaii's Best Bed & Breakfasts, and can set up your accommodations throughout the islands.

4 The Hamakua Coast

Luana Ola B&B Cottages. P.O. Box 430 (45-3474 Kawila St.), Honokaa, HI 96727. ☎ **800/357-7727** or 808/775-7727. Fax 808/775-0949. www.island-hawaii.com. 2 studio cottages (each sleeps up to 4; 1 cottage wheelchair accessible). TV TEL. $95 double. Rate includes continental breakfast. Extra person $18; children $10. 2-night minimum. MC, V. From Honokaa's main street, go makai (toward the sea) on Maile St.; take the 2nd left on Kawila St., and go 2 blocks to the cottages on the left.

These cottages are hard to find, but you'll be delighted once you do find them. They're tiny treasures off the tourist trail, at the end of a cul-de-sac in Honokaa town. The tin-roofed, plantation-style cottages are newly built in a romantic 1940s style and furnished in rattan and wicker. The 180°-views take in cane fields, the Hamakua coastline, the turquoise waters of the Pacific, the island of Maui across the channel, and some terrific sunsets. Check out the hut housing the laundry facilities—even it has a great view. Your genial hosts, Tim and Jeannie Mann (who live nearby) provide breakfast every morning. The town, within walking distance, is worth exploring for its Hawaiian craft shopping and genuine, unspoiled old Hawaii feeling.

○ **Waipio Wayside B&B Inn.** P.O. Box 840, Honokaa, HI 96727. ☎ **800/833-8849** or 808/775-0275. Fax 808/775-0275. www.stayhawaii.com/wayside.html. E-mail wayside@ilhawaii.net. 5 units (2 with shared bathroom). $95–$115 double. Rates include full breakfast. Extra person $25. MC, V. On Hwy. 240, 2 miles from the Honokaa Post Office; look on the right for a long white picket fence and sign on the ocean side of the road; the 2nd driveway is the parking lot.

Jackie Horne's restored Hamakua Sugar supervisor's home, built in 1938, sits nestled among fruit trees and surrounded with sweet-smelling ginger, fragile orchids, and blooming bird-of-paradise. The comfortable house, done in old Hawaii style, abounds with thoughtful touches, such as the help-yourself tea-and-cookies bar with 26 kinds of tea. A sunny lanai with hammocks overlooks a yard lush with five kinds of banana trees plus lemon, lime, tangerine, and avocado trees; a cliffside gazebo has views of the ocean 600 feet below. There are five vintage rooms to choose from: Our favorite is the master bedroom suite (dubbed the "bird's-eye" room) with double doors that open onto the deck; we also love the Library Room, which has an ocean view, hundreds of books, and a skylight in the shower. Jackie's friendly hospitality and excellent breakfasts (such as pesto scrambled eggs with blueberry muffins) really round out the experience.

5   Hilo

The Bay House. 42 Pukihae St., Hilo, HI 96720. ☎ and fax **808/961-6311.** E-mail thebayhouse@interpac.net. 2 units. TV. $95 double. Rates include continental breakfast. No credit cards.

Overlooking Hilo Bay, this brand-new bed and breakfast offers immaculate rooms (with oak wooden floors, king beds, sofas, TVs, private bath, refrigerator, microwave, coffeemaker, and ocean-view lanais) at reasonable prices. A continental breakfast (fruits, yogurt, hard boiled eggs, granola, muffins, and so on) is set out in a common area every morning; you can take all you want to eat back to your lanai and watch the sun rise over Hilo Bay. The only minus is that there are no laundry facilities (but there are plenty in nearby Hilo).

Dolphin Bay Hotel. 333 Iliahi St., Hilo, HI 96720. ☎ **808/935-1466.** Fax 808/935-1523. www.dolphinbayhilo.com. 18 units. TV TEL. $59–$69 studio single; $66–$76 studio double; $86 one-bedroom apt for 2; $98 two-bedroom apt. for 2. Extra person $10. From Hwy. 19, turn mauka (toward the mountains) on Hwy. 200 (Waianuenue St.), then right on Puueo St.; go over the bridge, and turn left on Iliahi St.

This two-story motel-like building, on a rise four blocks from downtown, is a clean, family-run property that offers good value in a quiet garden setting. Ripe starfruit hang from the trees, flowers abound, and there's a jungly trail by a stream. The tidy concrete-block apartments are small and often breezeless, but they're equipped with ceiling fans and jalousie windows. Rooms are brightly painted and outfitted with rattan furniture and Hawaiian prints. There are no phones in the rooms, but there's one in the lobby. You're welcome to all the papayas and bananas you can eat.

○ **Hale Kai Bjornen.** 111 Honolii Pali, Hilo, HI 96720. ☎ **808/935-6330.** Fax 808/935-8439. 5 units. TV. $90–$110 double. Rates include lavish gourmet breakfast. Extra person $15. 2-night minimum. No credit cards.

An eye-popping view of the ocean runs the entire length of the house. You can sit on the wide deck and watch the surfers slide down the waves. Staying here is like a visit to your favorite aunt and uncle's house. Only in this case your uncle is a Hawaiian who knows the island and its best deals inside and out (and will get on the phone to make sure you are treated like royalty). All the rooms have that fabulous ocean view through sliding glass doors. There's one suite, with living room, kitchenette, and separate bedroom. Guests have access to the pool, hot tub, large living room, bar room, and small family room with VCR, movies, small refrigerator, and library. For $3 a load, hostess Evonne will do your laundry. Breakfast is home-made macadamia nut waffles or banana pancakes.

Hawaii Naniloa Resort. 93 Banyan Dr. (off Hwy. 19), Hilo, HI 96720. ☎ **800/367-5360** or 808/969-3333. Fax 808/969-6622. www. planethawaii.com/sand/naniloa. 325 units. A/C TV TEL. $100–$240 double. Rates include airport shuttle. AE, CB, DC, DISC, JCB, MC, V.

Hilo's biggest hotel has nice rooms with lanais and enjoys a quiet, leafy Banyan Drive setting, with the ocean just across the road. There are restaurants and lounges, pools, a spa, and shops. Popular with Asian tour groups, this is a generally characterless place to stay but, in terms of comfort and amenities, it's one of the best that Hilo has to offer. The rack rates here are on the high side, but it's usually pretty easy to secure one of the cheapest rooms (which have only partial ocean views and no balconies). The general manager told us that getting a $100 room is usually not a problem, except during Merrie Monarch Hula Festival (the week after Easter).

○ **Shipman House Bed and Breakfast.** 131 Kaiulani St., Hilo, HI 96720. ☎ **800/627-8447** or 808/934-8002. Fax 808/935-8002. www. hilohawaii.com. E-mail bighouse@bigisland.com. 5 units. $140–$160 double. Rate includes continental breakfast and afternoon tea. Extra person $25. AE, MC, V. From Hwy. 19, take Waianuenue Ave.; turn right on Kaiulani St. and go 1 block over the wooden bridge; look for the large house on the left.

Built in 1900, the Shipman House is on both the national and state registers of historic places. This Victorian mansion has been totally restored by Barbara Andersen, the great-granddaughter of the original owner, and her husband Gary. Despite the home's historic appearance, Barbara has made sure that its conveniences are strictly 21st century: full baths with all the amenities, ceiling fans, and small refrigerators in each room (TVs are available on request). In addition to a large continental breakfast buffet, Barbara serves afternoon tea with nibbles on the enclosed lanai.

Uncle Billy's Hilo Bay Hotel. 87 Banyan Dr. (off Hwy. 19), Hilo, HI 96720. ☎ **800/367-5102** or 808/961-5818. Fax 808/935-7903. www.unclebilly.com. 144 units. A/C TV TEL. High season, $92–$112 double, $102–$112 studio with kitchenette; low season, $84–$104 double, $94–$104 studio with kitchenette. Car/room packages and special senior rates available. Extra person $10. Children 18 and under stay free in parents' room. AE, DC, DISC, MC, V.

Uncle Billy's is the least-expensive place to stay along Hilo's hotel row, Banyan Drive. This is an oceanfront budget hotel in a dynamite location, and the car/room package offers an extra incentive to stay here. You enter via a tiny lobby, gussied up Polynesian style; it's slightly overdone, with sagging fishnets and tapa-covered walls. The rooms are simple: bed, TV, phone, closet, and soap and clean towels in the bathroom—that's about it. The walls seem paper thin, and it can get very noisy at night (you may want to bring ear plugs), but at rates like these, you're still getting your money's worth. There's a pool on the property, and kitchenette studios are available.

6 Hawaii Volcanoes National Park & Volcano Village

Other excellent choices in Volcano include the ✪ **Guest House at Volcano** (☎ **808/967-7775;** fax 808/967-8295; www. volcanoguesthouse.com), a terrific cottage that rents for just $60 double. It's an ideal place to stay with the kids: completely childproofed and complete with toys, a basketball hoop, and a swing set. The upstairs bedroom has two twin beds and one queen, and the couch in the living room pulls out into a double bed. The room is outfitted with a full kitchen. There's even a forest trail in the backyard, which goes all the way through 2 miles of tropical rain forest to the Thurston Lava Tube in Hawaii Volcanoes National Park.

Hiiaka House (☎ **800/967-7960** or 808/967-7960; www.volcanoplaces.com) is a three-bedroom home from the 1930s that sleeps up to six. It's tucked in the rain forest and rents for $95 double (2-night minimum). The **Log Cabin** (☎ **808/262-7249**) is a century-old ohia log cabin for the young at heart, starting at $100. And there's the **Volcano Teapot Cottage** (☎ **800/ 670-8345** or 808/967-7112), a quaint, renovated, 1914, two-bedroom cottage decorated with one-of-a-kind antiques and renting for $105 double.

Volcano Area Accommodations

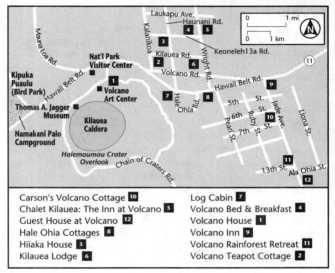

Carson's Volcano Cottage **10**	Log Cabin **7**
Chalet Kilauea: The Inn at Volcano **5**	Volcano Bed & Breakfast **4**
Guest House at Volcano **12**	Volcano House **1**
Hale Ohia Cottages **8**	Volcano Inn **9**
Hiiaka House **3**	Volcano Rainforest Retreat **11**
Kilauea Lodge **6**	Volcano Teapot Cottage **2**

EXPENSIVE

✪ **Chalet Kilauea: The Inn at Volcano.** P.O. Box 998 (off Hwy. 11, ³/₄ mile up Wright Rd.), Volcano, HI 96785. ☎ **800/937-7786** or 808/967-7786. Fax 800/577-1849 or 808/967-8660. www.volcano-hawaii.com. 6 units. TV TEL. $125–$395 double. Rates include full gourmet breakfast and afternoon tea. Extra person $15. AE, DC, DISC, JCB, MC, V.

Owner Brian Crawford and his wife, Lisha, may be the Conrad Hiltons of Volcano. Theirs was the first small property to get the prestigious triple Diamond Award from AAA. From the personal service at check-in to the afternoon tea to the rich two-course breakfast served on the finest china and linens, this place is worth the price (though it may be a bit formal for some). Nestled in the forest just a mile from Hawaii Volcanoes National Park, the inn features two rooms, three suites, and a separate elegant mountain cottage. These fabulous units are filled with art and furniture the Crawfords have collected during their travels. Most rooms have private hot tubs, but there's also a giant hot tub on the grounds.

In addition to this luxury B&B and two others (see below), Brian and Lisha Crawford have six vacation homes ranging in price from $125 a night for a two-bedroom cottage to $225 a night for a house that sleeps six. The homes are spacious and nicely furnished, and all have private phones, TV/VCRs, and fully equipped kitchens.

MODERATE

✪ **Carson's Volcano Cottage.** P.O. Box 503 (in Mauna Loa Estates, 501 Sixth St., at Jade Ave.), Volcano, HI 96785. ☎ **800/845-5282** or 808/ 967-7683. Fax 808/967-8094. www.carsonscottage.com. 3 units (with showers only), 6 cottages (3 with shower only). $95 double. $115–$185 cottages double. Rates include full breakfast. Extra person $15. AE, DISC, MC, V.

In 1988, friends of Tom and Brenda Carson came to visit from Alaska, so the Carsons renovated their 1925 tin-roofed cabin, under giant tree ferns in the rain forest, to accommodate them. That was the beginning of the Carson's B&B business, and today they're quite a success story. They have six units on their $1^1/2$ acres in the rain forest: three guest rooms with private entrances and private baths, done in Oriental, 1940s, and 1950s Hawaiiana themes; and three cottages, each with its own decor (Asian, American, and a quaint Victorian English cottage), plus another three houses in the neighborhood. The property also has a hot tub tucked under the ferns for guests' use. Several of the "deluxe" cottages even have their own hot tubs and free- standing fireplaces. Tom and Brenda serve a hearty breakfast in the dining room.

Kilauea Lodge. P.O. Box 116 (1 block off Hwy. 11 on Volcano Rd.), Volcano, HI 96785. ☎ **808/967-7366.** Fax 808/967-7367. www.planet-hawaii.com/ k-lodge. 12 units, 1 cottage. $110–$145 double. Rates include full breakfast. Extra person $15. AE, MC, V.

This crowded and popular roadside lodge, built in 1938 as a YMCA camp, sits on 10 wooded and landscaped acres. Its rooms offer heating systems and hot-towel warmers (Volcano Village is located at 3,700 feet), beautiful art on the walls, fresh flowers, and, in some, fireplaces. There's also a 1929 two-bedroom cottage with a fireplace and a full kitchen just a couple of blocks down the street. A full gourmet breakfast is served to guests only at the restaurant, which is open to the public for dinner.

INEXPENSIVE

Hale Ohia Cottages. P.O. Box 758 (Hale Ohia Rd., off Hwy. 11), Volcano, HI 96785. ☎ **800/455-3803** or 808/967-7986. Fax 808/967-8610. www. sugarnet.com/haleohia. 3 units, 3 cottages. $85–$125 double. Rates include continental breakfast. Extra person $15. CB, DC, DISC, MC, V.

Take a step back in time to the 1930s. Here you'll have the choice of three suites, all with private entrances, including one located in the main residence. There are also three guest cottages, ranging from one bedroom to three. The surrounding botanical gardens contribute to the overall tranquil ambiance of the estate. They were groomed in the 1930s by a resident Japanese gardener, who retained the natural volcanic terrain but gently tamed the flora into soothing shapes and designs. The lush grounds are just a mile from Hawaii Volcanoes National Park.

✪ **Volcano Bed & Breakfast.** P.O. Box 998 (on Keonelehua St., off Hwy. 11 on Wright Rd.), Volcano, HI 96785. ☎ **800/736-7140** or 808/967-7779. Fax 800/577-1849 or 808/967-8660. www.volcano-hawaii.com. 6 units (none with private bath). $45–$65 double. Rates include continental breakfast. Extra person $15. AE, DC, DISC, JCB, MC, V. From Hwy. 11, turn north onto Wright Rd.; go ¹/₂ mile; turn left on Keonelehua St.; the B&B is the 5th driveway on the right.

It's not as luxurious as Chalet Kilauea (see above), but this B&B (also owned by Brian and Lisha Crawford) is comfortable, clean, quiet, and quite a bargain. This restored 1912 historic home on its beautifully landscaped grounds is charming. The rooms are small, but Brian and Lisha have made sure that they're clean and inviting; all share bathrooms. The common rooms include a living room with TV/VCR and a piano, a reading room, and a sunroom. Hawaii Volcanoes National Park is just 5 minutes away.

Volcano House. P.O. Box 53 (Hawaii Volcanoes National Park), HI 96785. ☎ **808/967-7321.** Fax 808/967-8429. 42 units. TEL. $79–$105 double. AE, DC, DISC, JCB, MC, V.

Volcano House has a great location—and that's about all. This mountain lodge, which evolved out of a grass lean-to in 1865, is Hawaii's oldest visitor accommodation. It stands on the edge of Halemaumau's bubbling crater, and while its edgy view of the crater is still an awesome sight, the hotel has seen better days. The rooms have native koa-wood furniture, but service is inconsistent, and the lobby and public rooms look forlorn. This historic hotel deserves better. A novel treat: Rooms are heated with volcanic steam. A major drawback: The lodge is a major tour bus lunch stop. The food is edible but forgettable; you might want to stop for ohelo berry pie and coffee (or something stronger) at Uncle George's Lounge and bring it back to enjoy in front of the eerie crater.

Volcano Inn. Jade Ave./2nd St., Volcano. For reservations, write to 200 Kanoelehua Ave., Suite 103-301, Hilo, HI 96720. ☎ **800/628-3876** or 808/ 967-7773. Fax 808/967-8067. www.commercial-directory.com/volcano. 5 units (2 with shower only), 1 two-bedroom house. $55–$80 double, $95 for 4 in house. MC, V.

The Volcano Inn is the place to go for peace and quiet. All the units have exposed-beam ceilings and large windows overlooking a fern-tree forest. Cooking facilities in the rooms range from a breakfast bar to fully equipped kitchens. The one-bedroom cottage is perfect for families with children; not only does it have twin beds and a sleeping sofa in the living room, but it's stocked with puzzles and games. Volcano's two grocery stores are just a 5-minute drive away.

Volcano Rainforest Retreat. P.O. Box 957 (12th St., off Jade Ave.), Volcano, HI 96785. ☎ **800/550-8696** or 808/985-8696. E-mail volcanorainforest@ naturalhawaii.com. 3 units (1 with half bath). $95 double studio, $125–$155 double cottage. Rates include continental breakfast. 2-night minimum on cottages. Extra person $15. No credit cards.

This charming property is on an acre of fern-filled land. The guest cottage has a full kitchen, a sleeping loft, and a bathroom that looks right into the jungle. The eight-sided "Forest Hale" studio is a new addition with private forest entrance, queen bed, gas fireplace, kitchenette, skylight dome, and private bathroom. Another eight-sided building started out as a mediation house, but once guests saw it, they begged the Goldens to rent it out. The only drawback to this studio is the half-bath, but next door, open to the forest, is a handcrafted Japanese *furo* (hot tub) with an outdoor shower.

7 South Point

Becky's Bed & Breakfast at Naalehu. P.O. Box 673 (on Hwy. 11 in Naalehu Village, across from the Texaco Station), Naalehu, HI 96772. ☎ **800/235-1233** or 808/929-9690. Fax 808/929-9690. 3 units. TV. $65 double. Rates include full breakfast. MC, V.

Your evening respite at this charming restored doctor's home from 1937 will be a pleasant one. Becky and Chuck McLinn traded Alaska glaciers for volcanoes and the chance to welcome guests to Naalehu, a sleepy country village that happens to be the southernmost town in the United States. The rooms are fresh and comfy, and the McLinns are friendly country folks. Becky's is 64 miles south of Hilo and 56 miles south of Kailua-Kona on Hwy. 11—it's a perfect midway point for bicyclists on Circle Island treks.

✪ **Bougainvillea Bed & Breakfast.** P.O. Box 6045, Ocean View, HI 96737. ☎ **800/688-1763** or 808/929-7089. Fax 808/929-7089. E-mail peaceful@interpac.net. 4 units. $59 double. Rates include full breakfast. Extra person $15. 3% extra for credit cards. AE, CB, DC, DISC, MC, V.

Don and Martie Jean Nitsche bought this 3-acre property in the Hawaiian Rancho subdivision of Ocean View and had a *Field of Dreams* experience: They decided that if they built a bed-and-breakfast, people would come. Where some people just saw lava, the Nitsches saw the ancient Hawaiian path that went from the mountain to the sea. So they built. And out of the lava came gardens—first colorful bougainvillea, then flowers, a pineapple patch, then a fishpond to add to the pool and hot tub. A satellite for TV reception was added. Word got out. Martie's breakfast—her secret-recipe banana-nut pancakes, plus sausage, fruit, and coffee—drew people from all over. Things got so good, they had to add more rooms (all with their own private entrances) and expand the living room (complete with TV/VCR and video library) and dining room. Guests usually take their breakfast plates and sit on the lanai to look at the ocean view.

✪ **Macadamia Meadows Bed & Breakfast.** 94-6263 Kamaoa Rd., Naalehu, HI 96772. ☎ **888/929-8118** or 808/929-8097. Fax 808/929-8097. www.stayhawaii.com/macmed/macmed.html. 3 units. TV. $75–$120. Rates include continental breakfast. Extra person $15, children $10. AE, JCB, MC, V.

Near the most southern point in the United States and just 45 minutes from Volcano National Park lies one of the Big Island's most welcoming bed-and-breakfast accommodations. It's located on an 8-acre working macadamia nut farm, in a great place for star-gazing. The warmth and hospitality of hosts Charlene and Cortney Cowan is unsurpassed: each guest is treated like a favorite relative. The accommodations include a two-bedroom suite, a private room, and a honeymoon suite, which has an antique claw-foot tub on a private lanai. All rooms have private entrances and cable TV. Guests can use the full tennis court and in-ground swimming pool. Charlene had her own cleaning business for 20 years, so the facilities are immaculately clean. Laundry costs $2.50 a load.

✪ **South Point Banyan Tree House.** At Hwy. 11 and Piano St., Waiohinu. c/o Greg & Janette LeGault, Nature's Nitche, HC1-778, Gurney, WI 54559. ☎ **888/451-0880** or 715/893-2419. www.ifb.com/hawaii-banyan/. 1 cottage. TV. $110 double, $135 for 4. 2-night minimum. No credit cards.

Couples looking for an exotic place to nest should try this treehouse, nestled inside a huge Chinese banyan tree. The cottage comes complete with see-through roof that lets the outside in and a comfy, just-for-two hot tub on the wraparound deck. Inside, there's a queen bed and a kitchen with microwave, two-burner stove, refrigerator, and coffeemaker. The sweet scent of ginger brings you sweet dreams at night, and the twitter of birds greets you in the morning.

5

Dining

by Jocelyn Fujii

*T*he Big Island's cuisine is anchored in its fertile soil and the labors of its tireless farmers and fishermen. The island has produced its share of celebrity chefs, but it's also known for its home-style flair and its abundance of small neighborhood ethnic restaurants, especially in Hilo. You'll find an extraordinary diversity of dining choices here. Every time we visit the island of Hawaii, we sing praises to the kitchen gods as we make plans for the next day's hike, a necessary sequel to the typical day's culinary excesses.

Dining here has become an authentic island attraction, rather than an afterthought. The volcanic soil of the island continues to produce fine tomatoes, lettuce, beets, beans, fruit, and basic herbs and vegetables that were once difficult to find locally. Along with the lamb and beef from Big Island ranches and seafood from local fishermen, the freshness of the produce forms the backbone of ethnic cookery and Hawaii Regional Cuisine.

Among the star chefs who claim their roots here, or who have cut their teeth on the island, are Peter Merriman (the visionary behind the eponymous Merriman's in Waimea), Sam Choy (the Kona chef who prepares local food with a gourmet twist), and Alan Wong (who put the Mauna Lani's CanoeHouse on the map before moving to open his own place, now Honolulu's most popular). They are just a few of the hugely talented artists who have honed and shaped Hawaii Regional Cuisine, giving it culinary muscle and credibility.

Kailua-Kona is teeming with restaurants for all pocketbooks; although most of them are touristy and many overpriced, there are some recommendable restaurants in town. Hopes run high for the Keauhou Beach Resort in Kailua, soon to open (at this writing) with Sam Choy at the helm of all food and beverage operations, including a signature Sam Choy restaurant. The new Huggo's On the Rocks on Alii Drive, adjoining Huggo's, is the local hot spot, a sunset oasis with beach chairs, mai tais, and sizzling appetizer menu for the barefoot-in-the-sand crowd. Nearby on Alii Drive, the new Coconut Grove Marketplace, a stone's throw from the waves, is the hub for all ages, with the very popular Lu Lu's and a seawall lined with under-25s at sunset. Next door to the Grove, Lava Java in the Alii Sunset Plaza is abuzz with javanistas on their way to or from the new Hard Rock Café.

The haute cuisine of the island is concentrated in the Kohala Coast resorts, where the 3-year-old Hualalai Resort and its tony Four Seasons Resort at Hualalai, the Mauna Lani Bay Hotel and Bungalows, the Orchid at Mauna Lani, the Mauna Kea Beach Hotel, and the Hapuna Beach Prince Hotel claim their share of the action for deep pockets and special-occasion tastes.

Waimea, also known as Kamuela, is a thriving upcountry hot spot, a haven for yuppies and retirees who know a good place when they see one. Two new restaurants have sprouted in Waimea, including Parker Ranch Grill, a meat-and-potatoes place in the Parker Ranch Center. It opened too recently for us to visit, but initial reports were not good. In Hawi, North Kohala, expect bakeries, neighborhood diners, and one tropical-chic restaurant. In Hilo in eastern Hawaii, you'll find pockets of trendiness among the precious old Japanese and ethnic restaurants that provide honest, tasty, and affordable meals in unpretentious surroundings.

In the listings below, reservations are not required unless otherwise noted.

1 The Kona Coast

IN & AROUND KAILUA-KONA

Note: Hualalai Club Grille, Pahu i'a, and Beach Tree Bar & Grill are located north of Kailua-Kona in North Kona, just south of the Kohala Coast.

EXPENSIVE

Chart House. Waterfront Row, 75-5770 Alii Dr. ☎ **808/329-2451.** Reservations recommended. Main courses $16.50–$31. Seafood at market price. AE, DC, DISC, MC, V. Sun–Thurs 5–9:30pm, Fri–Sat 5–10pm. STEAK/SEAFOOD.

The Chart House formula–baked potato, salad bar, steak, prime rib, and seafood—endures in this open-air restaurant on Kailua Bay. The view is paramount, and the filet mignon, catch of the day, lobster choices, and familiar surf-and-turf offerings keep this popular chain restaurant among the Kona institutions. But Chart House has added to the formula a few new favorites, including filet mignon with brandy cabernet sauce, ponzu shrimp, and shrimp coconut. The mud pie (Kona coffee ice cream, a chocolate wafer crust, fudge, almonds, and whipped cream) is famous.

Edward's at Kanaloa. The Kanaloa at Kona, 77-261 Manukai St. ☎ **808/ 322-1003.** Reservations recommended. Main courses $16.50–$30. AE, DC, MC, V. Daily 8am–2pm, 5–9pm; bar open 8am–9pm. MEDITERRANEAN.

If you're willing to drive the 10 extra minutes south from Kona to Keauhou, this stellar spot, located on a breathtaking point at the ocean, could very well make your day. Edward's at Kanaloa (it's the dining room for the Kanaloa condominiums) is an oasis without walls, where you can look for whales and dolphins and take in the ocean breeze over an excellent ragout of mushrooms, or salmon or shrimp with angel-hair pasta and exotic glazes. The macadamia nut–banana waffle is a hit at breakfast. At lunch, try the salade Niçoise, a mound of fresh local greens topped with 4 ounces of fresh, grilled ahi. At lunch or dinner, Edward's is known for innovative selections in fresh fish, grains, and mushrooms.

Hualalai Club Grille. In the Hualalai Resort, Queen Kaahumanu Hwy., Kaupulehu-Kona. ☎ **808/325-8525.** Reservations recommended. Lunch main courses $10–$14, dinner main courses $18–$32. AE, CB, DC, JCB, MC, V. Daily 11am–3pm, bar menu served 3–9pm, dinner 5–9pm. PACIFIC RIM.

The Grille is a part of the golf clubhouse, but even non-golfers make a special trip to the open-air dining room for lunch and dinner. The food is excellent. Start with the Kona lobster and shrimp cake with a sweet chili glaze, roasted corn relish, and lemon butter. The onion flower in Cajun aïoli, a signature item, is a flamboyant dazzler. Fresh fish in several presentations competes with the brick-oven pizzas, and the choice isn't easy. Toppings such as Italian sausage, rock shrimp, Kona lobster, and smoked duck are a cut above standard pizzas, and so are the sandwiches and pasta. At dinner, tuck into pan-seared ahi, local lobster, seafood, lamb chops, and other meats (perhaps even ostrich) and then sit back for some after-dinner entertainment or an occasional impromptu hula by friends.

✪ **Huggo's.** 75-5828 Kahakai Rd. ☎ **808/329-1493.** Reservations requested. Main courses $7.95–$13.95 at lunch, $19.95–$36.95 at dinner. AE, CB, DC, DISC, JCB, MC, V. Mon–Fri 11:30am–2:30pm and 5:30–10pm, Sat–Sun 5:30–10pm (light menu Mon–Fri 11:30am–10pm. PACIFIC RIM/SEAFOOD.

The main Huggo's dining room still hums with diners murmuring dreamily about the view, but it's the new thatched-bar fantasy that's *really* on the rocks. Huggo's On the Rocks, a mound of thatch, rock, and grassy-sandy ground right next to Huggo's, is a sunset-lover's nirvana. At sunset, On the Rocks is choked with people either on chaises or at the 50-seat, square thatched bar, sipping mai tais and noshing on pizza, poke, or kalua chicken–quesadillas. Island-style pupus are offered here from 11:30 to 10pm. At the senior Huggo's, fresh fish remains the signature, as does the coral-strewn beach with tide pools just beyond the wooden deck. The tables are so close to the water you can see the entire curve of Kailua Bay. Nosh on Kona Caesar salad with Waimea greens, quesadillas, burgers, pizza, prime-rib sandwiches, hot dogs, and the fresh catch for lunch. The evening's offerings feature specialties such as ono with rock shrimp and garlic-basic aïoli, pan-charred ahi, pasta, and prime rib.

Kona Inn Restaurant. In the Kona Inn Shopping Village, 75-5744 Alii Dr. ☎ **808/329-4455.** Reservations recommended at dinner. Main courses $12.95–$22.95; Cafe Grill $4.95–$10.95. AE, MC, V. Cafe Grill daily 11:30am–10:30pm; dinner menu served daily 5:30–10:30pm. AMERICAN/SEAFOOD.

Even in a string of waterfront restaurants, the Kona Inn stands out. The large, open terrace on the ocean and panoramic view of the Kailua shoreline are its most attractive features, especially for sunset cocktails and appetizers. Touristy as the place is (it's impossible not to be, in Kona), it still delivers decent fresh seafood for lunch and dinner, from sandwiches to grilled and sautéed entrees. The ubiquitous seafood, sandwiches, and salads dominate the Cafe Grill menu; the more upscale dinner menu is heavier on pricier fresh catches, chicken, and steaks. Watch for the daily specials on the Cafe Grill menu.

La Bourgogne. Hwy. 11 (3 miles south of Kailua-Kona). ☎ **808/329-6711.** Reservations required. Main courses $18.50–$30. AE, CB, DC, DISC, MC, V. Mon–Sat 6–10pm. CLASSIC FRENCH.

Come to this cozy French inn to satisfy your Gallic urgings. An intimate inn of 10 tables, La Bourgogne serves classic French fare with simple, skillful elegance. Baked Brie in puff pastry, a classic onion soup, the fresh catch of the day (market price), venison in sherry and pomegranate glaze, and a straightforward selection of French offerings give La Bourgogne a special distinction. Osso bucco, formerly an occasional special, has been added to the menu by popular demand while steamed New Zealand mussels, in a broth of apple cider, thyme, shallots, cognac, and a hint of cream, are a welcome addition to the roster of specials. Chef Ron Gallaher, a classically trained French cook, expresses his allegiance to *la cuisine Française* down to the last carefree morsel of crème brûlée, chocolate Grand Marnier soufflé, cherries jubilee, baked caramel apple, and chocolate mousse.

Pahu'a. In Four Seasons Resort at Hualalai, Queen Kaahumanu Hwy., Kaupulehu-Kona. ☎ **808/325-8000.** Reservations recommended. Breakfast

$9–$23.50, dinner main courses $19–$43. AE, DC, DISC, MC, V. Daily 6–11:30am (buffet 7–11:30am) and 5:30–10pm. FRESH ISLAND SEAFOOD/ INTERNATIONAL.

A small bridge leads to the oceanfront dining room, where views on three sides expand on the aquatic theme (*pahu i'a* is Hawaiian for "aquarium," and there's a large one at the entrance). Executive chef Michael Goodman, who can be seen cycling along the hotel's pathways in his toque and crisp white uniform, loves seafood and features the rare *moi* (threadfish, a Hawaiian delicacy), caught fresh daily from aquaculture pools on the premises. Guests begin their day here with the excellent breakfast buffet, the coast's most elegant presentation of omelets, meats, fresh fruit and regional specialties. On the à la carte menu, the vegetarian sampler is gourmet fare (black bean salsa with slices of fresh asparagus, spinach, and mushrooms). At dinner, part of the menu changes daily and always includes several fresh seafood preparations, while Asian influences prevail on the rest of the menu.

Sam Choy's Restaurant. In the Kaloko Light Industrial Park, 73-5576 Kauhola St. ☎ **808/326-1545.** Reservations recommended for dinner. Main courses $4.50–$9 at lunch, $17.95–$30 at dinner. DISC, MC, V. Mon–Sat 6am–2pm, Tues–Sat 5–9pm, Sun 7am–2pm. HAWAII REGIONAL.

An informal atmosphere, humongous servings, and high-volume local food with a gourmet twist are the Sam Choy trademarks. His restaurant, recently doubled in size, has turned a nondescript industrial area into a dining mecca. Hearty breakfasts and lunchtime favorites include fried poke, saimin, bentos made to order, and burgers. Choy's legendary dinners include seafood laulau, his signature dish of fresh fish with julienned vegetables and seaweed, wrapped and steamed with spinach in a pouch of ti leaves. Among other classics are an old-fashioned rib-eye steak with sautéed onions, Chinese-style honey duck, sautéed pork loin, and unforgettable mashed potatoes. Keep in mind that the servings, always too big for mere mortals, can astonish the uninitiated. Thank goodness there's a children's menu. On the other side of Kailua-Kona, in the Keauhou Beach Resort, Choy is, at this writing, poised to open a new eatery that will include the Big Island Open Farmer's Market Buffet, featuring the products of Big Island farmers and ranchers.

MODERATE

✪ **Beach Tree Bar and Grill.** In the Four Seasons Resort at Hualalai, Queen Kaahumanu Hwy., Kaupulehu-Kona. ☎ **808/325-8000.** Reservations recommended for dinner. Main courses $9.75–$15. AE, CB, DC, JCB, MC, V. Daily 11am–8pm. CASUAL GOURMET.

Here is an example of outstanding cuisine in a perfect setting—without being fancy, expensive, or fussy. The thatched bar on the sand is a sunset paradise, and the sandwiches, seafood, and grilled items at the casual outdoor restaurant (a few feet from the bar) are in a class of their own—simple, excellent, prepared with imagination and no shortcuts. The menu, the same for lunch and dinner, features the MLT (wild mushrooms, lettuce, and tomato sandwich with roasted eggplant and a hint of pesto), a brilliant vegetarian take on the BLT; an albacore tuna sandwich that merits space on the postcard home; coconut marinated chile prawns; and grilled catch of the day as sandwich or entrée. You could thrive on the appetizers alone. The Saturday evening barbecue on the beach is frequently sold out, with guests lining up at the flaming grills and bountiful tables of fish, oysters, and clams. An added attraction: entertainment from 5 to 8pm nightly.

Bianelli's Pizza. Pines Plaza, 75-240 Nani Kailua Dr. ☎ **808/326-4800.** Reservations recommended for dinner. Pizzas $8.95–$22.95; main courses $7.95–$22.95. CB, DC, DISC, MC, V. Mon–Fri 11am–10pm, Sat–Sun 5–10pm. PIZZA/ITALIAN.

This is Kona's finest pizza, made with wholesome ingredients and cheeses and no sacrifice in flavor. Everything is fresh: the herbs—straight from the farmers—the handmade dough, the homemade pasta, the organic lettuces and produce. The full bar features an international beer selection, including the local Kona Brew. The sensational Ricotta pizza is dripping with garlic, Parmesan, and ricotta, yet it's 40% less fatty than most pizzas. The house specialty, the Buffala, is redolent with garlic and buffalo-milk mozzarella. Bianelli's delivers everything on the menu except alcoholic beverages.

Cassandra's Greek Taverna. 75-5719 Alii Dr. ☎ **808/334-1066.** Main courses $12.95–$28.95. AE, DISC, JCB, MC, V. Mon–Sat 11:30am–2:30pm and 5–10pm, Sun 5–9pm. GREEK.

Saunter over to this indoor-outdoor cafe for an outstanding Greek salad, melt-in-your-mouth pita bread, and perfectly seasoned spanakopita and stuffed grape leaves. Other choices include scallop-stuffed mushroom caps and prawns uvetsi, a Mediterranean fantasy baked with fresh tomatoes, spinach, and feta cheese. Whether you're up for moussaka or pasta, comfort-food casseroles or plain old steak and lobster, you'll find a menu of cross-cultural delights here.

Kona Ranch House. Hwy. 11 (at the corner of Kuakini and Palani). ☎ **808/329-7061.** Reservations recommended for dinner. Complete breakfast from $5.25, lunch $5.95, dinner $9.95. AE, DC, DISC, MC, V. Daily 6:30am–9pm. AMERICAN.

The Kona Ranch House remains the local favorite for its good quality and high value. The turn-of-the-century plantation-style decor is as comfortable as the cuisine, which includes children's menus and generous, inexpensive platters of steak, shrimp, pork, ribs, and chicken. There's breakfast, too, with hefty favorites that include eggs Benedict and its crab counterpart, with tomatoes and onions. The family-style dining menu includes stews, spaghetti, and broiled fish for less than $11, plus sandwiches. In the wicker-accented Plantation Lanai, ranch-house favorites—complete steak, seafood, and prime-rib dinners for less than $20—are big sellers and still a value, especially when accompanied by the cornbread, baked beans, and mashed potatoes. Another plus: the service, always friendly.

Lu Lu's. In the Coconut Grove, 75-5819 Alii Drive. ☎ **808/331-2633.** Reservations not accepted. Main courses $9.95–$13.95. AE, DISC, MC, V. Daily 11am–10pm, appetizers until midnight, bar until 2am. AMERICAN.

This place is casual, noisy, and corny (black velvet paintings at the entrance!), but it's popular as heck, with open-air dining, ocean views, and international flags waving cheerily in the breeze on the wraparound deck. At night, fairy lights add a festive touch. It's kitschy—there are concrete floors, capiz-shell lamps, clam-shell sconces, and a life-size cartoon of a hula girl—but it's basically a sports bar and restaurant, with television sets galore and a billiards table in the mauka (inland) corner. The offerings: appetizers, sandwiches, salads, burgers, burrito ("as big as your head"), fresh fish tacos, and fresh fish and meats in the evening. Okay for certain folks, but not for romantics in search of a quiet, intimate evening.

✪ **Oodles of Noodles.** In the Crossroads Shopping Center (Ste. 102), 75-1027 Henry St. ☎ **808/329-9222.** Noodle dishes $7–$25. AE, DC, JCB, MC, V. Mon–Sat 10am–9pm, Sun 10am–8pm. NOODLES.

Udon, cake noodles, saimin, ramen, spaghetti, orzo, somen, spring rolls, chow mein, linguine, vermicelli—you name it, you'll find it here. If you're looking for the world's best macaroni and cheese, saimin made with Peking duck broth, summer rolls, Pad Thai chicken, coconut tapioca, or shaved ice with fresh fruit or azuki beans, go no further than Oodles of Noodles. The former executive chef at the Hotel Hana Maui and the former Ritz-Carlton Mauna Lani, Amy Ferguson-Ota hit upon a winning concept: creative noodle dishes from all over the world, served informally and affordably. East meets West here, with everything from dim sum to saimin to Vietnamese pho, summer rolls, and pasta in all incarnations. Creative sauces, broths, and eclectic presentations in Ota's inimitable style carry the menu—everything tasty and from scratch. Pizza takes a bow on the menu too, with mushrooms, pesto, Peking duck, grilled chicken with red onion and mozzarella, and other fusion toppings.

Quinn's Almost By the Sea. 75-5655A Palani Rd. ☎ **808/329-3822.** Main courses $7–$19. MC, V. Mon–Sat 11am–2am, Sun 11am–midnight. STEAK/ SEAFOOD.

Quinn's, located at the northern gateway to town, is a great place to stop at for decompression after coming in from the airport. Pleasant without being overwhelming, Quinn's offers casual alfresco dining in a garden lanai that takes advantage of the balmy Kona weather. The menu covers all the bases: steak, seafood, and vegetarian fare. From the pier across the street comes fresh fish, prepared several ways and served with salad, vegetables, and potatoes or rice. Fresh ahi sandwiches are among the lunchtime values.

Tropics Café. Royal Kona Resort, 75-5852 Alii Drive. ☎ **808/329-3111.** Reservations recommended. Buffets $16.95–$21.50. AE, DC, JCB, MC, V. Daily 6:30–10:30am, 6–9pm. THEME BUFFETS.

If you're a buffet-basher, read no further. But if terrific ocean views and top-value buffets appeal to you, Tropics is a find. The Royal Kona Resort's circular, high-ceiling dining room is on the water, with stunning views of the Kailua coastline and a surprisingly pleasant seafood buffet. You'll sit on plastic lanai chairs at the edge of the terrace, but you'll be so close to the water that you won't notice. Tako and fish poke, snow crab, mahimahi, prime rib, lomi salmon, peel-and-eat shrimp, clams, seafood pasta, roasted potatoes, and a large salad bar are some of the offerings at the seafood buffet on Friday evenings. Pasta and steak, shrimp tempura, and Asian food are featured on weeknights, but it's the seafood buffet that draws the crowds.

INEXPENSIVE

For an inexpensive meal, also consider the more casual room at the **Kona Inn Restaurant,** the Cafe Grill (see "Expensive," above).

Basil's Pizzeria. 75-5707 Alii Dr. ☎ **808/326-7836.** Individual pizzas $5.95– $9.95; main courses $7.95–$14.95. JCB, MC, V. Daily 11am–10pm. PIZZA/ ITALIAN.

Two dining rooms seat 100 in a garlic-infused atmosphere where pizza is king, sauces are sizzling, and pasta is cheap. The ocean-view restaurant is redolent with the smells of cheeses, garlic, zesty sauces, and fresh organic herbs (a big plus). Shrimp pesto and the original barbecue-chicken pizzas are long-standing favorites, and so is the artichokes-olive-capers version, a Greek-Italian hybrid.

Kona Coffee Mania!

Despite ups and downs in coffee prices, coffeehouses are booming on the Big Island. Why not? This is, after all, the home of Kona coffee, and it's a wide-open field for the dozens of vendors competing for your loyalty and dollar. Although we often wince at the plethora of T-shirts and mugs that make up the visual merchandising of the coffee world, it seems to come with the turf. Kona coffee co-ops, offering steaming cups of fresh brew or coffee by the bag to go, are ubiquitous.

The real activity, though, is concentrated in the North and South Kona districts, where coffee remains a viable industry. Here are some names to watch for. ✪ **Bong Brothers** (☎ 808/ 328-9289) thrives with its coffees, roadside fruit stand, B&B, and natural-foods deli that sells smoothies and healthy foods that feature local produce. Aficionados know that **Langenstein Farms** ☎ 808/328-8356), a name associated with quality and integrity, distributes excellent Kona coffee and macadamia nuts in the town of Captain Cook. ✪ **Rooster Farms** (☎ 808/328-9173), in Honaunau, has an excellent reputation for the quality of its organic coffee beans. The **Kahauloa Coffee Company,** Highway 11 in Captain Cook (☎ 808/328-9555), sells its own coffee and coffee beans in a gift shop adjoining its wonderful open-air deli, The Coffee Shack. Stop for a final boost before the long drive down and around the south end of the island; although the deli is fairly new, Kahauloa coffees have been around for 25 years. South Kona also has the **Royal Aloha Coffee Mill** (☎ 808/328-9851), the largest coffee cooperative around, with 300 farmers. The **Bad Ass Coffee Co.** has franchises in Kainaliu, Kawaihae, Honokaa, Keauhou, and two locations in Kailua-Kona, all selling its 100%

Ocean View Inn. 75-5683 Alii Dr. ☎ **808/329-9998.** Main courses $7.50–$10.75. No credit cards. Tues–Sun 6:30am–2:45pm and 5:15–9pm. AMERICAN/ CHINESE/HAWAIIAN.

The Hawaiian food, rare in this town, and the local color are reason enough to come here, although the quality of the food is less than outstanding. But you can't beat the prices, and the Ocean View Inn is as much a Kona fixture as the sunsets that curl around Kailua Pier across the street. Give it a go if you feel like trading your

Kona as well as coffees from Molokai, Kauai, and other tropical regions.

In Holualoa, upcountry from Kailua-Kona, the ✪ **Holualoa Kona Coffee Company** (☎ **808-322-9937**) purveys organic Kona: unsprayed, hand-picked, sun-dried, and carefully, precisely roasted. Not only can you buy premium, unadulterated Kona coffee here, but you can also witness the hulling, sorting, roasting, and packaging of beans from 8am to 4pm weekdays. Also in this upcountry village, the **Holuakoa Cafe,** Highway 180 (☎ **808/322-2233**), is famous for its high-octane espresso at a deli owned by Meggi Worbach, who grinds fresh-roasted pure Kona beans from Holualoa.

In Waimea, the ✪ **Waimea Coffee Company,** Parker Square, Highway 19 (☎ **808/885-4472**), a deli/coffeehouse/retail operation, is a whirl of activity. Coffee is heady stuff here: pure Kona from Rooster Farms, pure organic from Sakamoto Estate, pure water-processed decaf—an impressive selection of the island's best estate-grown coffees. The homemade quiches, sandwiches, and pasta specials are wholesome and affordable, drawing a lively lunch-time crowd. Island-made gourmet foods (pastas, muffin mixes, dipping oils) make great gift baskets, and local Hawaii artists display their work on the walls.

A good bet in Hilo is **Bears' Coffee,** 106 Keawe St. (☎ **808/935-0708**), the quintessential sidewalk coffeehouse. In this world of fleeting pleasures, Bears' is a Hilo stalwart that has weathered storms and sunny days, good times and bad. Regulars love to start their day here, with coffee and specialties such as souffléed eggs, cooked light and fluffy in the espresso machine and served in a croissant. It's a great lunchtime spot as well.

gourmet standards for serviceable food in a casual and endearing atmosphere. Stew and rice, roast pork, a vegetarian selection, and local staples such as shoyu chicken and broiled ahi appear on a menu with dozens of Chinese dishes. A refreshing change, definitely, from the more touristy waterfront eateries, but don't expect epicurean fare.

Sibu Cafe. In Banyan Court, 75-5695 Alii Dr. ☎ **808/329-1112.** Most items less than $12. No credit cards. Daily 11:30am–3pm and 5–9pm. INDONESIAN/ SOUTHEAST ASIAN.

An affordable favorite for many years, Sibu offers curries, homemade condiments, and a very popular, spicy, grilled Balinese chicken served with peanut sauce. Other great choices: garlic shrimp with pasta, vegetable curry, Indonesian-style shrimp laksa (with vegetables, rice noodles, coconut milk, lemongrass, and spices); and beef sate. Weekday lunch specials are a good value: $6.25 buys you the Kona Combo, a spring roll, chicken or beef satay, vegetable stir-fry, and a cucumber salad with rice. For $5.95 you can order a vegetarian combo or a small gado gado (actually a large Indonesian salad). The Indonesian decor, courtyard dining, and excellent *sates* (traditional grilled skewers of vegetables, seafood, and meats), are the Sibu signature. The larger combination plates pamper all palates, while the vegetable curries and stir-fries appeal to vegetarians. Top off your order with the homemade three-jalapeño, red-chile, or spicy coconut condiment (or all three). Wine and beer are available; no white sugar or MSG on the premises.

Thai Rin. 75-5799 Alii Dr., Kona. ☎ **808/329-2929.** Main courses $6.95–$12.95. AE, DC, DISC, JCB, MC, V. Sun–Fri 11am–2:30pm, nightly 5–9pm. THAI.

Kona's most popular Thai eatery offers more than great curries and spicy salads. Because everything here is made to order, virtually any item can be prepared for vegetarians. Most popular are the pad Thai noodles, spicy *tom yum kung* (spicy, sweet-sour lemongrass soup with shrimp), curries (red, green, yellow, and panang), bountiful salads, and spring roll appetizers. Stunning sunset and ocean views are a part of the deal. Patchara Suntharo, owner and manager, grows many of her own herbs, including basil, mint, lemongrass, kaffir lime leaves, and the Thai ginger called *kalanga*.

SOUTH KONA

Aloha Cafe. Hwy. 11, Kainaliu. ☎ **808/322-3383.** Reservations recommended for large parties. Most items less than $7 daytime, $6.50–$17.95 evenings. MC, V. Mon–Thurs 8am–3pm, Fri–Sat 8am–9pm, Sun 8am–2pm. ISLAND CUISINE.

There have been changes in the menu, but the Aloha Cafe's trademarks remain: large portions, the best carrot cake in the area, heroic burgers and sandwiches, and a mix of items for vegetarians and carnivores. Place your order at the counter and grab a seat on the veranda that wraps around the old Aloha Theatre. The view sweeps down the coffee fields to the shoreline. The cheaper daytime staples include omelets, breakfast burritos, tostadas, quesadillas, and home-baked goods. Most of the produce is organic, and fresh-squeezed orange juice and fresh-fruit smoothies are served daily. Sandwiches, from fresh fish to tofu-avocado, are heaped with vegetables on tasty whole-wheat buns, still generous after all these years.

The Coffee Shack. Hwy. 11 (1 mile south of Captain Cook). ☎ **808/ 328-9555.** Most items less than $6.75. AE, MC, V. Mon–Sat 7am–5pm. COFFEEHOUSE/DELI.

Great food, crisp air, and a sweeping ocean view make the Coffee Shack one of South Kona's great finds. It's an informal place, with counter service, pool chairs, and white trellises on the deck framed by ferns, palms, and banana trees. A cheerful assortment of imported beers; excellent sandwiches on home-baked breads; and fresh, hearty salads made with organic lettuces are only a few of the taste treats. Let the kids order peanut-butter-and-jelly or grilled-cheese sandwiches while you head for the smoked Alaskan salmon sandwich (on whole wheat, French, rye bread or focaccia) or the hot corned-beef Reuben with sauerkraut, cheese, and a tangy Russian dressing. The breakfast pizza is inches high and topped with cheese, juicy-fresh mushrooms, olives, ruby-red tomatoes, and artichoke hearts. Not a bad start to the day, especially on the charming wooden deck near a towering old tree that droops with the weight of its avocados. Next door in the gift shop and coffee-tasting room, you can sample some of the many 100% Kona coffees grown and sold here.

✪ **Keei Cafe.** Hwy. 11 (about 25 minutes south of Kailua). ☎ **808/328-8451.** Main courses $9–$16. No credit cards. Tues–Sat 5–9pm. MEDITERRANEAN/ LATINO/ISLAND.

Formerly Stan's Fishmarket, the Keei Cafe is the darling of this coastline. It's the restaurant farthest south from Kailua before you hit the South Point area on the main highway, and people drive long distances to get here. A friendly ambiance, great food, and affordable prices are only part of its appeal; we only wish it were open for lunch. The concrete floors, plastic chairs, and nine tables create a quirky setting, highlighted by local art. The menu roams the globe, from sashimi from local fishermen down the road to Greek food and Thai specials. The fresh catch and grilled chicken are highlights, sometimes accompanied by caramelized onions and whipped potatoes. Everything is made from scratch, and virtually everything is grown or harvested in the Honaunau Valley area—meats from the local butcher, fish from down the street, tomatoes grown down the road. Save room for dessert: the bread pudding and coconut flan, made by the owner's mother-in-law from Portugal, are to die for.

⭐ **Manago Hotel Restaurant.** In the H. Manago Hotel, Hwy. 11, Captain Cook. ☎ **808/323-2642.** Reservations recommended for dinner. Main courses $6.50–$11.50. DISC, MC, V. Tues–Sun 7–9am, 11am–2pm, and 5–7:30pm. AMERICAN.

The dining room of the decades-old H. Manago Hotel is a local legend, greatly loved for its unpretentious, tasty food at family prices. At breakfast, $4.50 buys you eggs, bacon, papaya, rice, and coffee. At lunch or dinner, you can dine handsomely on local favorites: a 12-ounce T-bone, fried ahi, opelu, or the house specialty, pork chops, for $10.75 and less. Manago T-shirts announce "the best pork chops in town": the restaurant serves 1,300 pounds monthly. When the akule or opelu are running, count on a rush by the regular customers. This place is nothing fancy, mind you, and there's a lot of frying going on in the big kitchen, but the local folks would riot if anything changed after so many years.

Ted's Kona Theater Cafe. Hwy. 11 (across from the Captain Cook Post Office), Captain Cook. ☎ **808/328-2244.** Most items less than $7, dinners $8.50–$14.95. No credit cards. Tues–Sun 7:30am–3:30pm; Fri–Mon 5–9pm. MEDITERRANEAN.

More commonly known as the Kona Theater Cafe, this place is famous for its award-winning, made-from-scratch garden burger. It's phenomenal—perfectly seasoned, with a sprinkling of dates, served with banana chutney on homemade bread. You can have the veggie burger at breakfast, too, in the $6.25 Farmer John's special with three eggs and other choices. The fresh-fish, baked chicken, and vegetarian plate lunches are other legends in the area, but you can also order Italian and Greek specialties, such as pasta marinara and Greek chicken. Although there are vegetarian choices aplenty, meat roasts and lamb pita are available too—and the fresh catch, including the fresh ahi sandwich, is a find. All sandwiches are served with local organic lettuce, onions, tomatoes, and sprouts.

Teshima's. Hwy. 11, Honalo. ☎ **808/322-9140.** Reservations recommended for large parties. Complete dinners $14.95 and less. No credit cards. Daily 6:30am–1:45pm and 5–9pm. JAPANESE/AMERICAN.

This is local style all the way. Shizuko Teshima has a strong following among those who have made her miso soup and sukiyaki a local staple. The early-morning crowd starts gathering while it's still dark for omelets or Japanese breakfast (soup, rice, and fish). As the day progresses, the orders pour in for shrimp tempura and sukiyaki. By dinner, Number 3 teishoku trays—miso soup, sashimi, sukiyaki, shrimp, pickles, and other delights—are streaming out of the kitchen; at $12.25, it's a steal. Other combinations include steak and shrimp tempura; beef teriyaki and shrimp tempura; and the deep-sea trio of shrimp tempura, fried fish, and sashimi. Original art hangs on the walls of the elongated dining room.

2   The Kohala Coast

✪ **Batik.** In the Mauna Kea Beach Hotel, Kawaihae. ☎ **808/882-7222.** Reservations required; collared shirts with buttons all the way down the front are required. Prix fixe $65 and $75. AE, DC, JCB, MC, V. Sun, Mon, Wed–Fri 6–9pm. EURO-ASIAN.

This is a room of hushed tones and great restraint, with dark-wood ceilings, sedate (and loyal) guests, and sensitive lighting—a shrine to fine dining. Executive chef Goran Streng is doing a first-rate job of showcasing the agricultural products of the island and his finely honed culinary skills. The artichoke salad is one of many standouts on the appetizer menu. Other choices: Maine lobster and avocado napoleon; ahi carpaccio; crisp salmon with saffron pepper; grilled mahimahi with tomato-seaweed-herb sauce; fresh local flounder in a ginger-sesame glaze; and a favorite held over from previous menus, the fresh snapper with Kona mushrooms and lobster ragout. If your tastes run hotter, the curry selection has expanded. Naan bread from the tandoori oven comes warm and fresh.

Brown's Beach House. In The Orchid at Mauna Lani, One North Kaniku Drive. ☎ **808/885-2000.** Reservations recommended for dinner. Main courses $25–$37. AE, DC, DISC, MC, V. Daily 11:30am–5pm, 6:30–10pm. HAWAII REGIONAL.

David Reardon, executive chef of The Orchid at Mauna Lani, quickly turned this new dining room into a household word on the Kohala Coast. Take your pick from lobster-taco appetizers, mango–black bean crab cakes, free-range chicken in kaffir lime, blackened ahi with wasabi mashed potatoes, herb-crusted moonfish, orange-horseradish–crusted salmon, and jumbo sea scallops cradled in Szechwan pepper. Informal, with an open-air room that takes in the ocean view, Brown's takes full advantage of the Kohala Coast sunsets.

Cafe Pesto. Kawaihae Shopping Center, at Kawaihae Harbor, Pule Hwy. and Kawaihae Rd. ☎ **808/882-1071.** Main courses $6.95–$16.95. AE, DC, DISC, MC, V. Mon–Thurs 11am–9pm, Fri–Sat 11am–10pm. PIZZA/ITALIAN.

You can always count on Cafe Pesto to serve fresh organic greens, sizzling sauces on great pizza crust, and world-class dressings. Fans drive long miles to this harborside pizza house for gourmet pizzas, calzones, and fresh organic greens grown from Kealakekua to Kamuela. Lobsters from the aquaculture farms on Keahole Point (south on the coastline); shiitake mushrooms from a few miles mauka (inland); and fresh fish, shrimp, and crab adorn the herb-infused Italian pies. Honey-miso crab cakes, Santa Fe chicken pasta, sweet roasted peppers, and herb-garlic Gorgonzola dressing are favorites.

✪ **CanoeHouse.** In the Mauna Lani Bay Hotel and Bungalows. ☎ **808/ 885-6622.** Reservations recommended. Main courses $27–$48. AE, CB, DC, DISC, JCB, MC, V. Daily 5:30–9:30pm. HAWAII REGIONAL.

Dining at the CanoeHouse is like living in a Don Blanding sketch—sunsets, stars, rustling palm fronds, waves lapping a few feet away from the terrace. In the open-air dining room, a koa canoe hangs from the ceiling. Corked decanters on the table hold soy sauce and chili water, two staples of modern local culture that Alan Wong, who opened CanoeHouse, thrust into gourmet status. Lobster tempura, baby-back ribs, and nori-wrapped ahi remain staples here, but there are always new surprises. Seafood is a good bet, but if you'd like a change, try the hibachi-grilled chicken in sesame vinegar.

Coast Grille. In the Hapuna Beach Prince Hotel. ☎ **808/880-3011.** Reservations recommended. Main courses $20–$36. AE, DC, JCB, MC, V. Daily 6–9:30pm. STEAK/SEAFOOD/HAWAII REGIONAL CUISINE.

You'll work up an appetite during the 3-minute walk from the main lobby to the open-air Grille, but the view is nothing to complain about. The split-level dining room has banquettes and wicker furniture. The wide seafood selection includes fresh oysters, poke, and clams at the Oyster Bar, as well as such pleasures as pistachio-crusted opah, aquacultured *moi* (threadfish), Kona lobster tempura sushi, and the best clam chowder on the coast. The Grille features only the finest cuts of beef, lamb, and veal.

✪ **Roy's Waikoloa Bar & Grill.** 250 Waikoloa Beach Dr., Waikoloa Beach Resort. ☎ **808/886-4321.** Main courses $7.95–$13.75 at lunch, $21.95–$26.95 at dinner; prix-fixe menu $37.95. AE, DC, DISC, JCB, MC, V. Daily 11:30am–2pm, 5:30–9:30pm. PACIFIC RIM/EURO-ASIAN.

Despite its location in a shopping mall, Roy's Waikoloa has several distinctive features: a golf course view, large windows looking out over part of a 10-acre lake, and the east-west cuisine and upbeat service that are the Roy Yamaguchi signatures. This is one of the stellar clones of his Oahu restaurant, with the signature dishes we have come to love: Szechwan baby-back ribs, blackened island ahi, and at least six other types of fresh fish prepared charred, steamed, seared, and topped with exotic sauces of shiitake miso and gingered lime-chile butter. Always in demand are the roasted wild mushroom polenta gratin and the four-cheese, sun-dried tomato ravioli. Yamaguchi's tireless exploration of local ingredients and traditions from around the world produces food that keeps him at Hawaii's culinary edge.

The Terrace. In the Mauna Kea Beach Hotel, Kawaihae. ☎ **808/882-7222.** Reservations recommended. Sunday buffet $29.50. AE, DC, JCB, MC, V. Sun 11am–2pm. BUFFET LUNCH.

The Mauna Kea introduced the concept of the lavish luncheon buffet decades ago and continues the tradition in the Terrace, the most casual of its restaurants. Sunday brunch is still an occasion, with a cornucopia of salads, gourmet breakfast items (eggs Benedict, fresh omelets, Belgian waffles), cheeses, salads, American classics (prime rib, sautéed fresh catch, roast turkey, sautéed chicken), pasta, seafood (sashimi, shrimp cocktail, crab claws), and local favorites (shrimp and vegetable tempura, sushi).

3 North Kohala

Bamboo. Hwy. 270, Hawi. ☎ **808/889-5555.** Reservations recommended. Main courses $8.95–$20.95 (full- and half-size portions available). DC, JCB, MC, V. Tues–Sat 11:30am–2:30pm and 6–9pm, Sun 11am–2pm (brunch). PACIFIC RIM.

Serving fresh fish and Asian specialties in a turn-of-the-century building, Hawi's self-professed "tropical saloon" is a major attraction on the island's northern coastline. The exotic interior is a nod to nostalgia, with high wicker chairs from Waikiki's historic Moana Hotel, works by local artists, and old Matson liner menus accenting the walls. The fare, island favorites in sophisticated presentations, is a match for all this style: imu-smoked pork quesadillas, fish prepared several ways, sesame nori-crusted or tequila-lime shrimp, and herb-roasted leg of lamb. Produce from nearby gardens and fish fresh off the chef's own hook are among the highlights. At Sunday brunch, diners gather for eggs Bamboo (eggs Benedict with a lilikoi-hollandaise sauce) and the famous passion-fruit margaritas. Hawaiian music wafts through the Bamboo from 7pm to closing on weekends. Next door is a gallery of furniture and arts and crafts, some very good and most locally made.

Jen's Kohala Café. Hwy. 270, Kapaau, in front of the King Kamehameha Statue. ☎ **808/889-0099.** Main courses $2.50–$5.75. MC, V. Daily 10am–6pm. GOURMET DELI.

Jen's is loved for its healthy fare and made-with-care wraps. Fresh soups and salads, homemade burgers and veggie burgers, an award-winning black-bean and red-onion chili served with fresh homemade corn bread—it's all good stuff. But most in demand are Jen's wraps, herb-garlic flatbread filled with local organic baby greens and vine-ripened organic tomatoes, with cheese and various fillings. The Kamehameha Wrap (Jen's is across the street from the famous statue) features kalua pork, two different cheeses, and a Maui onion dressing; There are about 30 seats indoors and a few outdoors.

ICE CREAM

Kohala Coffee Mill and Tropical Dreams Ice Cream. Hwy. 270, Hawi. ☎ **808/889-5577.**

No longer under a single ownership, Tropical Dreams ice creams are spreading out over the island. North Kohala is where the line began. Across the street from Bamboo, this coffee shop serves the upscale ice creams along with a wide selection of island coffees, including 100% Kona. Jams, jellies, herb vinegars, Hawaiian honey, herbal salts, and macadamia nut oils are among the gift items at the Coffee Mill. The ice creams at Bamboo, Sam Choy's, the Kohala Coast resorts, and most Kohala Coast restaurants are made by Tropical Dreams.

4 Waimea

Aioli's. Opelo Plaza, Hwy. 19. ☎ **808/885-6325.** Lunch main courses $3.95–$8.95, dinner main courses $11.95–$17.95. MC, V. Tues–Thurs 11am–8pm, Fri–Sat 11am–9pm, Sun 8am–2pm. AMERICAN ECLECTIC.

Most of the breads for the sandwiches are homemade, the turkey is roasted in Aioli's own kitchen, the prices are reasonable, and on Saturday mornings, the scent of fresh-baked cinnamon rolls wafts through the neighborhood. Specialty salads, homemade cookies and desserts, and daily hot sandwich specials (fresh catch on fresh bread can hardly be beat!) have kept the diners coming. The evening bistro menu changes every two weeks; recent offerings include herb-crusted Black Angus prime rib with baked potato and vegetables, grilled shrimp marinated in herbs and citrus, mahimahi en papillote, lemon chicken, and vegetarian items. It's an informal room, with patio chairs on tile.

Edelweiss. Kawaihae Rd. ☎ **808/885-6800.** Lunch $6.50–$10.50; complete dinners $17.50–$46 (most around $21). MC, V. Tues–Sat 11:30am–1:30pm and 5–9pm. CONTINENTAL.

Diners with a hankering for Wiener schnitzel, bratwurst, sauerkraut, Black Forest cake, and richly adorned fowl and meats are known to drive all the way from Kona and Hilo for the traditional German offerings at this chalet-like bistro. The upscale ranch burgers and chicken aux champignons may require siesta time after lunch, but they do have a following. In the evening, complete dinners include sautéed veal, rack of lamb, roast pork, roast duck, and other continental classics. Although heavy on the meats and sauces, and certainly not a magnet for vegetarians or folks on a low-fat diet, Edelweiss has anchored itself firmly in the hearts of Hawaii islanders. "We do not believe in all these changes," sniffs chef/owner Hans Peter Hager. "When you enjoy something, you come back for it." The menu has barely changed in his 14 years in Waimea, and the tables are always full, so who's arguing? Edelweiss is closed every September for 5 weeks.

Koa House Grill. Hwy. 19. ☎ **808/885-2088.** Reservations suggested. Sandwiches $6.50–$7.95, dinner main courses $12.50–$29.95. MC, V. Mon–Sat 11am–11pm, Sun 10am–11pm. AMERICAN.

Waimea's newcomer is paniolo-themed (what in Waimea isn't?) and popular, with dark paneled walls, a large window looking out over the chef's herb garden, and pictures of paniolo filling the walls. At lunch, the catch of the day and the fresh fish sandwich, with garlic, lemon, and spicy chipotle aioli, are good values. Even with the all-American items (burgers and Philly-style prime rib sandwich), the Pacific Rim influence prevails: There's seared ahi with wasabi-lilikoi vinaigrette, lilikoi barbecue spare ribs, and fresh fruit glazes on the meats and fish. There are four specials a night, fresh fish daily, grilled steaks galore, roasted chicken, pastas, and a salad bar in the evening. We found the food quality to be uneven, but here's hoping that the kinks have been worked out.

The Little Juice Shack. Parker Ranch Shopping Center, Hwy. 19. ☎ **808/885-1686.** Most items less than $5.25. No credit cards. Mon–Fri 7am–6pm, Sat 9am–4pm. JUICE BAR/DELI.

The smoothies and sandwiches here are wholesome and the produce fresh, green, and varied. All juices are made fresh to order: orange, pear, apple, pineapple, carrot, tomato, and many combinations, including vegetable drinks and spirulina powder to order. Smoothies (Bananarama, Nutty Monkey, Hawaii 5-0) are witty, creamy, and healthy, made with low-fat yogurt milk. Bagels and luscious toppings (pesto, smoked salmon, tapenade); vegetarian chili; and hearty soups, salads, and sandwiches (Thai curry vegetable soup, Greek salad, local organic spinach salad, ahi-tuna sandwich) are guiltless and guileless. *Tip:* When locally grown ✪ **Ka'u oranges** are in season, they're used for the fresh-squeezed orange juice—the best. Mainland fruit is a last resort here.

✪ **Maha's Cafe.** Spencer House, Hwy. 19. ☎ **808/885-0693.** Main courses $6–$13.50. MC, V. Wed–Mon 8am–4:30pm. COFFEEHOUSE/SANDWICHES.

The smallest kitchen on the island—the size of a closet, literally—serves impressive sandwiches in a tiny, wood-floored room of Waimea's first frame house, built in 1852. Harriet-Ann Namahaokalani (Maha) Schutte, who cut her culinary teeth in a large Hawaiian family before making her mark at Mauna Lani Resort's Knickers, dispenses hotcakes and granola for breakfast, delectable sandwiches at lunch, and cookies all day long. The menu reads like a map of the island: smoked-ahi sandwiches with lilikoi salsa, fresh roasted turkey with mushroom stuffing and squaw bread, fresh fish with Waipio taro and Kahua greens, vine-ripened tomatoes with locally made feta cheese and bread made from Waimea sweet corn. Lunch has never been grander, served at cozy wooden tables on lauhala mats and enlivened with a sublime pesto, tangy with a hint of green olive. At the other end of the room is Cook's Discoveries (see "Shops & Galleries," in chapter 7).

✪ **Merriman's.** Opelu Plaza, Hwy. 19. ☎ **808/885-6822.** Reservations recommended. Lunch main courses $5.95–$14.95, dinner main courses $12.95–$22.95 (market price for ranch lamb or ahi). AE, MC, V. Mon–Fri 11:30am–1:30pm, daily 5:30–9pm. HAWAII REGIONAL.

In Waimea and throughout the island, Merriman's is peerless. Although founder/owner/chef Peter Merriman now commutes between the Big Island and Maui, where he runs the Hula Grill, he has managed to maintain the sizzle that made Merriman's a premier Hawaii attraction. Order anything from saimin to poisson cru for lunch, and for dinner, Merriman's signature wok-charred ahi, grilled scallops *ume* (plum), kung pao shrimp, lamb from nearby Kahua Ranch, and a noteworthy selection for vegetarians. Peter's Caesar with sashimi, Pahoa corn and shrimp fritters, and his sautéed, sesame-crusted fresh catch with spicy lilikoi sauce are among our many favorites. An organic spinach salad (like most things on the menu, grown nearby), Lokelani tomatoes, goat cheese and kalua pig quesadillas, and his famous platters of seafood and meats are among the many reasons Merriman's is *the* dining spot in Waimea.

5   The Hamakua Coast

Cafe Il Mondo. Mamane St., Honokaa. ☎ **808/775-7711.** Pizzas $7.50–$17.25; sandwiches $3.95–$4.50; pasta $7.95. AE, MC, V. Mon–Sat 11am–9pm. PIZZA/ESPRESSO BAR.

A tiny cafe with a big spirit has taken over the Andrade Building in the heart of Honokaa. Tropical watercolors and local art, the irresistible aromas of garlic sauces and pizzas, and a 1924 koa bar meld gracefully in Sergio and Dena Ramirez' tribute to the Old World. A classical and flamenco guitarist, Sergio plays solo guitar regularly in his restaurant and often rehearses with his group, Adaggio Latino, while contented drinkers tuck into the stone oven–baked pizzas. The vegetable pizza, Waipio, is a best seller, but the Sergio—pesto with marinated artichokes and mushrooms—is the one folks remember. Sandwiches come cradled in fresh French, onion, and rosemary buns, all made by local bakeries. Fresh pasta has been added to the menu, and all greens are fresh, local, and organic.

Jolene's Kau Kau Korner. At Mamane St. and Lehua, Honokaa. ☎ **808/775-9498.** Plate lunches $5.95–$7.95, dinner main courses $7.95–$18.95. MC, V. Mon– Wed and Fri 10am–8pm, Thurs, Sat 10am–3pm. AMERICAN/LOCAL.

It's homey and friendly, with eight tables and windows that look out into a scene much like an old Western town, but for the cars. The Hawaiian food has been dropped from the menu, leaving us with saimin, sandwiches (including a good vegetarian tempeh burger), and plate lunches—mahimahi, fried chicken, shrimp, beef stew, and familiar selections of local food. Nothing fancy, although Jolene's has upped the choices (and prices) for dinner, with New York steak, chicken katsu, combination "kau kau plates," and the usual American fare with a local twist, such as the shrimp tempura/New York steak special.

Mamane Street Bakery. Mamane St., Honokaa. ☎ **808/775-9478.** Most items less than $3. MC, V. Mon–Sat 7am–5:30pm. BAKERY/CAFE.

Honokaa's gourmet bake shop serves espresso, cappuccino, sandwiches, and snacks, including a legendary focaccia. Most sandwich lovers on the island have tasted their breads, because the Mamane Street Bakery also wholesales breads and pastries, including its well-known burger buns, to the island's most prominent eateries. Portuguese sweet bread and honey-nut muffins are the big sellers in this easygoing, informal coffeehouse with lower-than-coffeehouse prices: Breads sell for $2.25 to $2.95, but most pastries are less than $1.25. Very Honokaa: no marble, wing tips, or pretense, but danishes to die for.

Simply Natural. Mamane St., Honokaa. ☎ **808/775-0119.** Deli items $3–$6. JCB, MC, V. Mon–Sat 9am–4pm, Sun 10am–4pm. HEALTH FOOD/SANDWICH SHOP.

Simply Natural is a superb find on the main street in Honokaa. We love this charming deli, with its friendly staff, delicious food, and vintage interior. It offers a counter and a few small tables with bright tablecloths and fresh anthuriums. Don't be fooled by the unpretentiousness of the place; we had the best smoked chicken sandwich we've ever had here. The owner's mother proudly displayed the gloriously plump whole chicken, smoked by her neighbor in Honokaa, before slicing and serving it on freshly baked onion bread from the Big Island Bakery. The menu is wholesome, with no sacrifice in flavor: sautéed mushroom/onion sandwich with salad, tempeh burger, veggie-mushroom sandwich, avocado sandwich, and breakfast delights that include taro-banana pancakes. You can choose between squaw, onion, or rosemary bread and top it off with premium ice creams by Hilo Homemade (another favorite). The place is connected to Decorative Arts, the gallery/shop next door where koa artist and gifted furniture maker Susan Sanders can be found.

Tex Drive In & Restaurant. Hwy. 19, Honokaa. ☎ **808/775-0598.** Main courses $5.95–$8.25. CB, DC, DISC, MC, V. Daily 6am–8:30pm. AMERICAN/LOCAL ETHNIC.

When Ada Lamme bought the old Tex Drive In, she made significant changes, including improving upon an ages-old recipe for Portuguese *malassadas,* a cake-like doughnut without a hole. Tex sells close to 50,000 of these sugar-rolled morsels a month, including malassadas filled with pineapple/papaya preserves, pepper jelly, or Bavarian cream. The menu has a local flavor and features ethnic specialties: Korean chicken, teriyaki meat, kalua pork with cabbage, and Filipino specials. Hamburgers, on buns by Mamane Street Bakery, are a big seller. Many changes are planned for this roadside attraction, including a large new retail store/coffee bar that will carry Hawaiian crafts, local coffees and gift items, and, in a nod to her native Holland and Honokaa's large Portuguese community, European chocolates, Dutch wooden shoes, and fine pottery from Portugal.

What's Shakin'. 27-999 Old Mamalahoa Hwy. (on the 4-mile scenic drive), Pepeekeo. ☎ **808/964-3080.** Most items less than $6.95; smoothies $3.65–$4. No credit cards. Daily 10am–5:30pm. HEALTH FOOD.

Look for the cheerful plantation-style wooden house in yellow and white, with a green roof, 2 miles north of the Hawaii Tropical

Botanical Garden. This is where many of the bananas and papayas from Patsy and Tim Withers' 20-acre farm end up: in fresh-fruit smoothies with names like Papaya Paradise, an ambrosial blend of pineapples, coconuts, papayas, and bananas. If you're in the mood for something more substantial, try the Blue Hawaii blue-corn tamale with homemade salsa, or the teriyaki-ginger tempeh burger (made with the best tempeh in the world, by Lean Green Foods of Hilo). Every plate arrives with fresh fruit and a fresh green salad topped with Patsy's Oriental sesame dressing. You can sit outdoors in the garden, where bunches of bananas hang for the taking and the ocean view is staggering.

6 Hilo

EXPENSIVE

Pescatore. 235 Keawe St. ☎ **808/969-9090.** Reservations recommended for dinner. Main courses $6.95–$11.95 at lunch, $15.95–$28.95 at dinner. CB, DC, MC, V. Daily 11am–2pm; Sun–Thurs 5:30–9pm, Fri–Sat 5:30–10pm. SOUTHERN ITALIAN.

This is a special-occasion restaurant, dressier and pricier than the standard neighborhood cafe or mom-and-pop diner. It's ornate, especially for Hilo, with gilded frames on antique paintings, chairs of vintage velvet, koa walls, and a tile floor. The fresh catch is offered five ways, from reduced-cream and Parmesan to capers and wine. The paper-thin ahi carpaccio is garnished with capers, red onion, garlic, lemon, olive oil, and shaved Parmesan—and it is superb. Chicken, veal, and fish Marsala, a rich and garlicky scampi Alfredo, and the Fra Diavolo, a spicy seafood marinara, are the headliners on a long and satisfying menu. At lunch, pasta marinara is simple and satisfying and rivals the chicken Parmesan as one of the values of the day.

MODERATE

Harrington's. 135 Kalanianaole. ☎ **808/961-4966.** Reservations recommended. Lunch main courses $6.25–$14.75, dinner main courses $15.50–market price. MC, V. Mon–Fri 11am–2:30pm; Mon, Tues, Thurs–Sat 5:30–9:30pm, Sun 5:30–9pm. SEAFOOD/STEAK.

The house specialty, thinly sliced Slavic steak swimming in butter and garlic, is part of the old-fashioned steak-and-seafood formula that makes the Harrington's experience a predictable one. The meunière-style fresh catch, sautéed in white wine and topped with a lightly browned lemon-butter sauce, is popular, but it's not for the calorie-conscious. Lobster, scallops in chardonnay sauce, chicken

Marsala, and New York peppercorn steak are among the American classics on this conscience-busting menu. The strongest feature of Harrington's is the tranquil beauty of Reeds Pond (also known as Ice Pond), one of Hilo's visual wonders. With the open-air restaurant perched on the pond's shore, the ambiance eclipses the menu.

Nihon Restaurant & Cultural Center. Overlooking Liliuokalani Gardens and Hilo Bay, 123 Lihiwai St. ☎ **808/969-1133.** Reservations recommended. Main courses $8.95–$19.95. AE, CB, DC, DISC, MC, V. Mon–Sat 11am–1:30pm, 5–8pm. JAPANESE.

The room offers a beautiful view of Hilo Bay on one side and the soothing green sprawl of Liliuokalani Gardens on the other. This is a magnificent part of Hilo that's often overlooked because of its location away from the central business district. The reasonably priced menu features steak-and-seafood combination dinners and selections from the sushi bar, including the innovative poke and lomi salmon hand rolls. In the "Businessman's Lunch," you make two choices from among butterfish, tempura, sashimi, chicken, and other morsels, and they come with sushi, potato salad, soup, and vegetables—all for $10.95. This isn't inexpensive dining, but the return on your dollar is high, with a presentation that matches the serenity of the room and its stunning view of the bay.

Ocean Sushi Deli. 239 Keawe St. ☎ **808/961-6625.** Sushi boxes $3.75–$19.95; all-you-can-eat sushi lunch $15.95; all-you-can-eat sushi dinner $19.95; sushi family platters $16.95–$43.95. MC, V. Daily 9am–9pm. SUSHI.

My goodness, it can be busy. We tried three times before we finally got in, but then we returned as soon as we could. Lines down the street announced the popularity of this tiny take-out sushi shop, Hilo's newest sensation. And no wonder. The sushi is good, inexpensive, and imaginative. Local-style specials stretch purist boundaries but are so much fun: lomi salmon, oyster nigiri, opihi nigiri, unagi avocado hand roll, ahi poke roll. For traditionalists, there are ample shrimp, salmon, hamachi, clam, and other sushi delights—a long menu of them, including handy ready-to-cook sukiyaki and shabu-shabu sets.

Queen's Court Restaurant. Hilo Hawaiian Hotel, 71 Banyan Dr. ☎ **808/935-9361.** Reservations recommended. Wed and Fri Hawaiian lunch buffet 11:15am–1:15pm, $12.50; Mon–Thurs prime rib/crab buffet $22.50; Fri–Sat seafood buffet $25.50; Sun Hawaiian seafood buffet $24.25, Sun brunch 10:30am–1:30pm, $22.50; breakfast buffet 6–9:30am Mon–Sat, Sun 6:30–9am, $9.50. AE, DC, DISC, MC, V. Dinner buffets daily 5:30–9pm. AMERICAN/BUFFET.

Many of those with a "not me!" attitude about buffets have been disarmed by the Hilo Hawaiian's generous and well-rounded offerings at budget-friendly prices. À la carte menu items are only offered Monday to Thursday, but the Hawaiian, seafood, and Dungeness-crab/prime-rib buffets throughout the week, particularly the seafood buffet, cover the bases and draw throngs of local families. Hawaiian food lovers also come for the Wednesday and Friday Hawaiian lunch buffet. The weekend seafood buffets are generous.

Restaurant Miwa. In the Hilo Shopping Center, 1261 Kilauea Ave. ☎ **808/ 961-4454.** Reservations recommended. Main courses $8.75–$36.50. AE, CB, DC, DISC, JCB, MC, V. Mon–Sat 11am–2pm and 5–10pm; Sun 5–9pm. JAPANESE.

Duck around a corner of the shopping center and discover sensational seafood in this quintessential neighborhood sushi bar. This self-contained slice of Japan is a pleasant surprise in an otherwise unremarkable shopping mall. Shabu-shabu (you cook your own ingredients in a heavy pot), tempura, fresh catch, and a full sushi selection are among the offerings. The top-of-the-line dinner, the steak-and-lobster combination, is a splurge you can enjoy without dressing up. Some items, such as the fresh catch, may be ordered American style. The haupia (coconut pudding)–cream-cheese pie is a Miwa signature, but is not offered daily; blueberry cream-cheese is the alternative.

✪ **Seaside Restaurant.** 1790 Kalanianaole Hwy. ☎ **808/935-8825.** Reservations recommended. Main courses $10.50–$20. DC, MC, V. Tues–Sun 5–8:30pm. AMERICAN/LOCAL.

How fresh are the trout, catfish, mullet, golden perch, and *aholehole*, the silvery mountain bass devoured passionately by island fish lovers? Fished out of the pond shortly before you arrive, that's how fresh. The restaurant has large windows overlooking the glassy ponds that spawned your dinner, so you can't be sentimental. Colin Nakagawa raises the fish and cooks them in two unadorned styles: steamed in ti leaves with lemon juice and onions, or fried. Daily specials include steamed opakapaka, onaga, or parrot fish; steak and lobster; paniolo-style prime rib; salmon encrusted with a nori-wasabi sprinkle; New York steak; and shrimp. The fried *aholehole*, which often sells out, has been known to lure diners on the next plane from Honolulu. You must call ahead, so your order can be fished from the ponds and whisked from kitchen to table. With children's portions at $6.95 to $7.95 for a complete dinner (rice, salad, hot vegetable, and dessert), and free tours of the surrounding aquaculture ponds between 9am and 3pm, this is a terrific stop for families.

INEXPENSIVE

✪ **Cafe Pesto Hilo Bay.** In the S. Hata Building, 308 Kamehameha Ave. ☎ **808/969-6640.** Pizzas $6.95–$17.95. AE, CB, DC, DISC, JCB, MC, V. Mon–Thurs 11am–9pm, Fri–Sat 11am–10pm. PIZZA/PACIFIC RIM.

The Italian brick oven burns many bushels of ohia and kiawe wood to turn out its toothsome pizzas, topped with fresh organic herbs and island-grown produce. The high-ceilinged 1912 room, with windows looking out over Hilo's bayfront, is filled with seductive aromas. It's difficult to resist the wild mushroom–artichoke pizza or the chipotle and tomato-drenched Southwestern, but go with the Four Seasons—dripping with prosciutto, bell peppers, and mushrooms, it won't disappoint. Other personal favorites are the Milolii, a crab-shrimp-mushroom sandwich with basil pesto; the smoked salmon minipizza appetizer; the chili-grilled shrimp pizza; and the flash-seared poke salad on a bed of spinach. There are many raves on this tried-and-true menu.

Canoes Cafe. In the S. Hata Building, 308 Kamehameha Ave. ☎ **808/935-4070.** Most items less than $6.95. CB, DC, DISC, MC, V. Mon–Sat 7:30am–3pm, Sun 10am–2pm. SANDWICH/AMERICAN.

Totally hip and totally Hilo, Canoes does all the right things: it uses fresh organic produce, keeps the food quality up and the prices down, and serves zesty, homemade dressings and bread fresh from the bakery next door. Tandoori chicken, five-cheese, BLT, the Hilo Paddler grinder (lean roast beef, pastrami, or ham), and the Kamehameha Italian deli grinder sandwich (salami, ham, Maui onion, cheeses, the works) are among the imaginative offerings. You can try any of seven sandwich creations—and they *are* creations. From roast beef to turkey to vegetarian, the sandwiches are made with homemade mayonnaise, mustard, and dressings on rye, sour-dough French, focaccia, herbed carrot, or whole-grain bread. Don't be intimidated by the unfamiliar names (Ihoe Wa'akau, Puna Ihoe)—these are American classics, the familiar made new with Hilo ingredients. There are only a few tables and a take-out counter; we like to order take-out for across the street, where we can sit serenely on a bayfront bench and watch fishermen and surfers on Hilo Bay.

Fiascos. In Waiakea Square, 200 Kanoelehua Ave. ☎ **808/935-7666.** Reservations recommended for parties of 5 or more. Main courses $6.95–$15.95. AE, DC, DISC, MC, V. Sun–Thurs 11am–10pm, Fri–Sat 11am–11pm. AMERICAN/MEXICAN/ECLECTIC.

All the makings of fantastic fajitas arrive on sizzling cast-iron platters so you can build your own at the table. Although best known
for this Mexican dish, Fiascos also offers a huge selection of soups
and salads at its $7.95 soup-and-salad bar. There are also four dif-
ferent soups daily, fresh-fish sandwiches, bountiful salads, pastas,
burgers, steaks, seafood, "honey-stung" fried chicken, chimichangas,
vegetarian tempeh burgers, blackened-chicken sandwiches, meat
loaf, pasta—something for everyone. Prime-rib specials every Friday
and Saturday night, blackened fresh catch, and the blackened-ahi
salad are among the popular features here.

Honu's Nest. 270 Kamehameha Ave. ☎ **808/935-9321.** Main courses
$4.75–$7.95. No credit cards. Mon–Sat 10am–4pm. JAPANESE/AMERICAN.

Home-cooked Japanese fare at budget-friendly prices and a location
on the bayfront of Hilo make this newcomer a solid hit. There are
only four tables and a small wooden counter, so the place is usually
full, and you'll see why. It's not just the prices that are winning—
this is good home cooking, tasty without being greasy, light on the
pocketbook as well as the waistline. The teishoku dishes—served
with a fresh salad, miso soup, and rice—are unbelievably inexpensive; they include broiled fresh fish, tofu steak, sautéed squid, sautéed
vegetables, broiled spicy chicken, sesame chicken, teriyaki chicken,
and other worthy choices. Tempura is also a top value, not just for
the price, but for the quality. The rice dishes called donburi come
in nine varieties (we like the ahi donbori), the curries in four, and
the soups in seven, including chicken soup and udon.

Island Grinds. On Hilo's Bayfront Beach, opposite old Hilo Iron Works (the first
right onto the beach after the bridge north of Suisan Fish Market). ☎ **808/
895-0625.** Burgers and plate lunches $3.50–$6.95. No credit cards. Mon,
Wed–Fri 10am–2pm. LUNCH WAGON.

Look for the wooden Island Grinds lunch wagon, as tiny as a closet,
under the willowy ironwood trees on Hilo Bay. The plastic table and
few chairs are a charming sight on the sand. Paper plates notwith-
standing, the dishes that Lisa Werner and Norina Page serve meet all
the standards of gourmet fare. The fresh-fish plate ($5.50 regardless
of market price—a steal!) comes perfectly sautéed; the turkey is smoky,
lean, and shredded; and the grilled lime chicken is fork-
tender. Fresh island produce appears in such marvels as taro-red potato salad, lilikoi-macadamia nut cole slaw, lasagna filled with fresh
vegetables and cheese, salads, burritos and rellenos, and submarine
sandwiches with an Island twist. Everything is served with a smile. Island Grinds is a local treasure and the consummate find for visitors.

Ken's House of Pancakes. 1730 Kamehameha Ave. ☎ **808/935-8711.**
Most items less than $9.50. AE, DC, DISC, MC, V. Daily 24 hours. AMERICAN.

You never know who you'll bump into at Ken's after an important
convention, concert, or the Merrie Monarch Hula Festival. The only
24-hour coffee shop in Hilo, Ken's fulfills basic dining needs simply and efficiently (but watch out for the calories: there are 13 different pies!). Omelets, pancakes, French toast with Portuguese sweet
bread, saimin, sandwiches, soup—what they call a "poi dog
menu"—stream out of the busy kitchen. Other affordable selections
include fried chicken, steak, grilled fish, and hamburgers with salad
and all the accompaniments. Most popular is the Mauna Kea hamburger, big as a mountain, topped with pineapple and the works
between sweet-bread buns—very local, very Hilo.

Kuhio Grille. Prince Kuhio Plaza. ☎ **808/959-2336.** Main courses $4.95–
$8.95. MC, V. Mon–Thurs 5am–10pm, Fri 5am–Sun 10pm (24 hours on week-
ends). AMERICAN/HAWAIIAN.

The "home of the one-pound laulau" is quite the local hangout, a
coffee/saimin shop with a few tables outdoors and a bustling business indoors. Taro from Waipio Valley is featured in the popular
Hawaiian plate, but there are other local specialties: saimin, miso-
saimin, crab omelets with mushrooms, yakitori, burgers, fried rice
(a specialty), and eclectic selections such as nacho salad and chicken
yakitori.

✪ **Miyo's.** At Waiakea Villas, 400 Hualani St. ☎ **808/935-2273.** Lunch main
courses $4.50–$8.95, combinations $7.50–$9.25; dinner main courses $4.75–
$10.50, combination dinners $8.50–$10.75. No credit cards. Tues–Sat 11am–
2pm and 5:30–8:30pm. JAPANESE.

Miyo's legacy is home-cooked, healthy Japanese food, served in an
open-air room on Wailoa Pond, where an idyll of curving footpaths
and greenery fills the horizon. Sliding shoji doors bordering the dining area are left open so you can take in the view and gaze at Mauna
Kea on a clear day. This is clearly the environment of someone to
whom cooking and dining are a meditation. Although sesame
chicken (deep-fried and boneless with a spine-tingling sesame sauce)
is a bestseller, the entire menu is appealing. For vegetarians, there are
constantly changing specials like vegetable tempura, vegetarian
shabu-shabu (cooked in a chafing dish at your table, then dipped in
a special sauce), and noodle and seaweed dishes. There are also
mouth-watering selections of sashimi, beef teriyaki, fried oysters,
many different types of tempura, ahi donburi (seasoned and steamed
in a bowl of rice), sukiyaki, and generous combination dinners. The
miso soup is a wonder, and the ahi tempura plate is one of Hilo's

stellar buys. Special diets (low-sodium, sugarless) are cheerfully accommodated, and no MSG is used.

Naung Mai. 86 Kilauea Ave. ☎ **808/934-7540.** Reservations recommended. Main dishes $4.50–$8.50. MC, V. Mon–Fri 11am–2pm and 5–8:30pm. THAI.

This tiny eatery (three main booths, two tables) fills up quickly. In a short time, Naung Mai has gained a good reputation among Hilo residents for its curries and Pad Thai noodles and its use of fresh local ingredients. The flavorings are commendable, the produce is fresh from the Hilo Farmers Market, and the chef adheres to high standards. The four curries—green, red, yellow, and Indian-style—go with the jasmine, brown, white, and sticky rice. The Pad Thai rice noodles, served with tofu and fresh vegetables, come with a choice of chicken, pork, beef, or shrimp, and are sprinkled with fresh peanuts. You can order your curry Thai-spicy (incendiary) or American-spicy (moderately hot), but even mild, the flavors are outstanding.

✪ **Nori's Saimin & Snacks.** 688 Kinoole St. ☎ **808/935-9133.** Most items less than $7.95. MC, V. Sun–Mon 10:30am–9:30pm, Tues–Thurs 10:30am–midnight, Fri–Sat 10:30am–1am. SAIMIN/NOODLE SHOP.

Nori's requires some looking but is worth it. Unmarked on Kinoole Street and not visible from the street, it's located across from the Hilo Lanes bowling alley, down a short driveway into an obscure parking lot. You'll wonder what you're doing here, but stroll into the tiny noodle house with the neon sign of chopsticks and a bowl, plywood booths and Formica tables, and prepare to enjoy the best saimin on the island. Saimin comes fried or in a savory homemade broth—the key to its success—with various embellishments, from seaweed to Chinese dumplings called wonton. Ramen, soba, udon, and a Korean noodle soup, called *mundoo,* are among the 16 varieties of noodle soups. Barbecued chicken or beef sticks are part of the saimin ritual, smoky and marvelous. Cold noodles, plate lunches (teriyaki beef, ahi, Korean short ribs), and sandwiches give diners ample choices from morning to late night, but noodles are the star. Hilo residents come here after the movies or a game and wouldn't think of leaving without a bag of Nori's famous chocolate mochi cookies or cakes.

Reuben's Mexican Restaurant. 336 Kamehameha Ave. ☎ **808/961-2552.** Most items less than $9.50. MC, V. Mon–Fri 11am–9pm, Sat noon–9pm. MEXICAN.

Reuben's is Hilo's south-of-the-border outpost, with serapes, sombreros, Mexican doilies, and rainbow colors everywhere you look.

The juxtaposition of Hilo Bay outside and the dark, funky, margarita-infused atmosphere inside makes for a flamboyantly campy dining experience. The tacos, enchiladas, and hefty combination plates are authentic, as are the award-winning Reuben's margaritas, served in frothy, bountiful pitcherfuls that grease the wheels of conviviality. The free-flowing margaritas are a good match for the moist, tasty tortillas, cilantro-laden salsa, and chile rellenos, a Reuben's specialty.

Royal Siam Thai Restaurant. 70 Mamo St. ☎ **808/961-6100.** Main courses $4.95–$8.95. AE, CB, DC, DISC, MC, V. Mon–Sat 11am–2pm and 5–8:30pm. THAI.

One of Hilo's most popular neighborhood restaurants, the Royal Siam serves consistently good Thai curries in a simple room just off the sidewalk. Fresh herbs and vegetables from the owner's gardens add an extra zip to the platters of noodles, soups, curries, and specialties that pour out of the kitchen in clouds of spicy fragrance. The Buddha Rama, a wildly popular concoction of spinach, chicken, and peanut sauce, is a scene-stealer and a personal favorite. The Thai garlic chicken, in sweet basil with garlic and coconut milk, is equally superb.

ICE CREAM

Hilo Homemade Ice Cream. 1477 Kalanianaole Ave. (Keaukaha area of Hilo). ☎ **808/959-5959.**

Fresh, creamy, homemade ice cream made in paradise flavors fresh from the island: That's Hilo Homemade. Young Hilo ginger is used for the ginger ice cream, a bestseller; other winners include mango, lilikoi (passion fruit) sherbet, local banana, green tea, Kona coffee, macadamia nut, coconut-crème, banana-poha (gooseberry), and many others. Some loyalists come daily or several times weekly for the same flavor.

7 Volcano Village & Hawaii Volcanoes National Park

Kilauea Lodge. Hwy. 11 (Volcano Village exit). ☎ **808/967-7366.** Reservations recommended. Main courses $14.75–$28.50. AE, MC, V. Daily 5:30–9pm. CONTINENTAL.

Diners travel long distances to drive through the lava-rock pillars lined with hydrangeas and escape from the crisp upland air into the warmth of the high-ceilinged room. The sofa in front of the 1938 fireplace is inviting, especially when the fire is roaring. The decor is a cross between chalet-cozy and volcano-rugged. The European cooking is a fine culinary act on the big volcano. Favorites: the fresh catch, hasenpfeffer, potato-leek soup (all flavor and no cream), and Alsatian soup. All dinners come with soup, a loaf of warm, freshly baked bread, and salad.

Lava Rock Café. Hwy. 11 (Volcano Village exit, next to Kilauea Kreations). ☎ **808/967-8526.** Lunch main courses $4.50–$6.99, dinner main courses $7–$17.50. MC, V. Sun–Tues 7:30am–5pm, Wed–Sat 7:30am–9pm. AMERICAN.

Surprise! Volcano Village's newest favorite spot isn't a rocky cave, but a cheerful, airy oasis in knotty pine, with tables and booths indoors and semi-outdoors, under a clear corrugated-plastic ceiling. The menu includes everything from chow fun to fajitas. Wednesday night is Mexican night, Friday is for Hawaiian food, and the rest of the time the choices include teriyaki beef and chicken, meat or vegetable lasagna, grilled mahimahi, fresh catch, T-bone steak, and steak-and-shrimp combos. The lunchtime winners are the "seismic sandwiches" (which they also pack for hikers), chili, quarter-pound burgers, and a host of salads, plate lunches, and "volcanic" heavies such as southern-fried chicken and grilled meats. If you order the pancakes, the lilikoi syrup they serve you is homemade and scrumptious.

Rainbow Moon Pizza. Delivery only, Volcano area. ☎ **808/967-8617.** Regular pizzas $10.50–$16.50, more for double. CB, DISC, MC, V. Wed–Sun 4–9pm. PIZZA.

What a find! "The best pizza we've ever had" is how many describe the roasted garlic pizza with fresh local tomato and the "Big Kahuna," with its generous layers of cheese, roasted garlic, onions, and about 10 other ingredients. You can get regular or thin crust, hand rolled and topped with fresh sauces and a special nine-spice seasoning, and topped also with imaginative combinations with names like Rainbow Warrior, Vegetarian Villager, Lava Land, and Mauna Kea. Crater pockets are a unique offering, with smoked sausage, smoked marlin, and other ingredients baked inside the pocket. Every pizza is personally made by Bea Arnopole, a German living in Hawaii making Italian food—and doing it well. Rainbow Moon offers free delivery to the Kilauea Lodge and other B&Bs in Volcano. Many hikers place their orders before venturing out into lavaland, and time their deliveries for their return. After a full day of hiking, nothing can beat sinking into the sofa in front of a fire and having a Rainbow Moon pizza delivered to your door.

Steam Vent Cafe. Haunani Rd. (between mile markers 26 and 27 on Hwy. 11). ☎ **808/985-8744.** Sandwiches and salads $4.95–$7.95, salads $4.95–$8.95. AE, DC, DISC, MC, V. Daily 6:30am–8:30pm. DELI/COFFEE BAR.

Never mind that the Italian Lavazza coffee beans are impressing all of Volcano, or that the self-service espresso and cappuccino machine makes a potent cup of brew in 20 seconds, or that the gourmet sandwiches, salads, and delectable pastries are worth a special stop. Those are details. The big news is that the ATM machine here was the first to be installed in Volcano Village and is still quite an attraction. Steam Vent serves excellent coffees and teas and sweet dessert breads, and also sells postcards, gift items, raincoats, polos and tees and, most important, flashlights for lava walks at night or treks through lava tubes by day. The breads are made by Hilo's O'Keefe & Sons Bakery.

Surt's. Old Volcano Road, off of Hwy 11. ☎ **808/967-8511.** No reservations accepted between 6–7:30pm. Lunch main courses $7.95–$14.95; dinner main courses $9.95–$24.95. AE, DC, DISC, MC, V. Daily 11am–9:30pm. ASIAN-EUROPEAN.

A cozy bistro with a couple of tables on the deck fronting the Volcano Store, Surt's is a popular stop for fresh fish and curries prepared with a fusion touch. It's wonderful to enter the Euro-upcountry ambience of this cheery cocoon (white tablecloths and candles, smartly dressed servers), where wildlife artist Marian Berger's acrylic paintings adorn the knotty-pine walls. We applaud the menu's ambitiousness, but calorie-watchers, beware: Surt's is more French than Asian, with butter a primary ingredient. The choices usually include five or six different fishes (opakapaka, hebi, opah, kajiki, ahi), in several fusion preparations.

Volcano Golf & Country Club. Hwy. 11 (at mile marker 30). ☎ **808/967-8228.** Reservations recommended for large groups. Breakfast under $6, lunch under $9. AE, DC, DISC, MC, V. Daily 7–10am and 10:30am–2pm. Bar open until 4pm. AMERICAN/LOCAL.

This golf course clubhouse is one of the few places to eat in the Volcano area, so if the Kilauea Lodge is closed, you don't have much choice but to head here—unless you're up for a long drive. Thankfully, the food ranges from okay to good. The room looks out over a fairway, which isn't as clichéd as it sounds, especially when the mists are rolling in and the greens and grays assume an eye-popping intensity. We have even seen nene geese from our table. In the typically cool Volcano air, local favorites such as chili, saimin, and Hawaiian stew with rice become especially comforting. Also featured are prime rib on special occasions, teriyaki beef or chicken, stir-fry, and a corned beef and cabbage (also on occasion) that's better than it sounds.

8 Naalehu/South Point

✪ **Mark Twain Square**. Hwy. 11, Waiohinu. ☎ **808/929-7550.** Most items less than $4.95. AE, DC, JCB, MC, V. Mon–Fri 8:30am–8pm, Sat 8:30am–6pm. AMERICAN/LOCAL.

This is a charming stop in a remote village whose most distinctive feature is the row of monkeypod trees that Mark Twain planted. Two of those trees remain, and you can have lunch under one of them. Imagine dining on a turkey sandwich or tuna melt on home-made sweet bread on a shaded veranda in the lap of history. Friendly service and homemade breads (banana, guava, sweet bread), accompanied by Kona coffee and trendy new coffee drinks, add to the appeal. Look for the poi sticks, a Mark Twain Square original. Made with poi and roasted macadamia nuts, they're the best biscotti ever to be dipped into your Kona coffee.

Naalehu Fruit Stand. Hwy. 11, Naalehu. ☎ **808/929-9009.** Most items less than $10. No credit cards. Mon–Sat 9am–6:30pm, Sun 9am–5pm. AMERICAN/PIZZA.

This little roadside attraction is a bright spot on the long southern route, the liveliest nook in pleasingly sleepy Naalehu. You can buy sandwiches, pizza, fresh salads, and baked goods—the best-loved items here—and then nosh away at one of the few tables on the front porch while panting canines from truck beds stare longingly. Big Island macadamia nuts, hefty quiches, fresh local papayas, and Ka'u navel oranges are usually good here, and the pastries are famous, especially the macadamia-nut pie made with whole nuts, like grandma's old-fashioned pecan pie.

Shaka Restaurant. Hwy. 11, Naalehu. ☎ **808/929-7404.** Reservations recommended for dinner. Lunch main courses $5.50–$7.95, dinner main courses $8.85–$18.95. AE, DC, DISC, JCB, MC, V. Tues–Sun 8am–8pm. AMERICAN/LOCAL.

You can't miss the Shaka sign from the highway. This new 52-seat restaurant has white tile floors, long tables, an espresso machine, and a friendly, casual atmosphere. The serviceable menu of plate lunches and American fare seems like foie gras on the long drive through the Ka'u desert. The servings are humongous, especially the Mauna Loa–sized burrito, brimming with cheese, beans, olives, onions, and zucchini—highly recommended. Residents come here for the plate lunches, sandwiches (the shaka burger is very popular), and honey-dipped fried chicken, and at dinner, for the fresh catch, grilled or deep fried. The fried foods are popular, and the french fries are delicious.

South Point Bar & Restaurant. Hwy. 11 (at mile marker 76), South Point. ☎ **808/929-9343.** Main courses $5.95–$7.95 at lunch, $7.95–$17.95 at dinner. DC, MC, V. Mon–Sat noon–3pm, 5:30–9pm, Sun 9am–2pm; bar Mon–Thurs and Sat 11am–10pm, Fri 11am–midnight. AMERICAN.

This 40-seat diner has ocean views from the deck, a surf-and-turf menu, and a separate bar with a piano. Whether it's agony or ecstasy at the ivories, a party mood often prevails, a point made at the outset with the hand-painted parrots and flamingos at the entrance. This is a frontier outpost where area residents know one another and travelers drop by for burgers, enchiladas, Reubens, fresh fish, eggplant lasagna, and vegetarian specials. The specials change daily, with prime rib on Friday and Saturday nights.

6

Fun in the Surf & Sun: Beaches & Active Pursuits

by Jeanette Foster

You can have some of the greatest outdoor adventures on earth on the Big Island. From snorkeling with clouds of kaleidoscopic fish to hiking into lush rainforests, there's something for everyone, no matter what your age or ability.

1 Beaches

Too young geologically to have many great beaches, the Big Island instead has an odd collection of unusual ones: brand-new black-sand beaches, green-sand beaches, salt-and-pepper beaches, and even a rare white-sand beach.

THE KONA COAST
KEKAHA KAI STATE PARK (KONA COAST STATE PARK)
You'll glimpse this beach as your plane makes its final approach to Kona Airport. It's about 2 miles north of the airport on Queen Kaahumanu Highway; turn left at a sign pointing improbably down a bumpy road. You won't need a four-wheel–drive vehicle to make it down to the beach—just drive slowly and watch out for potholes. What you'll find at the end is 5 miles of shoreline with a half-dozen long, curving beaches and a big cove on Mahaiula Bay, as well as archaeological and historical sites. The series of well-protected coves is excellent for swimming, and there's great snorkeling and diving offshore; the big winter waves attract surfers. Facilities include rest rooms, picnic tables, and barbecue pits; you'll have to bring your own drinking water. Since it's a state park, the beach is open daily from 8am to 8pm (the closing is strictly enforced, and there's no overnight camping).

WHITE SANDS BEACH
As you cruise Alii Drive, blink and you'll miss White Sands Beach. This small, white-sand pocket beach about 4¹/₂ miles south of

Beaches & Outdoor Activities on the Big Island

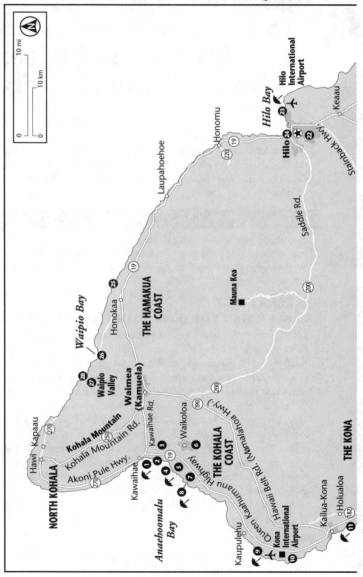

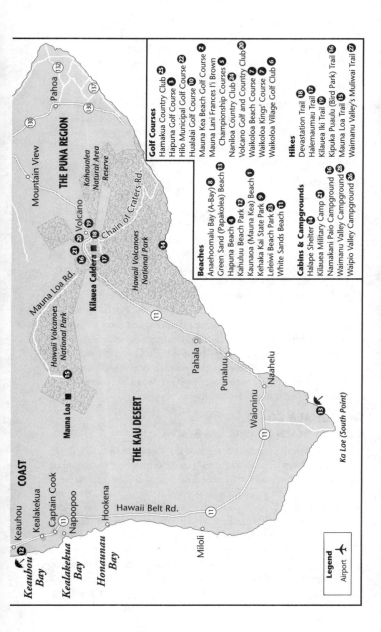

Golf Courses

Hamakua Country Club 25
Hapuna Golf Course 3
Hilo Municipal Golf Course 22
Hualalai Golf Course 10
Mauna Kea Beach Golf Course 2
Mauna Lani Frances I'i Brown Championship Courses 5
Naniloa Country Club 24
Volcano Golf and Country Club 20
Waikoloa Beach Course 7
Waikoloa Kings' Course 7
Waikoloa Village Golf Club 6

Hikes

Devastation Trail 18
Halemaumau Trail 17
Kilauea Iki Trail 19
Kipuka Puaulu (Bird Park) Trail 16
Mauna Loa Trail 15
Waimanu Valley's Muliwai Trail 27

Beaches

Anaehoomalu Bay (A-Bay) 8
Green Sand (Papakolea) Beach 13
Hapuna Beach 4
Kahulu Beach Park 12
Kaunaoa (Mauna Kea) Beach 1
Kehaka Kai State Park 9
Leleiwi Beach Park 23
White Sands Beach 11

Cabins & Campgrounds

Halape Shelter 14
Kilauea Military Camp 21
Namakani Paio Campground 16
Waimanu Valley Campground 28
Waipio Valley Campground 26

109

Kailua-Kona—very unusual on this lava-rock coast—is sometimes called Disappearing Beach because it does just that, especially at high tide or during storms. It vanished completely when Hurricane Iniki hit in 1991, but it's now back in place. (At least it was the last time we looked.) Locals use the elementary waves here to teach their children how to surf and boogie board. On calm days, the water is perfect for swimming and snorkeling. In winter, the waves swell to expert levels, attracting both surfers and spectators. Facilities include rest rooms, showers, lifeguards, and a small parking lot.

✪ KAHALUU BEACH PARK

This is the most popular beach on the Kona Coast; these reef-protected lagoons attract 1,000 people a day almost year-round. Kahaluu is the best all-around beach on Alii Drive, with coconut trees lining a narrow salt-and-pepper–sand shore that gently slopes to turquoise pools. The schools of brilliantly colored tropical fish that weave in and out of the well-established reef make this a great place to snorkel. It's also an ideal spot for children and beginning snorkelers to get their fins wet; the water is so shallow that you can literally stand up if you feel uncomfortable. Be careful in winter, though: The placid waters become turbulent, and there's a rip current when high surf rolls in; look for the lifeguard warnings.

Kahaluu isn't the biggest beach on the island, but it's one of the best equipped, with off-road parking, beach-gear rentals, a covered pavilion, and a food concession. It gets crowded, so come early to stake out a beach blanket–sized spot.

THE KOHALA COAST
KAUNAOA BEACH (MAUNA KEA BEACH)

For 25 years, this gold-sand beach at the foot of Mauna Kea Beach Hotel has been the top vacation spot among America's corporate chiefs. Everyone calls it Mauna Kea Beach, but its real name is Hawaiian for "native dodder," a lacy, yellow-orange vine that once thrived on the shore. A coconut grove sweeps around this golden crescent, where the water is calm and protected by two black-lava points. The sandy bottom slopes gently into the bay, which often fills not only with schools of tropical fish but green sea turtles and manta rays, especially at night, when the hotel lights flood the shore. Swimming is excellent year-round, except in rare winter storms. Snorkelers prefer the rocky points, where fish thrive in the surge. Facilities include rest rooms, showers, and ample parking, but there's no lifeguard.

✪ HAPUNA BEACH

Just off Queen Kaahumanu Highway, south of the Hapuna Beach Prince Hotel, lies this crescent of gold sand—big, wide, and a half-mile long. In summer, when the beach is widest, the ocean calmest, and the crowds biggest, this is the island's best beach for swimming, snorkeling, and bodysurfing. But beware Hapuna in winter, when its thundering waves, strong rip currents, and lack of lifeguards can be dangerous. Facilities include A-frame cabins for camping, pavilions, rest rooms, showers, and plenty of parking.

ANAEHOOMALU BAY (A-BAY)

The Big Island makes up for its dearth of beaches with a few spectacular ones, like Anaehoomalu, or A-Bay, as the locals call it. This popular, peppered, gold-sand beach, fringed by a grove of palms and backed by royal fishponds still full of mullet, is one of Hawaii's most beautiful. It fronts the Outrigger Waikoloa Beach Resort and is enjoyed by guests and locals alike. The beach slopes gently from shallow to deep water; swimming, snorkeling, diving, kayaking, and windsurfing are all excellent here. Equipment rental and snorkeling, scuba, and windsurfing instruction are available at the north end of the beach. At the far edge of the bay is a rare-turtle cleaning station, where snorkelers and divers can watch endangered green sea turtles line up, waiting their turn to have small fish clean them. There are rest rooms, showers, picnic tables, and plenty of parking.

HILO
LELEIWI BEACH PARK

Hilo's beaches may be few, but Leleiwi is one of Hawaii's most beautiful. This unusual cove of palm-fringed black-lava tide pools fed by freshwater springs and rippled by gentle waves is a photographer's delight—and the perfect place to take a plunge. In winter, big waves can splash these ponds, but the shallow pools are generally free of currents and ideal for families with children, especially in the protected inlets at the center of the park. Leleiwi often attracts endangered sea turtles, making this one of Hawaii's most popular snorkeling spots. The beach is 4 miles out of town on Kalanianaole Avenue. Facilities include rest rooms, showers, lifeguards, picnic pavilions, and paved walkways. There's also a marine-life facility here.

SOUTH POINT
GREEN SAND BEACH (PAPAKOLEA BEACH)

Hawaii's famous green-sand beach is located at the base of Puu o Mahana, an old cinder cone spilling into the sea. The place has its problems: it's difficult to reach; the open bay is often rough; there are no facilities, fresh water, or shade from the relentless sun; and howling winds scour the point. Nevertheless, each year the unusual emerald-green sands attract thousands of oglers, who follow a well-worn four-wheel–drive–only road for 2¹/₂ miles to the top of a cliff, which you have to climb down to reach the beach (the south end offers the safest path). The "sand" is actually crushed olivine, a green semiprecious mineral found in eruptive rocks and meteorites. If the surf's up, just check out the beach from the cliff's edge; if the water's calm, it's generally safe to swim and dive.

How to Get to Green Sand Beach: From the boat ramp at South Point, follow the 2¹/₂-mile four-wheel–drive trail; even if you have a four-wheel–drive vehicle, you may want to walk, as the trail is very, very bad in parts. Make sure you have appropriate close-toed footwear: tennis shoes or hiking boots. The trail is relatively flat, but you're usually walking into the wind as you head toward the beach. The beginning of the trail is lava. After the first 10 to 15 minutes, the lava disappears and the trail begins to cross pasture land. Then, after about 30 to 40 minutes, you'll see an eroded cinder cone by the water; continue to the edge, and there lie the green sands below.

The best way to reach the beach is to go over the edge from the cinder cone. (It looks as though walking around the south side of the cone would be easier, but it's not.) From the cinder cone, go over the overhang of the rock, and you'll see a trail.

Going down to the beach is very difficult and treacherous, as you'll be able to see from the top. You'll have to make it over and around big lava boulders, dropping down 4 to 5 feet from boulder to boulder in certain spots. And don't forget that you'll have to climb back up. Look before you start; if you have any hesitation, don't go down (you get a pretty good view from the top, anyway).

Warning: When you get to the beach, watch the waves for about 15 minutes and make sure that they don't break over the entire beach. If you walk on the beach, always keep one eye on the ocean and stick close to the rock wall. There can be strong rip currents here, and it's imperative to avoid them. Allow a minimum of 2 to 3 hours for this entire excursion.

2 Hitting the Water

BOATING

For fishing charters, see "Sportfishing: The Hunt for Granders," below.

Body Glove. Kailua Pier. ☎ **800/551-8911** or 808/326-7122. www.bodyglovehawaii.com. $44–$67 adults, $37 children 6–17, under 5 free; additional $30 for certified scuba divers with own equipment, additional $40 for certified scuba divers needing rental equipment; whale-watching with Greenpeace Hawaii Dec–April $44 adults, $24 children 6–17, under 5 free.

This 55-foot trimaran runs an adventurous sail-snorkel-dive cruise at a reasonable price. The boat carries up to 100 passengers. You'll be greeted with fresh Kona coffee, fruit, and breakfast pastries; then you'll sail north of Kailua to Pawai Bay, a marine preserve where you can snorkel, scuba dive, swim, or just hang out on deck for a couple of hours. After an all-you-can-eat lunch spread, you might want to take the plunge off the boat's waterslide or diving board before heading back to Kailua Pier. The *Body Glove* departs daily from the Kailua Pier at 9am and returns at 1:30pm. The only thing you need to bring is your towel, as snorkeling equipment (and scuba equipment, if you choose to dive) is provided. *Money-saving tip:* The afternoon trip is $23 cheaper for adults.

Captain Beans' Cruises. Kailua Pier. ☎ **800/831-5541** or 808/329-2955. $49 per person; you must be 21 to board the boat.

Captain Beans runs Kona's most popular dinner sails on a 150-foot catamaran, which can accommodate about 290 passengers. The 2-hour cruise includes dinner, cocktails, dancing, and Hawaiian entertainment.

✪ Captain Dan McSweeney's Year-Round Whale-Watching Adventures. Honokohau Harbor. ☎ **888/WHALE6** or 808/322-0028. Fax 808/322-2732. www.ilovewhales.com. $44.50 adults, $29.50 kids under 11.

Hawaii's most impressive visitors—45-foot humpback whales—return to the waters off Kona every winter. Captain Dan McSweeney, a whale researcher for more than 20 years, is always here to greet them, as well as other whales who spend the warmer months in Hawaiian waters. Since Captain Dan works daily with the whales, he has no problem finding them. Frequently, he drops an underwater microphone into the water so you can listen to their songs. If the whales aren't singing, he may use his underwater video camera to show you what's going on. In humpback season—roughly December to April—Dan makes two 3½-hour trips a day. The rest of the year, he schedules one morning trip daily to look for pilot, sperm, false killer, melon-headed, pygmy killer, and beaked whales. Capt. Dan guarantees a sighting, or he'll take you out again for free. There are no cruises from May to June, though; that's when he goes whale-watching in Alaska.

✪ Frommer's Favorite Big Island Experiences

Creep Up to the Ooze. Hawaii Volcanoes National Park is a work in progress, thanks to Kilauea Volcano, which pours red-hot lava into the sea and adds land to the already big Big Island every day. You can walk right up to the creeping lava flow for an up-close-and-personal encounter.

Go Underwater at Kealakekua Bay. At easily accessible, mile-wide Kealakekua Bay, an uncrowded marine preserve on the South Kona Coast, you can swim with dolphins, sea turtles, octopi, and every species of tropical fish that calls Hawaii's waters home.

Gawk at the Day's Catch in Honokohau Harbor. Every afternoon between 4 and 5pm, local fishermen pull into the fuel dock to weigh in their big-game fish. We're talking 1,000-pound blue marlins and 200-pound yellowfin tunas, plus plenty of scale-tipping mahimahi, ono (also known as wahoo), and other Pacific billfish.

Discover Old Hawaii at Puuhonua O Honaunau National Historical Park. This sacred Honaunau site was once a refuge for ancient Hawaiian warriors. Today, you can walk the consecrated grounds and glimpse a former way of life in a partially restored 16th-century village, complete with thatched huts, canoes, forbidding idols, and a temple that holds the bones of 23 Hawaiian chiefs.

Hang Out in Waipio Valley. Pack a picnic and head for this gorgeously lush valley that time forgot. Delve deep into the jungle on foot, comb the black-sand beach, or just laze the day away by a babbling stream, the tail-end of a 1,000-foot waterfall.

Stargaze from Mauna Kea. A jacket, beach mat, and binoculars are all you need to see the Milky Way from here. Every star and

---

Captain Zodiac. From Gentry's Marina, Honokohau Harbor. ☎ **808/ 329-3199.** www.planet-hawaii.com/zodiac/kona.html. $62 adults, $52 children 2–12.

If you'd prefer to take a **snorkel cruise to Kealakekua Bay** in a small boat, go in Captain Zodiac's 16-passenger, 24-foot inflatable rubber life raft. Pioneered by Jacques Cousteau, the boat takes you on a wild ride 14 miles down the Kona Coast to Kealakekua, where you'll spend about an hour snorkeling in the bay. Trips are twice daily, from 8:15am to 12:15pm and from 1 to 5pm. *Warning:*

planet shines brightly in this ultraclean atmosphere, where the visibility is so keen that 11 nations have set up telescopes (two of them the biggest in the world), to probe deep space.

Savor a Cup of Kona Coffee. Most of the coffee craze is centered around the North and South Kona districts, but for a truly authentic cup of java, head upcountry to **Holuakoa Cafe,** on Mamalahoa Highway in Holualoa (☎ **808/322-2233**), where owner Meggi Worbach buys green beans from local farmers, roasts them, grinds them, and then pours you the freshest cup of coffee you've ever had.

Hunt for Petroglyphs. Archaeologists still aren't sure who's responsible for these ancient rock carvings, but there are more than 3,000 in the 233-acre Puako Petroglyph Archaeological District, depicting canoes, paddlers, turtles, sails, marchers, dancers, and more. See how many you can spot!

Chase Rainbows at Akaka Falls. When the light is right, a perfect prism is formed and a rainbow leaps out of this spectacular 442-foot waterfall, located about 11 miles north of Hilo. Take some time to roam through the surrounding tropical rain forest, where you'll see exotic birds, aromatic plumeria trees, and shocking red-torch ginger.

Shop at the Hilo Farmers Market. For less than $10, you can buy a pound of *rambutan* (a sweet Indonesian fruit), a bouquet of tropical orchids, and a couple of tasty foot-long Hawaiian laulaus (pork, chicken, or fish steamed in ti leaves). Be sure to arrive early— the market opens at sunrise—as many of the 60 or so vendors quickly sell out of their Big Island specialties.

Pregnant women and people with bad backs should avoid this often-bumpy ride.

✪ **Fair Wind Snorkeling and Diving Adventures.** ☎ **800/677-9461** or 808/322-2788. www.fair-wind.com. Prices vary depending on cruise.

One of the best ways to snorkel Kealakekua Bay, the marine-life preserve that's one of the best snorkel spots in Hawaii, is on Fair Wind's half-day **sail-and-snorkel cruise to Kealakekua.** The company's 60-foot catamaran holds up to 100 passengers. The morning cruise, which leaves from Keauhou Bay at 9am and returns at 1:30pm, includes breakfast, lunch, snorkeling gear, and lessons; it's $75 for adults, $42 for children ages 6 to 17 (free for those 5 and under). The afternoon cruise is a little shorter and a little cheaper: It leaves at 2pm and returns at 5:30pm and includes snacks, sailing, and snorkeling; it's $48 for adults, $31 for kids ages 6 to 17.

Just added: the sunset snorkel and dinner cruise, a 3½ hour cruise with 1½ hours of snorkeling for $75 for adults and $42 for children ages 6 to 17. Dinner and all snorkeling gear are included.

Fair Wind also has a daily 4-hour **Zodiac snorkel cruise** from Kailua Pier aboard their 28-foot hard-bottom Zodiac boat. The trip includes stops at two snorkel sites (Kealakekua Marine Preserve and Honaunau), snacks, and a historical/cultural tour on the return (including stopping to look in sea caves and lava tubes). Only 14 people are booked at a time. The cost for the morning cruise is $61 for adults and $54 for children ages 8 to 17 (you must be 8 years or older to go); the afternoon cruise is $46 for adults and $35 for children 8 to 17.

Kamanu. Honokohau Harbor. ☎ **800/348-3091** or 808/329-2021. www.kamanu.com. $48 adults, $29 children under 12.

This sleek catamaran provides a laid-back sail-snorkel cruise from Honokohau Harbor to Pawai Bay. The 3½-hour trip includes a tropical lunch, snorkeling gear, and personalized instruction for first-time snorkelers. The *Kamanu* sails twice daily (weather permitting) at 9am and 1:30pm (no sails on Sunday) and can hold up to 24 people.

Nautilus II. Kailua Pier. ☎ **808/326-2003.** www.nautilussub.com. 1-hour tours daily at 9:30am, 10:30am, 11:30am, and 12:30pm. $59 adults, $39 children.

People who want to see the underwater world but don't want to get wet might opt for a ride on this semisubmersible 58-foot boat that cruises the waters off the Kona Coast. Claustrophobes and sun worshipers can enjoy the 1-hour trip from the deck, while more adventurous souls can ride below in the air-conditioned cabin, where magnificent sea creatures come to life through oversized windows. A scuba diver is on hand in the water to lure fish, turtles, and other aquatic critters close to the windows.

BODY BOARDING (BOOGIE BOARDING) & BODYSURFING

On the Kona side of the island, the best beaches for body boarding and bodysurfing are **Hapuna Beach, White Sands Beach,** and **Kekaha Kai State Park.** On the east side, try **Leleiwi Beach.**

You can rent boogie boards and fins from **Snorkel Bob's,** in the parking lot near Huggo's Restaurant, 75-5831 Kahakai Rd. (off Alii Drive), Kailua-Kona (☎ **800/262-7725** or 808/329-0770; www.snorkelbob.com), for $6.50 a day or $26 a week. No one offers formal boogie-boarding lessons, but the staff at Snorkel Bob's can give you pointers and tell you where waves appropriate for beginners are rolling in. If you're staying on the Kohala Coast, try **Red Sail Sports** (☎ **800/255-6425;** www.redsail.com), with locations at Hilton Waikoloa Village (☎ **808/885-2876**) and the Hapuna Beach Prince Hotel (☎ **808/880-1111,** ext. 3690). Body boards rent for $5 an hour, $10 for a half-day, or $15 for a full day.

KAYAKING

OCEAN KAYAKING   Imagine sitting at sea level, eye-to-eye with a turtle, a dolphin, even a whale—it's possible in an oceangoing kayak. Anyone can kayak: Just get in, find your balance, and paddle. After a few minutes of instruction and a little practice in a calm area (like the lagoon in front of the **King Kamehameha's Kona Beach Hotel**), you'll be ready to explore. Beginners can practice their skills in **Kailua** and **Kealakekua bays;** intermediates might try paddling from **Honokohau Harbor** to **Kekaha Kai Beach Park;** the **Hamakua Coast** is a challenge for experienced kayakers.

You can rent one- and two-person kayaks (and other ocean toys) from **Kona Beach Shack,** on the beach in front of the King Kamehameha's Kona Beach Hotel (☎ **808/329-7494**), starting at $15 for the first hour and $5 for each additional hour. The price is the same for both a one-person kayak and a two-person kayak.

✪ FRESHWATER FLUMING   Years ago, the best thing to do on a hot summer day was to grab an old inner tube and go "fluming" down the Kohala Sugar Plantation irrigation system. There were only two problems: You had to trespass to get to the elaborate ditch system, and the water was cold. But the opportunity to float past a pristine rain forest, over ravines, and under waterfalls was worth the risk of getting caught (and worth a numb rear end). You no longer have to worry about either problem. The **Kohala Mountain Kayak Cruise** (☎ **808/889-6922;** fax 808/889-6944; www.kohala.net/kayak) offers access to this North Kohala area (via four-wheel–drive, air-conditioned vans) and guided tours in high-tech, double-hulled, inflatable kayaks, with knowledgeable guides "talking story" about the history, culture, and legends of the area, followed by a swim in a waterfall-fed mountain pool, and snacks. Wear a swimsuit or bring a change of clothing, as the kayaks pass under waterfalls and through water pouring in from the intake systems—getting wet is part of the fun, and the whole experience is one you won't forget. The $2^{1}/_{2}$-hour cruises are $75 for adults, $55 for kids ages 5 to 18. No experience necessary, but children must be at least age 5.

SCUBA DIVING

The Big Island's leeward coast offers some of the best diving in the world, because the water is calm (protected by the two 13,000-foot volcanoes), warm (75–81°F), and clear (visibility is 100-plus-feet year-round). Want to swim with fast-moving game fish? Try **Ulua Cave** at the north end of the Kohala Coast. How about a dramatic underwater encounter with large, feeding manta rays? **Manta Ray Village,** located outside Keauhou Bay off the Kona Surf Resort, is a proven spot.

There are nearly two dozen dive operators on the west side of the Big Island, plus a couple in Hilo. They offer everything from scuba certification courses (you must be certified to dive, although some operators will offer an "intro" dive), to guided-boat dives. One of Kona's most popular dive operators is **Eco Adventures,** King Kamehameha's Kona Beach Hotel, Kailua-Kona (☎ **800/949-3483** or 808/329-7116; www.eco-adventure.com). A two-tank morning dive off either of their 26-foot, 36-foot, or 50-foot boats (ask for the 36-foot or the 50-foot boats, which have bathrooms and hot showers) costs $90 with your own gear, and includes lunch. The late afternoon two-tank dive, including a one-tank manta ray dive, is $95. Gear is available for $5 per item. Note that validated parking in the hotel parking lot is $4 for six hours.

Another popular dive operator is **Jack's Diving Locker,** 75-5819 Alii Dr. (☎ **800/345-4807** or 808/329-7585; www.divejdl.com), which offers two-tank morning or sunset dives off either a 23- or 30-foot boat, starting at $80 per person with your own gear; if you need to rent equipment the dives are $125. Jack's also offers intro dives for beginners from boat or shore; the cost is $45 per person from shore, plus gear rental.

In Hilo, contact **Nautilus Dive Center,** 382 Kamehameha Ave., between Open Market and the Shell Gas Station (☎ **808/935-6939**). The center offers one-tank and two-tank shore dives in Keakaha for $55 and $75, which includes all gear.

HOT LAVA DIVES Hilo's **Nautilus Dive Center** (☎ **808/935-6939**) also offers a very unusual diving opportunity for

advanced divers: diving where the lava flows into the (
each, four divers can take two-tanks dives where the mo...
into the ocean. "Sometimes you can feel the pressure from the sound
waves as the lava explodes," owner Bill De Rooy says. "Sometimes you
have perfect visibility to the color show of your life."

✪ **NIGHT DIVING WITH MANTA RAYS**   A little less risky—
but still something you'll never forget—is swimming with manta
rays on a night dive. These giant, totally harmless creatures, with
wingspans that reach up to 14 feet, glide gracefully through the
water and flock toward the lights off the Kona Surf Resort in
Keauhou Bay to feed on plankton. **Eco Adventures** (☎ **800/
949-3483** or 808/329-7116) will take you on a two-tank afternoon/
night dive for $95. **Sandwich Isle Divers,** 75-5729 Alii Dr., in the
back of the Kona Market Place (☎ **808/329-9188** or 888/
743-3483; www.aloha.net/~sandive), also offers manta dives for $70,
including equipment ($60 if you have your own gear).

WEEKLONG DIVES   If you're a serious diver looking for an all-
diving vacation, you might think about spending a week on the 80-
foot **Kona Aggressor II** (☎ **800/344-5662** or 808/329-8182;
www.pac-aggressor.com), a live-aboard dive boat that promises to
provide you with unlimited underwater exploration, including day
and night dives, along 85 miles of the Big Island's coastline. You
may spot harmless 70-foot whale sharks, plus not-so-harmless tiger
and hammerhead sharks, as well as dolphins, whales, monk seals,
and sea turtles. You'll navigate through caves and lava tubes, glide
along huge reefs, and take on the open ocean, too. Ten divers are
accommodated in five staterooms. Guided dives are available, but as
long as you're certified, just log in with the dive master and you're
free to follow the limits of your dive computer. It's $1,895 for 7 days
(without gear), which really isn't so bad when you consider the
excellent accommodations and that all meals are included. Rental
gear—from cameras (starting at $100 a week) to dive gear ($120)
to computers ($100)—is available.

SNORKELING

The year-round calm waters along the Kona and Kohala coasts are
home to spectacular marine life. Some of the best snorkeling areas
on the Kona-Kohala Coast include **Hapuna Beach Cove,** at the foot
of the Hapuna Beach Prince Hotel, a secret little cove where you can
snorkel not only with schools of yellow tangs, needlefish, and green
sea turtles, but also, once in a while, with somebody rich and
famous. But if you've never snorkeled in your life, **Kahaluu Beach**

Park is the best place to start. Just wade in and look down at the schools of fish in the bay's black-lava tide pools. Another "hidden" snorkeling spot is off the rocks north of the boat launch ramp at **Honaunau Bay.** Other great snorkel spots include **White Sands Beach,** as well as **Kekaha Kai State Park, Hookena, Honaunau, Puako,** and **Spencer** beach parks.

Beach concessions at all the resorts, tour desks, and dive shops offer equipment rentals and snorkel lessons for beginners. Gear rental is about $4.50 to $15 a day, or $10 to $39 a week (including mask, fins, and snorkel); prices go up slightly for prescription masks and high-end snorkels. Dive shops and marine operators who rent gear include **Kona Coast Divers,** 75-5614 Palani Rd., Kailua-Kona (☎ **808/329-8802**). But the best deal on snorkel gear on the Kona Coast is from ✪ **Snorkel Bob's,** in the parking lot of Huggo's Restaurant at 75-5831 Kahakai Rd., at Alii Drive (☎ **800/262-7725** or 808/329-0770; www.snorkelbob.com), where a mask, fins, and snorkel start at just $2.50 a day. In Hilo, get gear from **Planet Ocean Watersports,** 200 Kanoelehua Ave., ☎ **808/935-7277.**

✪ **SNORKELING CRUISES TO KEALAKEKUA BAY** Probably the best snorkeling for all levels is to be had in **Kealakekua Bay.** The calm waters of this underwater preserve teem with a wealth of marine life. Coral heads, lava tubes, and underwater caves all provide an excellent habitat for Hawaii's vast array of tropical fish, making mile-wide Kealakekua the Big Island's best accessible spot for snorkeling and diving. Without looking very hard, you can see octopi, free-swimming moray eels, parrot fish, and goat fish; once in a while, a pod of spinner dolphins streaks across the bay. Kealakekua is reachable only by boat; check out **Fair Wind Snorkeling and Diving Adventures** and **Captain Zodiac** under "Boating," above. If you'd like to kayak out to Kealakekua, see "Kayaking," above, for rentals.

SNUBA

If you're not quite ready to make the commitment to scuba but you want more time underwater than snorkeling allows, **Big Island Snuba** (☎ **808/326-7446;** www.hshawaii.com/kvp/snuba/bi.html) may be the answer for you. Just like in scuba, the diver wears a regulator and mask; however, the tank floats on the surface on a raft, and is connected to the diver's regulator by a hose that allows the diver to go 20 to 25 feet down. Snuba can actually be easier than snorkeling, because the water is calmer beneath the surface. With just 15 minutes of instruction, neophytes can be down under. It's $65 for a 45-minute dive from the beach, $50 aboard a boat (plus the cost of the boat ride).

○ SPORTFISHING: THE HUNT FOR GRANDERS

If you want to catch fish, it doesn't get any better than the Kona Coast, known internationally as the marlin capital of the world. Big-game fish, including gigantic blue marlin and other Pacific billfish, tuna, mahimahi, sailfish, swordfish, ono (also known as wahoo), and giant trevallies (ulua) roam the waters here. On any trip, it can be all or nothing, but you seldom come away empty-handed. When anglers here catch marlin that weigh 1,000 pounds or more, they call them *granders;* there's even a "wall of fame" on Kailua-Kona's Waterfront Row, honoring 40 anglers who've nailed more than 20 tons of fighting fish.

Nearly 100 charter boats with professional captains and crew offer fishing charters out of **Keauhou, Kawaihae, Honokohau,** and **Kailua Bay harbors.** If you're not an expert angler, the best way to arrange a charter is through a charter boat booking agency; for several years we have recommended **The Charter Desk at Honokohau Marina** (☎ **888/KONA 4 US** or 808/329-5735; fax 808/329-7960; e-mail charter@aloha.net). However, at press time the operation was for sale. Hopefully, the new owner will continue to give the same great service of sorting through the more than 40 different types of vessels, fishing specialties, and personalities to match the prospective angler with the right boat. Prices range from $59.95 for a half-day "share charter" (where you share the boat with strangers) to $850 for a full-day exclusive charter aboard a million-dollar yacht. Generally, sportfishing charters run about $325 for a full-day charter on a six-passenger boat.

Serious sportfishers should call the boats directly. They include *Northern Lights* (☎ **808/329-6522**), *Marlin Magic* (☎ **808/325-7138**), *Ihu Nui* (☎ **808/885-4686**), and the *Sundowner* (☎ **808/329-7253**), which is run by TV personality Capt. Norm Isaacs. If you aren't into hooking a 1,000-pound marlin or 200-pound tuna and just want to go out to catch some smaller fish and have fun, we recommend **Reel Action Light Tackle Sportfishing** (☎ **808/325-6811**). Light-tackle anglers and saltwater fly fishermen should contact *Sea Genie II* (☎ **808/325-5355**), which has helped several anglers to set world records. All these outfitters operate out of Honokohau Harbor.

Most big-game charter boats carry six passengers max. Half-day and full-day charters are available, and boats supply all equipment,

Using Activities Desks to Book Your Island Fun

If you want to head out with an outfitter or guide—especially if you're interested in an activity such as horseback riding, whale watching, or sportfishing—and you'd like to save some money, you might want to consider booking your outing through a discount activities center or activities desk. These agents can often get you a better price than you'd get by going directly to the outfitter—on average, a 10% discount.

Not only will they save you money, but good activities centers should also be able to help you find, say, the snorkel cruise that's right for you, or the luau that's most suitable for both you *and* the kids. But remember that it's in the activities agent's best interest to sign you up with outfitters from which they earn the most commission; some agents have no qualms about booking you into any activity if it means an extra buck for them. If an agent tries to push a particular outfitter or activity too hard, be skeptical. Conversely, they'll try to steer you away from outfitters who don't offer big commissions. For example, Trilogy, the company that offers Maui's most popular snorkel cruises to Lanai (and the only one with rights to land at Lanai's Hulopoe Beach), offers only minimum commissions to agents and does not allow agents to offer any discounts at all. As a result, most activities desks will automatically try to steer you away from Trilogy.

bait, tackle, and lures. No license is required. Many captains now tag and release marlins and keep other fish for dinner—that's Island style. If you want to eat your catch or have your trophy marlin mounted, tell the captain before you go.

SUBMARINE DIVES

This is the stuff movies are made of: venturing 100 feet below the sea in a high-tech, 65-foot submarine. On a 1-hour trip, you'll be able to explore a 25-acre coral reef that's teeming with schools of colorful tropical fish. Look closely, and you may catch glimpses of moray eels—or even a shark—in and around the reef. On selected dives, you'll watch as divers swim among these aquatic creatures, luring them to the viewports for face-to-face observation. Call **Atlantis Submarines,** 75-5669 Alii Dr. (across the street from the

Another important word of warning: Be careful to stay away from those activities centers offering discounts as fronts for time-share sales presentations. Using a free or discounted snorkel cruise or luau tickets as bait, they'll suck you into a 90-minute presentation—and try to get you to buy into a Hawaii time-share in the process. Not only will they try to sell you a big white elephant you never wanted in the first place, but—since their business is time-shares, not activities—they're not going to be as interested or as knowledgeable about which activities might be right for you. These shady deals seem to be particularly rampant on Maui. Just do yourself a favor and avoid them altogether.

Our favorite islandwide discount activities house is the **Activity Warehouse** (☎ 800/923-4004; www.travelhawaii.com). Activity Warehouse is able to offer discounts of up to 50% on all kinds of activities (although most discounts are in the 10% to 20% range), with lots of operators to choose from. The company has offices on the Big Island (☎ 808/334-1155). You'll see Activity Warehouse ads in many local publications. All in all, we've found them to be helpful and not too sales-y. Although Activity Warehouse does represent time-shares, we've never once had anyone pitch us in all the times we've used them.

You might also check out the **Activity Connection,** in the King Kamehameha Mall, on Kuakini Hwy. (behind the King Kamehameha Hotel), Kailua-Kona (☎ 808/329-1038).

Kailua Pier, underneath Flashback's Restaurant), Kailua-Kona (☎ 800/548-6262 or 888/REAL-SUB; www.goatlantis.com). Trips leave daily between 10am and 3pm. The cost is $79 for adults, $39 for children under age 12. *Note:* The ride is safe for everyone, but skip it if you suffer from claustrophobia.

SURFING

Most surfing off the Big Island is for the experienced only. As a general rule, the beaches on the north and west shores of the island get northern swells during the winter, and those on the south and east shores get southern swells in the summer. Experienced surfers should check out the waves at **Pine Trees** (north of Kailua-Kona), **Lyman's** (off Alii Drive in Kailua-Kona), and **Banyan's** (also off Alii Drive); reliable surfing spots on the east side of the island include **Honolii**

Point (outside Hilo), **Hilo Bay Front Park,** and **Keaukaha Beach Park.** But there are a few sites where beginners can catch a wave, too: You might want to try **Kahuluu Beach,** where the waves are manageable most of the year, other surfers are around to give you pointers, and there's a lifeguard on shore.

Ocean Eco Tours, P.O. Box 2901, Kailua-Kona, HI 96745 (☎ **808/937-0494**), owned and operated by veteran surfers Rob Hemshere and Steve Velonza, is the only company on the Big Island that teaches surfing. Private lessons cost $125 an hour (minimum of 2 hours, including equipment), and 2- to 3-hour group lessons go for $75, including lunch and equipment (maximum of 4 students). Both guys love this ancient Hawaiian sport, and their enthusiasm is contagious; it's a ball to go out with them. The minimum age is 8, and you must be a fairly good swimmer.

Your only Big Island choice for surfboard rentals is **Pacific Vibrations,** 75-5702 Alii Dr., Kailua-Kona (☎ **808/329-4140**), where they're $15 for a 10am to 6pm rental, $20 for 24 hours.

WHALE WATCHING

Humpback whales pass through waters off the Kona Coast every winter from December to April. To spot them from shore, head down to the Keahole National Energy Lab, just south of the Kona airport, and keep your eyes peeled as you walk the shoreline. Since humpbacks are so big—up to 45 feet—you can see them for miles when they come out of the water. To reach the Energy Lab, follow Queen Kaahumanu Highway (Hwy. 19) toward the Keahole Airport. About 6 miles outside of town, look for the sign NATURAL ENERGY LAB; turn left. Just after the road takes a sharp turn to the right, there's a small paved parking area with rest rooms and showers. Park in the lot; a beach trail is on the ocean side of the parking lot.

WINDSURFING

Anaehoomalu Bay, on the Kohala Coast, is one of the best beaches for windsurfing, because there are constant 5- to 25-knot winds blowing onshore (toward the beach)—so if you get into trouble, the wind brings you back to shore (instead of taking you out to sea). **Ocean Sports,** at the Royal Waikoloan Hotel (☎ **808/885-5555**), starts beginners on a land simulator to teach them how to handle the sail and "come about" (turn around and come back). Instruction is $45 an hour; after a half-hour or so of instruction on land, you're ready to hit the water. If you're up for more windsurfing after your lesson, get the package deal: a 1-hour lesson, plus an additional hour on the water for $55. Equipment rental is $20 an hour.

Advanced windsurfers should head to **Puako** and **Hilo Bay.**

3 Hiking & Camping

Camping equipment is available for rent from **Pacific Rent-All,** 1080 Kilauea Ave., Hilo (☎ **808/935-2974**). It's for sale at **C&S Cycle and Surf** in Waimea (☎ **808/885-5005**); **Gaspro** in Hilo (☎ **808/935-3341**), Waimea (☎ **808/885-8636**), and Kona (☎ **808/329-7393**); and **The Surplus Store** in Hilo (☎ **808/935-6398**) and Kona (☎ **808/329-1240**).

GUIDED DAY HIKES   If you'd like to discover natural Hawaii off the beaten path but don't necessarily want to sleep under a tree to do it, a day hike is your ticket. A long-time resident of Hawaii, Dr. Hugh Montgomery of **Hawaiian Walk-ways** (☎ and fax **800/457-7759** or 808/885-7759; www.21stcenturyhawaii.com/hawaiianwalkways) offers a variety of day hikes, on a scheduled or custom basis, ranging from excursions on shoreline trails past ancient Hawaiian petroglyphs to hikes on volcanic summits reaching over 13,000 feet. Scheduled hikes are $110 for adults, $80 for children under 12; custom trips are $125 adults, $95 children under 12. Prices include transportation to the trailhead, food, beverages, and equipment.

Naturalist and educator Rob Pacheco of **Hawaii Forest & Trail** (☎ **800/464-1993** or 808/322-8881; www.hawaii-forest.com), will take you out for day trips in his plush four-wheel–drive van to some of the Big Island's most remote, pristine, natural areas, some of which he has exclusive access to. Rob fully narrates his trips, offering extensive natural, geological, and cultural history interpretation (and not just a little humor). Since he only takes a maximum of 10 people, his trips are highly personalized to meet the group's interests and abilities. A day with Rob may just be the highlight of your Big Island experience. He offers waterfall adventures, rain forest discovery hikes, birding tours, and a volcano tour, where he takes you hiking through a pitch-black lava tube and right up to the oozing flow after dark, when the lava is most spectacular—conditions permitting, of course. Each tour has 2 to 4 hours of easy-to-moderate walking, over terrain manageable by anyone in average physical condition. Half-day trips, including snacks, beverages, water and gear, start at $89 adult, $79 children ages 5 to 12; children under 5 are free.

Call these outfitters ahead of time (even before you arrive) for a schedule of trips, as they fill up quickly.

HAWAII VOLCANOES NATIONAL PARK

This national park is a wilderness wonderland. Miles of trails not only lace the lava, but also cross deserts, rain forests, beaches, and in the winter, snow at 13,650 feet. **Trail maps** are sold at park headquarters and are highly recommended. Check conditions before you head out on a trail. It can be cool and rainy any time of the year; come prepared for hot sun, cold rain, and hard wind. Always wear sunscreen and bring plenty of drinking water.

Warning: If you have heart or respiratory problems, or if you're pregnant, don't attempt any hike in the park; the fumes will get to you.

TRAILS

KILAUEA IKI TRAILS   You'll experience the work of the volcano goddess, Pele, firsthand on this hike. The 4-mile trail begins at the visitor center, descends through a forest of ferns into still-fuming Kilauea Iki Crater, and then crosses the crater floor past the vent where a 1959 lava blast shot a fountain of fire 1,900 feet into the air for 36 days. Allow 2 hours for this fair-to-moderate hike.

HALEMAUMAU TRAIL   This moderate 3$^1/_2$-mile hike starts at the visitor center, goes down 500 feet to the floor of Kilauea crater, crosses the crater, and ends at Halemaumau Overlook.

DEVASTATION TRAIL   Up on the rim of Kilauea Iki Crater, you can see what an erupting volcano did to a once-flourishing ohia forest. The scorched earth with its ghostly tree skeletons stands in sharp contrast to the rest of the nearby lush forest that escaped the rain of hot molten lava, cinder, and debris. Everyone can—and should—take this half-mile hike on a paved path across the eerie bed of black cinders. The trailhead is on Crater Rim Road at Puu Puai Overlook.

KIPUKA PUAULU (BIRD PARK) TRAIL   This easy 1$^1/_2$-mile, hour-long hike lets you see native Hawaiian flora and fauna in a little oasis of living nature in a field of lava. For some reason (gravity or rate of flow, perhaps), the once red-hot lava skirted—perhaps even surrounded—this miniforest and let it survive. At the trailhead on Mauna Loa Road is a display of plants and birds you'll see on the walk. Go early in the morning or in the evening (or even better, just after a rain) to see native birds like the *apapane* (a small, bright-red bird with black wings and tail that sips the nectar of the red-blossom ohia lehua trees) and the *iiwi* (larger and orange-vermilion colored, with a curved orange bill). Native trees along the trail include giant ohia, koa, soapberry, kolea, and mamani.

MAUNA LOA TRAIL   Probably the most challenging hike in Hawaii, this 7¹/₂-mile trail goes from the lookout to a cabin at the Red Hill at 10,035 feet, then 11.6 more miles up to the primitive Mauna Loa summit cabin at 13,250 feet, where the climate is called sub-arctic, whiteouts are common, and overnight temperatures are below freezing year-round; there's often snow in July. This 4-day round-trip requires advance planning, great physical condition, and registration at the visitors center. Call ☎ **808/985-6000** for maps and details. The trailhead begins where Mauna Loa Road ends, 13¹/₂ miles north of Highway 11.

CAMPGROUNDS & WILDERNESS CABINS

The only park campground accessible by car is **Namakani Paio,** which has a pavilion with picnic tables and a fireplace (no wood is provided). Tent camping is free; no reservations are required. Stays are limited to 7 days per year. Backpack camping at hiker shelters and cabins is available on a first-come, sharing basis, but you must register at the visitors center.

Kilauea Military Camp is a rest-and-recreation camp for active and retired military personnel a mile from the visitors center. Facilities include 75 one- to four-bedroom cabins with fireplaces, 100-bunk dorm, cafeteria, bowling alley, bar, general store, weight room, and tennis and basketball courts. Rates range from $26 to $100 a night; call ☎ **808/967-8333** on the Big Island or 808/438-6707 on Oahu.

The following cabins and campgrounds are the best of what the park and surrounding area have to offer:

HALAPE SHELTER   This backcountry site, about 7 miles from the nearest road, is the place for people who want to get away from it all and enjoy their own private white-sand beach. The small, three-sided stone shelter, with a roof but no floor, can accommodate two people comfortably, but four's a crowd. You could pitch a tent inside, but if the weather is nice, you're better off setting up outside. There's a catchment water tank, but check with rangers on the water situation before hiking in (sometimes they don't have accurate information on the water level; bring extra water just in case). The only other facility is a pit toilet. Go on weekdays if you're really looking to get away from it all. It's free to stay here, but you're limited to 3 nights. Permits are available at the visitors center on a first-come, first-served basis, no earlier than noon on the day before your trip. For more information, call ☎ **808/985-6000.**

NAMAKANI PAIO CAMPGROUNDS & CABINS   Just 5 miles west of the park entrance is a tall eucalyptus forest where you can pitch a tent in an open grassy field. The trail to Kilauea Crater is just a half-mile away. No permit is needed for tent camping, but stays are limited to 7 days. Facilities include pavilions with barbecues and a fireplace, picnic tables, outdoor dishwashing areas, rest rooms, and drinking water. There are also 10 cabins that accommodate up to four people each. Each cabin has a covered picnic table at the entrance and a fireplace with a grill. Toilets, sinks, and hot showers are available in a separate building. In the town of Volcano, 4 miles away, you can get groceries and gas. Make cabin reservations through **Volcano House,** P.O. Box 53, Hawaii National Park, HI 96718 (☎ **808/967-7321**); the cost is $40 per night for two adults (and two children), $48 for three adults, $56 for four adults.

WAIMANU VALLEY'S MULIWAI TRAIL

This difficult 2- to 3-day hiking adventure—only for the hardy—takes you to a hidden valley some call Eden. It probably looks just as it did when Capt. James Cook first saw it, with virgin waterfalls and pools and spectacular views. The trail, which goes from sea level to 1,350 feet and down to the sea again, takes more than 9 hours to hike in and more than 10 hours to hike out. Be prepared for clouds of blood-thirsty mosquitoes, and look out for wild pigs. If it's raining, forget it: You'll have 13 streams to cross before you reach the rim of Waimanu Valley, and rain means flash floods.

You must get permission to camp in Waimanu Valley from the **Division of Forestry and Wildlife,** P.O. Box 4849, Hilo, HI 96720-0849 (☎ **808/974-4221;** fax 808/974-4226). Permits to the nine designated campsites are assigned by number. They're free, but you're limited to a 7-day stay. Facilities are limited to two composting pit toilets. The best water in the valley is from the stream on the western wall, a 15-minute walk up a trail from the beach. All water must be treated before drinking. The water from the Waimanu Stream drains from a swamp, so skip it. Be sure to pack out what you take in.

To get to the trailhead, take Highway 19 to the turnoff for Honokaa; drive 9¹/₂ miles to the Waipio Valley Lookout. Unless you have four-wheel drive, this is where your hike begins. Walk down the road and wade the Wailoa Stream; then cross the beach and go to the northwest wall. The trail starts here and goes up the valley floor, past a swamp, and into a forest before beginning a series of switchbacks that parallel the coastline. These switchbacks go up and down about 14 gulches. At the ninth gulch, about two-thirds of the way along the trail, is a shelter. After the shelter, the trail descends into Waimanu Valley, which looks like a smaller version of Waipio Valley, but without a sign of human intrusion.

WAIPIO VALLEY CAMPING

Camping is permitted on the east side of the Waipio Stream, which is on the ocean side of the mouth of lush Waipio Valley. There's a grove of ironwood trees that provides a nice shady spot. Permits, which are free but limited to 4 days, must be applied for at least 2 weeks in advance from **Kamehameha Schools,** 78-6831 Alii Dr., Suite 232, Kailua-Kona HI 96740 (☎ **808/322-5300;** fax 808/ 322-9446). Permits are granted on a first-come, first-served basis. There are no facilities in the valley, so you're required to have your own chemical toilet or port-a-john (available at camping supply stores and at Sears, starting at $80). Water is available from the stream, but be sure to treat it before drinking.

4 Golf & Other Outdoor Activities

BICYCLING & MOUNTAIN BIKING

For mountain-bike and cross-training bike rentals in Kona, see **Dave's Bike and Triathlon Shop,** 75-5669 Alii Dr., across from the Kailua Pier underneath Flashback's Restaurant, behind Atlantis Submarine (☎ **808/329-4522**). Dave rents Specialized, Caloi, and other brand-name mountain bikes for $15 a day or $55 a week (includes helmet and water bottle). If you rent two bikes for a week, Dave will drop the price to $50 for one and $55 for the other—it's the best deal around. He also rents triathlon road bikes for $25 a day or $110 a week. Feel free to ask Dave for riding advice (such as which roads are closed by lava) and local weather reports. To carry your rented bike around, be sure to get a bike rack for your rental cars ($10 a week); this way, you can drive and bike as your trip dictates.

If you're a little pickier about the kind of bike you rent, **Hawaiian Pedals,** Kona Inn Shopping Village, Alii Dr., Kailua-Kona (☎ **808/329-2294**), has a huge selection, from mountain bikes and hybrids ($20 a day, $70 a week) to racing bikes and front-suspension mountain bikes ($25 a day, $105 a week) to full-suspension mountain bikes ($30 a day, $140 a week). The company also rents bike racks for your rental car at $5 a day, using the honor system to figure out how many days you actually use the bike rack (so if you have the rack for a week but only use it for two days, they'll just charge you $10). The folks at the shop are friendly and knowledgeable about cycling routes all over the Big Island.

In Waimea, contact **Mauna Kea Mountain Bikes** (☎ **888/ MTB-TOUR** or 808/883-0130, or pager 808/925-0530). Grant Mitchell can set you up with a mountain bike, starting at $25 for 5 hours or $30 a day. He'll have it delivered free to your hotel room, helmet, pump, tube, and patch kit included. Mitchell also has guided bike tours (see below).

BIKING AROUND THE ISLAND   When was the last time you bicycled around a tropical island? Jump on a 21-speed mountain bike and do it here. A novice can do the 225-mile Circle Island tour in 6 days or less; serious bikers do it in two.

Here are some tips if you're going to try to make your way around the island: Plan your trip. Make advance reservations. Get a bike that fits. Go early in the day; just after sunrise is best. Wear lightweight bike togs and a helmet. Take two water bottles and sunscreen. Bring rain gear. Stay on the road, because razor-sharp lava and kiawe thorns cause blowouts. Bring a patch kit, cables, and a lock. But most important, have fun!

GUIDED TOURS   If you want to explore the wilder side of paradise by bike but don't want to head out alone, the best outfitter to ride with is **Chris' Adventures** (☎ **808/326-4600**), which offers a variety of biking and biking-hiking tours. A half-day adventure costs $49 to $69 and includes equipment, transportation, and a snack; a full-day tour (usually 6 to 8 hours) costs from $76 to $110 and includes equipment, breakfast, and lunch. We love the Kohala Mountain Venture; you bike downhill through spectacular volcanic mountains and lush pastures, pass intriguing historic landmarks, and catch phenomenal views from the Pololu Lookout. It costs $79— which includes equipment, breakfast, lunch, and snorkeling at a remote beach—and it's well worth it.

Another alternative for bike touring, from beginner to advanced, is **Mauna Kea Mountain Bikes, Inc.** (☎ **888/MTB-TOUR** or 808/ 883-0130, or pager 808/925-0530), which offers rides from

3-hour downhill cruises in the historic Kohala mountains to advanced rides down monstrous Mauna Kea. Prices range from $45 to $115.

Contact the **Big Island Mountain Bike Association,** P.O. Box 6819, Hilo, HI 96720 (☎ **808/961-4452;** www.interpac.net/ ~mtbike), for their free brochure, *Big Island Mountain Biking,* which has useful safety tips on biking as well as great off-road trails for both beginners and advanced riders, or check out www.bikehawaii.com for information on trails and access. Another good contact for biking information and maps is Ann Peterson, executive director of **PATH** (☎ **808/326-9495**).

BIRDING

Native Hawaiian birds are few—and dwindling. But although Hawaii may be the endangered bird capital of the world, it still offers extraordinary birding for anyone nimble enough to traverse tough, mucky landscape. And the best birding is on the Big Island; birders the world over come here hoping to see three Hawaiian birds in particular: *akiapolaau,* a woodpecker wannabe with a war club–like head; *nukupuu,* an elusive little yellow bird with a curved beak, one of the crown jewels of Hawaiian birding; and *alala,* the critically endangered Hawaiian crow that's now almost impossible to see in the wild.

Good spots to see native Hawaiian and other birds include the following:

HAWAII VOLCANOES NATIONAL PARK The best places for accomplished birders to go on their own are the ohia forests of this national park, usually at sunrise or sunset, when the little forest birds seem to be most active. You may also see native birds at the entrance to the Thurston Lava Tube. The Hawaiian nene goose can be spotted at the park's Kipuka Nene Campground, a favorite nesting habitat. Geese and pheasants sometimes appear on the Volcano Golf Course in the afternoon. The white-tailed tropic bird often rides the thermals caused by steam inside Halemaumau Crater.

HAKALAU FOREST NATIONAL WILDLIFE REFUGE The first national wildlife refuge established solely for forest bird management is on the eastern slope of Mauna Kea above the Hamakua Coast. It's open for birding by permit only on the last weekend of each month and can be reached only by four-wheel–drive vehicle. Contact Refuge Manager Richard Wass, Hakalau Forest, 32 Kinoole St., Room 101, Hilo, HI 96720 (☎ **808/933-6915**), e-mail Richard_Wass@mail.fws.gov.

HILO PONDS   Ducks, coots, herons (night and great blue), cattle egrets, even Canadian and snow geese fly into these popular coastal wetlands in Hilo, near the airport. Take Kalanianaole Highway about 3 miles east, past the industrial port facilities to Loko Waka Pond and Waiakea Pond.

THE SADDLE ROAD   Check your rental-car agreement to see whether you can take your rental car on the 53-mile Saddle Road (Hwy. 200) from Hilo to the Kohala Coast between Mauna Kea and Mauna Loa. It's a beautiful drive—especially at sunset—and one of the best places to see *iao,* the Hawaiian hawk, as it soars over the rolling grasslands. Along the way, you'll see *kipukas* (islands of old forest surrounded by young lava flows), which are natural native-bird preserves. To enter, you must pick your way across razor-sharp lava; then you sit and wait for the birds.

BIRDING TOURS

If you don't know an apapane from a nukupuu, go with someone who does. Even rank amateurs can see Hawaii's *rara avis* in the wild. Naturalist Rob Pacheco leads tours with **Hawaii Forest & Trail;** see "Hiking & Camping," above.

The full-day **McCandless Ranch Eco-Tour** (☎ **808/328-8246;** fax 808/328-8671; e-mail hicrow@aloha.net) travels all over the slopes of Mauna Loa through the rain forest, passing by endemic Hawaiian flora and various native birds. The only alala in the world still found in the wild are on the Ranch property, where care is taken to protect them. Tours leave early in the morning to ensure more time for sighting the native birds and stopping for a picnic lunch. Prices start at $400 for two, $150 each for the third and fourth person. You can also book an overnight stay at the ranch's B&B; see "South Kona" in chapter 4 for details.

GOLF

For last-minute and discount tee times, call ☎ **888/645-BOOK** or 808/322-BOOK between 7am and 11pm. Stand-by offers discounted (10 to 40%) guaranteed tee times for same-day or next-day golfing.

If you game's a little rusty, you might head for the **Swing Zone,** 74-5562 Makala Blvd (corner of Kuikuni Hwy., by the Old Airport Park), in Kailua-Kona (☎ **808/329-6909**), which has everything to polish up your game: 35-stall golf driving ranges, 25 mats, and 10 grass tee spaces. A bucket of balls is $5 (60 balls), and the practice putting green and chipping area is free with a bucket of balls. The

Pro Shop has limited golf supplies for sale, but rental clubs are available. In the works is an 18-hole putting course built in the shape of the Big Island; prices will be $6 adults and $2.50 for children age 12 and under.

In addition to the courses below, we love the fabulous ✪ **Hualalai Golf Course** at Four Seasons Resort Hualalai. Unfortunately, it's open to resort guests only—but for committed golfers, this Jack Nicklaus–designed championship course is reason enough to pay the sky-high rates.

THE KOHALA COAST

✪ **Hapuna Golf Course.** Hapuna Prince Beach Resort, off Hwy. 19 (near marker 69). ☎ **808/880-3000.**

Since its opening in 1992, this 18-hole championship course has been named Most Environmentally Sensitive Course and one of the Top 10 New Courses in the Nation by *Golf Magazine,* and Course of the Future by the U.S. Golf Association. Designed by Arnold Palmer and Ed Seay, this 6,027-yard links-style course extends from the shoreline to 700 feet above sea level, with views of the pastoral Kohala Mountains and sweeping vistas of the Kohala coastline. The elevation changes on the course keep it challenging (watch out for the wind at the higher elevations!). There are a few elevated tee boxes and only 40 bunkers. Greens fees are $85 for resort guests, $135 for nonguests; twilight rates (after 3pm) are $50 for guests, $85 for nonguests. Facilities include putting greens, driving ranges, lockers, showers, a pro shop, and restaurants.

✪ **Mauna Kea Beach Golf Course.** Mauna Kea Beach Resort, Hwy. 19 (near mile marker 68). ☎ **808/882-5400.**

This breathtakingly beautiful, par-72, 7,114-yard championship course, designed by Robert Trent Jones, Jr., is consistently rated one of the top golf courses in the U.S. The signature 3rd hole is 175 yards long (and a shocking par-3); the Pacific Ocean and shoreline cliffs stand between the tee and the green, giving every golfer, from beginner to pro, a real challenge. Another par-3 that confounds golfers is the 11th hole, which drops 100 feet from tee to green and plays down to the ocean, into the steady trade winds. When the trades are blowing, 181 yards might as well be 1,000 yards. Greens fees are $95 for hotel guests, $175 for nonguests. Facilities include putting greens, driving range, lockers and showers, pro shop, and restaurant. The course is very popular, especially for early weekend tee times, so book ahead.

✪ **Mauna Lani Frances I'i Brown Championship Courses.** Mauna Lani Dr., off Hwy. 19 (20 miles north of Kona Airport). ☎ **808/885-6655.**

The **Mauna Lani South Course,** a 7,029-yard, par-72, has an unforgettable ocean hole: the downhill, 221-yard, par-3 7th, which is bordered by the sea, a salt-and-pepper sand dune, and lush kiawe trees. Depending on the wind, you may need anything from a wood to a wedge to hit the green. The **North Course** may not have the drama of the oceanfront holes, but because it was built on older lava flows, the more extensive indigenous vegetation gives the course a Scottish feel. The hole that's cursed the most is the 140-yard, par-3 17th: It's absolutely beautiful but plays right into the surrounding lava field. Greens fees for both courses are seasonal. Winter rates (January–March) are $105 for resort guests, $200 for nonguests, with twilight rates at $60 for resort guests and $75 for nonguests. Off-season rates (April–December) are $95 for resort guests, $185 for nonguests, with twilight rates at $60 for resort guests and $75 for nonguests. Facilities include two driving ranges, a golf shop (with teaching pros), a restaurant, and putting greens.

Waikoloa Beach Course. 1020 Keana Pl. (adjacent to the Royal Waikoloan and Hilton Waikoloa Village), Waikoloa. ☎ **800/552-1422** or 808/886-6060.

This pristine 18-hole, par-70 course certainly reflects designer Robert Trent Jones, Jr.'s motto: "Hard par, easy bogey." Most golfers remember the par-5, 505-yard 12th hole, a sharp dogleg left with bunkers in the corner and an elevated tee surrounded by lava. Greens fees are $85 for resort guests, $120 for nonguests, including cart; twilight rates are half price after noon. Facilities include golf shop, restaurant, and a driving range.

Waikoloa Kings' Course. 600 Waikoloa Beach Dr., Waikoloa. ☎ **800/552-1422** or 808/886-7888.

This sister course to the Waikoloa Beach Course is about 500 yards longer. Designed by Tom Weiskopf and Jay Morrish, the 18-hole links-style tract features a double green at the third and sixth holes and several carefully placed bunkers that often come into play due to the ever-present trade winds. Greens fees are $85 for resort guests, $120 for nonguests, including cart; rates drop to $55 after 2pm. Facilities include a pro shop and showers. Every Friday, there's a **free golf clinic** at 4pm; call for reservations.

Waikoloa Village Golf Club. Waikoloa Rd., Waikoloa Village, off Hwy. 19 (18 miles north of Kona Airport). ☎ **808/883-9621.** Turn left at the Waikoloa sign; it's about 6 miles up, on your left.

This semiprivate 18-hole course, with a par-72 for each of the three sets of tees, is usually overshadowed by the glamour resort courses along the Kohala Coast. Hidden in the town of Waikoloa, this is not only a beautiful course with great views, but it also offers some great golfing. Like most Hawaii courses, wind can play havoc with your game here, so choose your clubs with caution. Robert Trent Jones, Jr., designed this challenging course, inserting his trademark sand traps, slick greens, and great fairways. We're particularly fond of the 18th hole: this par-5, 490-yard thriller doglegs to the left, and the last 75 yards up to the green are water, water, water—always a great way to end the day. To keep your sense of humor, take time to check out the fabulous views of Mauna Kea and Mauna Loa, and—on a very clear day—Maui's Haleakala in the distance. Greens fees are $70 before 1pm, $40 after 1pm.

THE HAMAKUA COAST

Hamakua Country Club. On the ocean side of Hwy. 19 (41 miles from Hilo), Honokaa. ☎ 808/775-7244.

As you approach the sugar town of Honokaa, you can't miss this funky nine-hole course, built in the 1920s on a very steep hill overlooking the ocean. It's a par-33, 2,520-yard course that really only has room for about 4¹/₂ holes; but somehow, architect Frank Anderson managed to squeeze in nine by crisscrossing holes across fairways—you may never see a layout like this again. The best part about Hamakua, though, is the price: $10 for nine holes. The course is open to nonmembers on weekdays only; you don't need a tee time—you just show up. If no one's around, simply drop your $10 in the box and head right to the first tee. Carts aren't allowed because of the steep hills.

HILO

Hilo Municipal Golf Course. 340 Haihai St. (between Kinoole and Iwalani sts.), Hilo. ☎ 808/959-7711. From Hilo, take Hwy. 11 toward Volcano; turn right at Puainako St. (at Prince Kuhio Shopping Center), left on Kinoole, then right on Haihai St.; the entrance is between Kinoole and Iwalani sts.

This is a great course for the casual golfer: it's flat, scenic, and often fun. *Warning:* Don't go after a heavy rain (especially during the winter months), as the fairways can get really soggy and play can slow way down. The rain does keep the course green and beautiful, though. Wonderful trees (monkeypods, coconuts, eucalyptus, banyans) dot the grounds, and the views—of Mauna Kea on one side and Hilo Bay on the other—are breathtaking. This is a course where you can challenge yourself. There are four sets of tees, with a par-71 from all; if you carry a medium handicap, go ahead and play from the back (black) tees (6,325 yards of play). Getting a tee time can be a challenge, since lots of golfers in Hilo love this course; weekdays are your best bet. Greens fees are $20 weekdays, $25 Saturday and Sunday; the cart fee is $14.50.

Naniloa Country Club. 120 Banyan Dr. (at the intersection of Hwy. 11 and Hwy. 19). ☎ **808/935-3000.**

At first glance, this semiprivate, nine-hole course looks pretty flat and short, but once you get beyond the first hole—a wide, pretty straightforward 330-yard, par-4—the challenges come. The tree-lined fairways require straight drives, and the huge lake on the second and fifth holes is sure to haunt you. This course is very popular with locals and visitors, who can play a quick nine holes in the morning and head off for some sightseeing in the afternoon. On weekdays, greens fees are $30 for nine holes, plus $7 for a cart. On weekends, if you can get a tee time, it's $40, plus $9 for the cart. Twilight rates are $5 less after 4pm. Rental clubs are available.

VOLCANO VILLAGE

Volcano Golf and Country Club. Hwy. 11. ☎ **808/967-7331.** On the right side of Hwy. 11, just after the entrance to Hawaii Volcanoes National Park.

While most visitors head up to the national park to see the lava flows, some come for the golf. Located at 4,200 feet, this public course got its start in 1922, when the Blackshear family put in a green, using old tomato cans for the holes. It now has three sets of tees to choose from, all with a par of 72. The course is unusually landscaped, making use of a few ancient lava flows among the pine and ohia trees. It's considered challenging by locals. *Some tips from the regulars:* Since the course is located at 4,200 feet, the ball travels farther than you're probably used to, so club down. If you hit the ball off the fairway, take the stroke—you don't want to look for your ball in the lava. Also, play a pitch-and-run game, as the greens are slick and your ball just won't stick. Greens fees are $62.50 and include a shared cart.

HORSEBACK RIDING

Kohala Na'alapa, on Kohala Mountain Rd. (Hwy. 250) at mile marker 11 (ask for directions to the stables at the security-guard station; ☎ **808/889-0022**), has unforgettable journeys into the rolling hills of Kahua and Kohala ranches, past ancient Hawaiian ruins, through lush pastures with grazing sheep and cows, and along mountain tops with panoramic coastal views. The horses and selection of riding areas are suited to a variety of riders, from first-timers to experienced equestrians. There are two trips a day: a 2¹/₂-hour tour at 9am for $75 ($65 for children 8–14) and a 1¹/₂-hour tour at 1:30pm for $55 (same price for kids). No riders over 230 pounds, no pregnant riders, and no children under 8.

Paniolo Riding Adventure, Kohala Mountain Rd. (Hwy. 250) at mile marker 13 (just past the entrance to Kohala Ranch Estates), Kohala (☎ 808/889-5354), has a range of different rides to suit any riding ability. This is not a trail ride, but a chance to canter across open range, trot up mountain sides to hidden Hawaiian ruins, and enjoy the experience of riding on an 11,000-acre working ranch. Beginners and children (as young as 6 years old) are welcome. The company provides leather chaps (for better grip and comfort), cowboy hats and boots, and fleece "seat savers" on the leather saddles. Rides begin at $85 for a 2¹/₂-hour trip that promises stellar views of the Kona and Kohala coasts; a 4-hour tour is $125.

Experienced riders should call **King's Trail Rides, Tack, and Gift Shop,** Hwy. 11 at mile marker 111, Kealakekua (☎ 808/323-2388; www.interpac.net/~hit/ktr.html). These rides, which are limited to four people, head down the mountain along Monument Trail to the Captain Cook Monument in Kealakekua Bay, where you'll stop for lunch and snorkeling. The $95 price tag isn't so bad when you consider that it includes both lunch and gear.

To see Waipio Valley on horseback, call **Waipio Na'alapa Trail Rides** (☎ 808/775-0419). The 2-hour horseback tours of this gorgeous tropical valley depart Monday through Saturday at 9:30am and 1pm (don't forget your camera). The guides are well versed in Hawaiian history and keep a running commentary going as you move through this very historical place. The cost is $75 for adults, $65 for children ages 8 to 14. No kids under 8, no pregnant riders, and no one weighing more than 230 pounds.

RIDING A MULE ON THE BIG ISLAND   Mule rides used to be done only on Molokai; then in 1998, the **Hawaii Forest & Trail Guided Nature Adventures,** P.O. Box 2975, Kailua-Kona, HI 96745 (☎ 800/464-1993 or 808/322-8881; www.hawaii-forest.com), began the Kohala Mule Trail Adventure. This unique tour into historic Pololu Valley, where teams of mules were once used as transportation, is not only a trail-riding adventure, but a rare opportunity to step back in history. The trip begins at the historic Kohala Ditch Company Mule Station. After a brief orientation, the riders head out of the Pololu Valley lookout, where you can see miles of towering seacliffs, cascading waterfalls, and the black-sand beach below. The mules then take riders down the 500-foot descent. There are two 3-hour trips a day, at 8:30am and 12:30pm. The cost is $95 for adults, $85 for children ages 8 to 15. Snacks, water, and rain gear are provided.

RIDING PARKER RANCH   To ride Parker Ranch is to be lost in time and space. It looks familiar and foreign all at once, stretching as it does under the volcano. The land, barren and rolling and dimpled by craters, looks positively lunar. You gain a scant clue to the ranch's vast grandeur on a 2-hour trail ride that begins at Mauna Kea Stables in the Old West town of Waimea. Parker Ranch doesn't have "nose-to-tail" trail rides—it's too big for that. Here, you can gallop to the horizon across scenic upland pastures dotted with volcanic cinder cones and strewn with bleached white cattle bones. Corrals hold Texas longhorns and lost heifers; the wide-open range even offers a rare glimpse of wild Kona donkeys. Always, the final surprise is that you really are way out West—in Hawaii. **Mauna Kea Riding Stables,** off Hwy. 19 at Puuakalani Rd. (look for the Ace Hardware Store on the corner; it's down about a half-mile), Waimea (☎/Fax **808/885-4288**), offers guided open-range rides daily except Sundays for beginners to experts; you must be age 8 or older and weigh less than 210 pounds. It's $40 for a 1-hour ride, $70 for 2 hours, including instruction and trail guide.

7

Exploring the Island: Sight-Seeing, Shopping & Nightlife

*I*f you want nothing more than a fabulous beach to lie on and a perfectly mixed Mai Tai, we have what you're looking for—some of the most spectacular beaches (not to mention the best Mai Tais) in the world. But the Big Island's wealth of natural wonders are hard to resist; the year-round tropical climate and spectacular scenery tend to inspire even the most committed desk jockeys and couch potatoes to get outside and explore.

1 Seeing the Sights

by Jeanette Foster

THE KONA COAST

GUIDED WALKS The **Kona Historical Society** (☎ 808/323-2005) hosts two historic walking tours in the Kona region. All walks must be booked in advance; call for reservations and departure locations. The 90-minute **Kailua Village Walking Tour** is the most comprehensive tour of the Kona Coast. It takes you all around historic Kailua-Kona, from King Kamehameha's last seat of government to the summer palace of the Hawaiian royal family and beyond, with lots of Hawaiian history and colorful lore along the way. Tours leave Tuesday through Thursday and Saturday at 9:30am, Friday at 9:30am and 1:30pm. Tickets are $10 for adults, $5 for children under age 12.

There's also a **Preservation in Progress** walking tour of historic Uchida Coffee Farm, which introduces you to life on a coffee farm. It's offered Tuesday and Thursday at 9am, at a cost of $15 for adults, $7.50 for kids.

A SELF-GUIDED DRIVE If you're interested in seeing how your morning cup of joe goes from beans to brew, get a copy of the **Coffee Country Driving Tour.** This self-guided drive will take you farm by farm through Kona's famous coffee country; it also features a fascinating history of the area, the lowdown on coffeemaking lingo, some inside tips on how to make a great cup, and even a recipe for Kona coffee macadamia nut chocolate chunk pie (goes great with a cup of java). The free brochure is available at the **Hawaii Visitors and Convention Bureau,** 75-5719 W. Alii Dr., Kailua-Kona (☎ **808/329-7787;** fax 808/326-7563).

HORSE-DRAWN CARRIAGE TOURS   For a private historical and botanical tour of Kailua town, try the **Hawaiian Dreams Carriage Service,** P.O. Box 5679, Kailua-Kona, HI 96745 (☎ **808/325-2280;** e-mail 4horse@get.net), which offers various rides in a white carriage with burgundy velvet upholstery. Four adults or six children can fit comfortably. The drivers, decked out in white tux shirts, with traditional kukui nut leis and woven hats, not only point out the historical sites, but also stop and pick flowers along the route to give the guests the sights and smells of Kailua. During the day, Chinese parasols are provided free for those who want protection from the sun. You can find the carriages lined up at the Kona Inn Shopping Village every day from 4pm to 11pm. The costs are $45 per carriage for a 30-minute ride, $65 for a 45-minute ride, and $85 for the hour ride. For no extra charge, the staff will provide an ice bucket and glasses for whatever beverage you bring with you.

IN & AROUND KAILUA-KONA

Ellison S. Onizuka Space Center. At Kona International Airport, Kailua-Kona. ☎ **808/329-3441.** Fax 808/326-9751. Admission $3 adults, $1 children 12 and under. Daily 8:30am–4:30pm. Parking: In Airport lot, $2 per hour.

This small museum has a real moon rock and memorabilia in honor of Big Island–born astronaut Ellison Onizuka, who died in the 1986 *Challenger* space shuttle disaster. Fun displays in the museum include a gravity well, which illustrates orbital motion, and an interactive rocket-propulsion exhibit, where you can launch your own miniature space shuttle.

Hulihee Palace. 75-5718 Alii Dr., Kailua-Kona. ☎ **808/329-1877.** Admission $5 adults, $1 students, 50¢ children under 12. Mon–Fri 9am–4pm, Sat–Sun 10am–4pm. Daily tours held throughout the day (arrive at least an hour before closing).

This two-story New England–style mansion of lava rock and coral mortar, erected in 1838 by the governor of the island of Hawaii, John Adams Kuakini, overlooks the harbor at Kailua-Kona. The largest, most elegant residence on the island when it was erected, Hulihee (the name means "turn and flee") was the gracious summer

Kailua-Kona Town

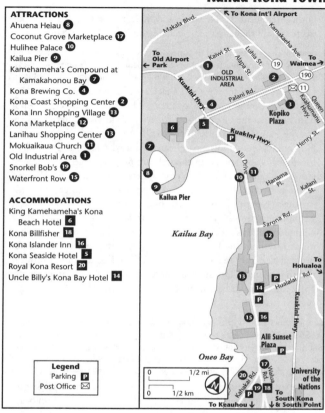

ATTRACTIONS
Ahuena Heiau **8**
Coconut Grove Marketplace **17**
Hulihee Palace **10**
Kailua Pier **9**
Kamehameha's Compound at
    Kamakahonou Bay **7**
Kona Brewing Co. **4**
Kona Coast Shopping Center **2**
Kona Inn Shopping Village **13**
Kona Marketplace **12**
Lanihau Shopping Center **13**
Mokuaikaua Church **11**
Old Industrial Area **1**
Snorkel Bob's **19**
Waterfront Row **15**

ACCOMMODATIONS
King Kamehameha's Kona
    Beach Hotel **6**
Kona Billfisher **18**
Kona Islander Inn **16**
Kona Seaside Hotel **5**
Royal Kona Resort **20**
Uncle Billy's Kona Bay Hotel **14**

Legend
Parking **P**
Post Office ✉

home of Hawaii's royalty, making it the other royal palace in the U.S. (the most famous being Oahu's Iolani Palace). Now run by Daughters of Hawaii, it features many 19th-century mementos and gorgeous koa furniture. You'll get lots of background and royal lore on the guided tour. No photography permitted.

The Palace hosts 12 **Hawaii music and hula concerts** a year, each dedicated to a Hawaiian monarch, at 4pm on the last Sunday of the month (except June and December, when the performances are held in conjunction with King Kamehameha Day and Christmas).

Across the street is **Mokuaikaua Church** (☎ 808/329-1589), the oldest Christian church in Hawaii. It's constructed of lava stones, but its architecture is New England–style all the way. The 112-foot steeple is still the tallest man-made structure in Kailua-Kona.

Kamehameha's Compound at Kamakahonu Bay. On the grounds of King Kamehameha's Kona Beach Hotel, 75-5660 Palani Rd., Kailua-Kona. ☎ **808/ 329-2911.** Free admission. Daily 9am–4pm; guided tours Mon–Fri at 1:30pm.

On the ocean side of the Kona Beach Hotel is a restored area of deep spiritual meaning to the Hawaiians. This was the spot that King Kamehameha the Great choose to retreat to in 1812 after conquering the Hawaiian islands. He stayed until his death in 1819. The king built a temple, Ahuena Heiau, and used it as a gathering place for his *kahunas* (priests) to counsel him on governing his people in times of peace. It was in this sacred ground in 1820 that Kamehameha's son Liholiho, as king, sat down to eat with his mother, Keopuolani, and Kamehameha's principal queen, Kaahumanu, thus breaking the ancient *kapu* (taboo) against eating with women; this act established a new order in the Hawaiian kingdom. Although the temple grounds are now just a third of their original size, they're still impressive. You're free to come and wander the grounds, envisioning the days when King Kamehameha appealed to the gods to help him rule with the spirit of humanity's highest nature.

Kaupulehu Petroglyphs. At Kona Village Resort, Queen Kaahumanu Hwy. ☎ **808/325-5555.** Free admission. Guided tours three times a week; reservations required. Turn off Hwy. 19 at the sign for Hualalai, then proceed 2.3 miles to the resort. The petroglyphs are reached via a footpath that passes the luau grounds, but you'll need a reservation to get past the gatehouse.

Here you can see some of the finest images in the Hawaiian islands. There are many petroglyphs of sails, canoes, fish, and chiefs in headdresses, plus a burial scene with three stick figures. Kite motifs—rare in rock art—similar to those found in New Zealand are also here.

Kona Brewing Co. 75-5629 Kuakini Hwy. (at Palani Rd.), Kailua-Kona. ☎ **808/334-1133.** E-mail konaale@aloha.net. Free tours and tastings. Tours Mon–Sat 10:30am and 3:30pm. Turn into Firestone's parking lot; the brewery is at the back of the shopping center (behind Zac's Photo)—look for the orange gecko on the door.

This microbrewery is the first of its kind on the Big Island. Spoon and Pops, a father-and-son duo from Oregon, brought their brewing talents here and now produce about 25 barrels (about 124,000 gallons) per year. Drop by at any time during their business hours and take a quick, informal tour of the brewery, after which you get to taste the product. A brew-pub, on the property, serves gourmet pizza, salads, and fresh-brewed Hawaiian ales.

Kona Pier. On the waterfront outside of Honokohau Harbor, Kailua-Kona. ☎ **808/329-7494.**

This is action central for water adventures. Fishing charters, snorkel cruises, and party boats all come and go here. Come by around 4pm, when the captains weigh in with the catch of the day, usually huge marlin—the record-setters often come in here. It's also a great place to watch the sunset.

Natural Energy Laboratory of Hawaii Authority. 73-4460 Queen Kaahumanu Hwy. (at mile marker 94), Kailua-Kona. ☎ **808/329-7341.** www.bigisland.com/nelha. Free guided tour Thurs 10am; reservations required.

Technology buffs should consider a visit to NELHA, the only site in the world where the hot, tropical sun, in combination with a complex pumping system that brings 42°F ocean water from 2,000 feet deep up to land, is used to develop innovations in agriculture, aquaculture, and ocean conservation. The interesting $1^1/_2$-hour tour takes in all areas of the high-tech ocean science and technology park, including the seawater delivery system, the energy-conversion process, and some of park's more interesting tenants, from Maine lobsters to giant clams.

UPCOUNTRY KONA: HOLUALOA

On the slope of Hualalai volcano above Kailua-Kona sits the small village of Holualoa, which attracts travelers weary of super resorts. Here you'll find a little art and culture—and shade.

This funky upcountry town, centered around two-lane Mamalaloa Highway, is nestled amid a lush, tropical landscape where avocados grow as big as footballs. Little more than a wide spot in the road, Holualoa is a cluster of brightly painted, tin-roofed plantation shacks enjoying a revival as B&Bs, art galleries, and quaint shops (see "Shops & Galleries" below, for details). In two blocks, it manages to pack in two first-rate galleries, a frame shop, a potter, a glassworks, a goldsmith, an old-fashioned general store, a vintage 1930s gas station, a tiny post office, a Catholic church, a library that's open 2 days a week, and the **Kona Hotel,** a hot-pink clapboard structure that looks like a Western movie set—you're welcome to peek in, and you should.

The cool upslope village is the best place in Hawaii for a coffee break. That's because Holualoa is in the heart of the coffee belt, a 20-mile-long strip at an elevation of between 1,000 and 1,400 feet, where all the Kona coffee in the world is grown in the rich volcanic soil of the cool uplands. Everyone's backyard seems to teem with glossy green leaves and ruby-red cherries (that's what they call

Big Island Highlights for Kids

Walking Through Thurston Lava Tube at Hawaii Volcanoes National Park (*see p. 167*)   It's scary, it's spooky, and it's perfect for any kid. You hike downhill through a rain forest full of little chittering native birds to enter this huge, silent black hole full of drips, cobwebs, and tree roots that stretches underground for almost a half-mile. At the end there's a fork in the tunnel, which leads either up a stairway to our world or—here's the best part—down an unexplored hole that probably goes all the way to China. Double dare you.

Snorkeling Kahaluu Beach Park (*see p. 120*)   The shallow waters off Kahaluu Beach are the perfect place to take kids snorkeling. The waters are shallow and calm, protected by a barrier reef, and the abundance of fish will keep the kids' attention.

Riding a Submarine into the Underwater World (*see p. 122*)   The huge viewing windows will have the kids enthralled as the high-tech sub leaves the surface and plunges 120 feet down through the mysterious Neptunian waters. The hour-long trip is just enough time to hold the young ones' attention as the sub passes through clouds of reef fish and past prehistoric-looking corals. Occasionally, way out in the deep, some lucky divers even spot Jaws!

coffee on the vine, because it's a fruit), and the air smells like a San Francisco espresso bar. The **Holuakoa Cafe** is a great place to get a freshly brewed cup.

To reach Holualoa, follow narrow, winding Hualalai Road up the hill from Hwy. 19; it's about a 15-minute drive.

SOUTH KONA

The Painted Church. Hwy. 19, Honaunau. ☎ **808/328-2227.**

Oh, those Belgian priests—what a talented lot. At the turn of the century, Father John Berchman Velghe borrowed a page from Michelangelo and painted biblical scenes inside St. Benedict's Catholic Church, so the illiterate Hawaiians could visualize the white man's version of creation.

✪ **Puuhonua O Honaunau National Historical Park.** Hwy. 160 (off Hwy. 11 at mile marker 104), Honaunau. ☎ **808/328-2288.** Fax 808/328-9485. www.nps.gov/puho. Admission $2, free for children 16 and under. Visitor center

Launching Your Own Space Shuttle (*see p. 140*) Okay, it's a model of a space shuttle, but it's close enough to the real thing to be a real blast. The Ellison S. Onizuka Space Center has dozens of interactive displays to thrill budding young astronauts, like a hands-on experience with gyroscopic stabilization. Great video clips of astronauts working and living in space may inspire your kids as well.

Hunting for Petroglyphs (*see p. 147*) There's plenty of space to run around and discover ancient stone carvings at either the Puako Petroglyph Archaeological District, at Mauna Lani Resort, or at the King's Trail by the Royal Waikoloan. And finding the petroglyphs is only part of the game—once you find them, you have to guess what the designs mean.

Watching the Volcano (*see p. 162*) Any kid who doesn't get a kick out of watching a live volcano set the night on fire has been watching too much television. Take hot dogs, bottled water, flashlights, and sturdy shoes and follow the ranger's instructions on where to view the lava safely. You might want to make the trip during daylight first so the kids can see the Technicolor difference in experiencing a lava flow in the dark.

open daily 7:30am–5:30pm; park open Mon–Thurs 6am–8pm, Fri–Sun 6am–11pm. From Hwy. 11, 3¹/₂ miles to park entrance.

With its fierce, haunting idols, this sacred site on the black-lava Kona Coast certainly looks forbidding. To ancient Hawaiians, however, it must have been a welcome sight, for Puuhonua O Honaunau served as a 16th-century place of refuge, providing sanctuary for defeated warriors and *kapu* (taboo) violators. A great rock wall—1,000 feet long, 10 feet high, and 17 feet thick—defines the refuge where Hawaiians found safety. On the wall's north end is Hale O Keawe Heiau, which holds the bones of 23 Hawaiian chiefs. Other archaeological finds include burial sites, old trails, and a portion of an ancient village. On a self-guided tour of the 180-acre site—which has been restored to its precontact state—you can see and learn about reconstructed thatched huts, canoes, and idols and feel the *mana* (power) of old Hawaii.

A cultural festival, usually held in June, allows you to join in games, learn crafts, sample Hawaiian food, see traditional hula, and experience life in the islands before outsiders arrived in the late 1700s. Every Labor Day weekend, one of Hawaii's major outrigger canoe races starts here and ends in Kailua-Kona, 18 miles away. Call for details on both events.

Kona Historical Society Museum. Hwy. 11, between mile markers 111 and 112 (park on grassy area next to Kona Specialty Meats parking lot), Captain Cook. ☎ **808/323-3222** or 808/323-2005. Fax 808/323-2398. www.ilhawaii.net/~khs. Mon–Fri 9am–3pm. Admission $2.

This well-organized pocket museum is housed in the historic Greenwell Store, built in 1875 by Henry Nicholas Greenwell out of native stone and lime mortar made from burnt coral. Inside, antiques, artifacts, and photos tell the story of this fabled coast. The museum is filled with items that were common to everyday life here in the last century, when coffee-growing and cattle-raising were the main industries. Serious history buffs should sign up for one of the museum's walking tours; see "Guided Walks," above.

A SIDE TRIP TO KAU

✪ **Kula Kai Caverns and Lava Tubes.** Off Hwy. 11, P.O. Box 6313, Ocean View. ☎808/929-7539. Tours by appointment. Between the 79 and 78 mile markers on Hwy 11, turn towards the ocean on Kula Kai Rd. Turn right on the 7th street down, Lauhala Rd. Look for thatched "yurt" field office on right.

Before you trudge up to Volcano to see Pele's volcanic eruption, take a look at her underground handiwork for the past 1,000 years or so. Ric Elhard and Rose Herrera have explored and mapped out the labyrinth of lava tubes and caves which crisscross their property on the southwest rift zone on the slopes of Mauna Loa near South Point. As soon as you enter their thatched yurt field office (which resembles something out of an Indiana Jones movie), you know you're in for an amazing tour. Your choices range from an easy one-hour tour on a well-lit underground route for $12 adults, $8 children ages 5 to 12; to a more adventuresome spelunking two-hour trip for $45 adults, $25 children ages 8 to 12; to the deluxe half-day explorations for $125 adults (minimum age 12 years), which includes lunch. Helmets, lights, gloves, and knee pads are all included. The Herreras recommend that you wear long pants and closed shoes.

THE KOHALA COAST
ANCIENT HAWAIIAN FISHPONDS

Like their Polynesian forefathers, Hawaiians were among the first aquaculturists on the planet. Scientists still marvel at the ways they developed of using the brackish ponds along the shoreline to stock and harvest fish. There are actually two different types of ancient fishponds (*loko i'a*). Closed ponds, inshore and closed off from the ocean, were used to raise mullet and milkfish; open ponds were open to the sea, with rock walls as a barrier to the ocean and sluice gates that connected the ponds to the ocean. The gates were woven vines, with just enough room for juvenile fish to swim in at high tide while keeping the bigger, fatter fish from swimming out. Generally, the Hawaiians raised mullet, milkfish, and shrimp in these open ponds; juvenile manini, papio, eels, and barracuda found their way in during high tides.

The **Kalahuipuaa Fishponds** at Mauna Lani Resort (☎ 808/ 885-6622) are great examples of both types of ponds in a lush tropical setting. South of the Mauna Lani Resort are **Kuualii** and **Kahapapa Fishponds** at the Royal Waikoloan Hotel (☎ 808/ 885-6789). Both resorts have taken great pains to restore the ponds to their original state and to preserve them for future generations; call ahead to arrange a free guided tour.

PETROGLYPHS

The Hawaiian petroglyph is a great enigma of the Pacific. No one knows who made them or why, only that they're here—hard physical evidence that early Hawaiians were gifted illustrators of their life and times. Petroglyphs appear at 135 different sites on six inhabited islands, but most of them are found on the Big Island.

At first glance, the huge slate of pahoehoe looks like any other smooth black slate of lava on the seacoast of the Big Island of Hawaii—until gradually, in slanting rays of the sun, a wonderful cast of characters leaps to life before your eyes. You see dancers and paddlers, fishermen and chiefs, hundreds of marchers all in a row. Pictures of the tools of daily life are everywhere: fish hooks, spears, poi pounders, canoes. The most common representations are family groups: father, mother, and child. There are also post–European contact petroglyphs of ships, anchors, goats, horses, and guns.

The largest concentration of these stone symbols in the Pacific lies within the 233-acre ✪ **Puako Petroglyph Archaeological District,** near Mauna Lani Resort. Once hard to find, the enigmatic graffiti is now easily reachable. The 1.4-mile **Malama Trail** starts north of Mauna Lani Resort; take Hwy. 19 to the resort turnoff and drive toward the coast on North Kaniku Drive, which ends at a parking lot; the trailhead is marked by a sign and interpretive kiosk. Go in the early morning or late afternoon when it's cool. A total of 3,000 designs have been identified, including paddlers, sails, marchers, dancers, and family groups, as well as dog, chicken, turtle, and deity symbols.

At the **Royal Waikoloan** (☎ 808/885-6789) is the **King's Trail,** an ancient footpath by the sea that leads to a place out by the golf course where the black lava swirls into a flat tablet. The rock art here along the well-marked trail is especially graphic and easy to see. Free, guided, 1-hour tours of the resort's petroglyphs are offered Monday through Friday at 8am; the King's Shops in Waikoloa also offers a free tour of the trail every Saturday at 8:30am, starting in front of the Food Pavilion.

Warning: The petroglyphs are thousands of years old and easily destroyed. Do not walk on them or attempt to take a "rubbing" (there's a special area in the Puako Preserve for doing so). The best way to capture a petroglyph is with a photo in the late afternoon, when the shadows are long.

A DRAMATIC TEMPLE

Puukohola Heiau National Historic Site. Hwy. 270, near Kawaihae Harbor. ☎ **808/882-7218.** Fax 808/882-1215. www.nps.gov/puhe. $1 admission. Daily 7:30am–4pm. The visitor center is on Hwy. 270, and the heiau is a short walk away; the trail is closed when it's too windy, so call ahead if you're in doubt.

This seacoast temple, called "the hill of the whale," is the single most imposing and dramatic structure of the ancient Hawaiians. It was built by Kamehameha I in 1790–91. The temple stands 224 feet long by 100 feet wide, with three narrow terraces on the seaside and an amphitheater to view canoes. Kamehameha built this temple of sacrifice with mortarless stone after a prophet told him he would conquer and unite the islands if he did so; 4 years later, he fulfilled his kingly goal. The site also includes the house of John Young, a trusted advisor of Kamehameha, and, offshore, the submerged ruins of Hale O Ka Puni, a shrine dedicated to the shark gods.

NORTH KOHALA

The Original King Kamehameha Statue. Hwy. 270, Kapaau.

Here stands King Kamehameha the Great, right arm outstretched, left arm holding a spear, as if guarding the senior citizens who have turned a century-old New England–style courthouse into an airy center for their golden years. The center is worth a stop just to meet the town elders, who are quick to point out the local sights, hand you a free *Guide to Historic North Kohala,* and give you a brief tour of the courthouse, where a faded photo of FDR looms over the judge's dais and the walls are covered with the faces of innocent-looking local boys killed in World War II, Korea, and Vietnam.

But the statue's the main attraction here. There's one just like it in Honolulu, across the street from Iolani Palace, but this is the original: an 8-foot, 6-inch bronze statue by Thomas R. Gould, a Boston sculptor. It was cast in Europe in 1880 but was lost at sea on its way to Hawaii. A sea captain eventually recovered and returned the statue, which was finally placed here, near Kamehameha's Kohala birthplace, in 1912.

Kamehameha was born in 1750, became ruler of Hawaii in 1810, and died in Kailua-Kona in 1819. His burial site remains a mystery.

Pololu Valley Lookout. At the end of Hwy. 270, Makapala.

At this end-of-the-road scenic lookout, you can gaze at the vertical jade-green cliffs of the Hamakua Coast and two islets offshore. The view may look familiar once you get here—it often appears on travel posters. Most people race up, jump out, take a snapshot, and turn around and drive off; but it's a beautiful scene, so linger if you can. For the more adventurous, a switchback trail leads to a secluded black-sand beach at the mouth of a wild valley once planted in taro; bring water and bug spray.

Lapakahi State Historical Park. Hwy. 270, Mahukona. ☎ **808/889-5566.** Free admission. Daily 8am–4pm. Guided tours by appointment.

This 14th-century fishing village, on a hot, dry, dusty stretch of coast, offers a glimpse into the lifestyle of the ancients. Lapakahi is the best-preserved fishing village in Hawaii. Take the self-guided, mile-long loop trail past stone platforms, fish shrines, rock shelters, salt pans, and restored *hale* (houses) to a coral-sand beach and the deep blue sea. Wear good hiking shoes or tennies; it's a hearty 45-minute walk. Go early or later in the afternoon, as the sun is hot and shade is at a premium. An attendant in a thatch hut, who hands out maps, also keeps a handy cooler of ice water available in case you didn't bring your own.

Mookini Luakini. On the north shore, near Upolu Point Airport.

On the coast where King Kamehameha the Great was born stands Hawaii's oldest, largest, and most sacred religious site, which is now a national historical landmark—the 1,500-year-old ✪ Mookini Heiau, used by kings to pray and offer human sacrifices. You need four-wheel–drive to get here, as the road is rough, but it's worth the trip. The massive three-story stone temple, dedicated to Ku, the Hawaiian god of war, was erected in A.D. 480; each stone is said to have been passed hand to hand from Pololu Valley, 14 miles away, by 18,000 men who worked from sunset to sunrise. Kamehameha, born nearby under Halley's Comet, sought spiritual guidance here before embarking on his campaign to unite Hawaii. Go in the late afternoon when the setting sun strikes the lava-rock walls and creates a primal mood.

WAIMEA (KAMUELA)

Kamuela Museum. At the junction of Hwy. 19 and Hwy. 250, Waimea. ☎ **808/885-4724.** Admission $5 adults, $2 children under 12. Daily 8am–5pm.

It only takes about an hour to explore tiny Kamuela Museum. Its eclectic collection includes an early Hawaiian dogtoothed death cup, which sits next to a piece of rope used on the *Apollo* mission, which in turn sits near ancient artifacts from the royal family.

PARKER RANCH

Consider the numbers: 225,000 acres, 50,000 head of cattle, 700 miles of fence, 400 working horses, 27 cowboys—together producing 80% of the beef marketed in Hawaii. The *paniolo* (cowboy) tradition began here in 1809, when John Parker, a 19-year-old New England sailor, jumped ship and rounded up wild cows for King Kamehameha. The tradition lives on with a skeleton posse of around 30 to 40 cowboys, each assigned about eight horses to patrol America's third largest (and Hawaii's biggest) ranch. There's some evidence that Hawaiian cowboys were the first to be taught by the great Spanish horsemen, the *vaqueros;* they were cowboying 40 years before their counterparts in California, Texas, and the Pacific Northwest.

The **Visitor Center,** located at the Parker Ranch Shopping Center on Hwy. 190 (☎ **808/885-7655**), is open daily from 9am to 5pm and houses the **Parker Ranch Museum,** which displays items that have been used throughout the ranch's history, dating back to 1847. The museum also illustrates the six generations of Parker family history. An interesting video takes you inside the ranch and captures the essence of day-to-day life there.

You can also tour two historic homes on the ranch. In 1989, the late Richard Smart—the sixth-generation heir who sought a career on Broadway (and danced with Nanette Fabray in *Bloomer Girl* at the Schubert Theater)—opened his 8,000-square-foot yellow Victorian home, **Puuopelu,** to art lovers. The French Regency gallery here includes 100 original works by impressionists, including Renoir, Degas, Dufy, Corot, Utrillo, and Pissarro. Next door is **Mana Hale,** built 140 years ago, a little New England saltbox made of koa wood.

Admission is $10 for both the museum and the tours of both homes; admission to the museum only is $5. If you're buying a dual

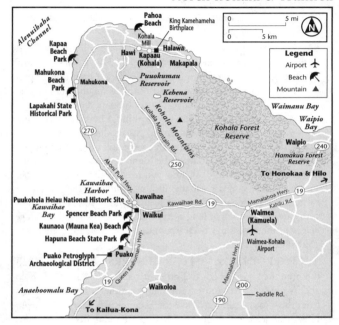

ticket, the last one is sold at 3pm; if you're visiting the museum only, you can arrive as late as 4pm. Allow about 1 1/2 hours to see everything.

See "Horseback Riding" in chapter 6 for details on riding tours of Parker Ranch.

MAUNA KEA

Some people just have to be on top of things. If you're one of those, head for the summit of Mauna Kea, which is the world's tallest mountain if you measure it from its base on the ocean floor.

Mauna Kea's summit is the best place on earth for astronomical observations, because its mid-Pacific site is near the equator and because it enjoys clear, pollution-free skies and pitch-black nights with no urban light to interfere. That's why Mauna Kea is home to the world's largest telescope. Needless to say, the stargazing from here is fantastic, even with the naked eye.

SETTING OUT You'll need a four-wheel–drive vehicle to climb to the peak, **Observatory Hill.** A standard car will get you as far as the visitors center, but check your rental agreement before you go;

some prohibit you from taking your car on the Saddle Road, which is narrow, rutted, and has a soft shoulder.

SAFETY TIPS   Always check the weather and Mauna Kea Road conditions before you head out (☎ **808/969-3218**). Dress warmly, as the temperatures drop into the 30s after dark. Other tips for preparing for your drive to the summit: Drink as much liquid as possible, avoiding alcohol and coffee, in the 36 hours surrounding your trip to avoid dehydration. Don't go within 24 hours of scuba diving—you could get the bends. Avoid gas-producing food the day before, such as beans, cabbage, onions, soft drinks, or starches. If you smoke, take a break for 48 hours before to allow carbon monoxide in your bloodstream to dissipate—you need all the oxygen you can get. Wear dark sunglasses to avoid snow blindness, and use lots of sunscreen and lip balm. Pregnant women and anyone under 16 or with a heart condition or lung ailment is advised to stay below. Once you're at the top, don't overexert yourself; it's bad for your heart. Take it easy up there.

ACCESS POINTS & VISITOR CENTERS   Before you climb the mountain, you've got to find it. It's about an hour from Hilo and Waimea to the visitors center, and another 30 to 45 minutes from there to the summit. Take the Saddle Road (Hwy. 200) from Hwy. 190; it's about 19 miles to Mauna Kea State Recreation Area, a good place to stop and stretch your legs. Go another 9 miles to the unmarked Summit Road turnoff, at the 28-mile marker (about 9,300 feet), across from the Hunter's Check-in Station. The higher you go, the more lightheaded you get, sometimes even dizzy; it usually sets in after the 9,600-foot marker (about 6.2 miles up the Summit Road), the site of the last comfort zone and the **Onizuka Visitor Center** (☎ **808/961-2180;** open Monday and Tuesday 10am to noon and 1pm to 4:30pm; Thursday 5:30pm to 10pm; Friday 9am to noon and 1 to 4:30pm; Saturday and Sunday 9am to 10pm; closed Wednesday), named in memory of Hawaii's fallen astronaut, a native of the Big Island and a victim of the *Challenger* explosion.

TOURS & PROGRAMS   If you'd rather not go it alone to the top, you can caravan up as part of a **free summit tour;** the tours, offered Saturday and Sunday at 1pm, start at the visitor center. You must be 16 years or older and have a four-wheel–drive vehicle. The tours explain the development of the facilities on Mauna Kea and include a walking tour of an observatory at 13,796 feet. Call ☎ **808/935-3371** if you'd like to participate.

On Thursday, Friday, Saturday, and Sunday nights from 6:30 to 10pm, you can do some serious **stargazing from the Onizuka Visitor Center.** There's a free lecture at 6:30pm. You'll have a chance to peer through an 11-inch telescope. Bring your own telescope or binoculars (with a red filter) as well, if you've got them, along with hot drinks and a snack. Dress for 30 to 40°F temperatures, but call for the weather report first (☎ **808/969-3218**). Families are welcome.

You can see a model of the world's largest telescope, which sits atop Mauna Kea, at the **Keck Control Center,** 65-1120 Mamalahoa Hwy. (Hwy. 19), across from the North Hawaii Community Hospital, Waimea (☎ **808/885-7887;** open Monday to Friday 8am to 4:30pm). Free brochures are available, and there's a 10-minute video explaining the Keck's search for objects in deep space.

If you don't have a four-wheel drive but still want to see the summit, consider **Mauna Kea Summit Tours** (☎ **808/775-7121;** fax 808/775-9911), offered Tuesday, Thursday, and Saturday. An experienced local guide will lead you on a 6-hour tour, which includes a stop at one of the observatories. Tours are limited to 10 people and leave from the Parker Ranch Shopping Center in Waimea. The cost is $80, which includes a picnic lunch.

MAKING THE CLIMB   If you're heading up on your own, stop at the visitor center for about a half-hour to get acquainted with the altitude, walk around, eat a banana, drink some water, and take deep breaths of the crystal-clear air before you press on upward, in low gear, engine whining. It takes about 30 to 45 minutes to get to the top from there. The trip is a mere 6 miles, but you climb from 9,000 to nearly 14,000 feet.

AT THE SUMMIT   Up there, 11 nations, including Japan, France, and Canada, have set up peerless infrared telescopes to look into deep space. Among them sits the **Keck Telescope,** the world's largest. Developed by the UC Berkeley and CalTech, it's eight stories high, weighs 150 tons, and has a 33-foot–diameter mirror made of 36 perfectly attuned hexagon mirrors, like a fly's eye, instead of one conventional lens.

Also at the summit, up a narrow footpath, is a **cairn of rocks;** from it, you can see across the Pacific Ocean in a 360° view that's beyond words and pictures. When it's socked in (and that can happen while you're standing there), you get a surreal look at the summits of Mauna Loa and Maui's Haleakala poking through the puffy white cumulus clouds beneath your feet.

Inside a cinder cone just below the summit is **Lake Waiau,** the only glacial lake in the mid-Pacific and the third highest lake in America (13,020 feet above sea level). The lake never dries up, even though it sits in porous lava where there are no springs and gets only 15 inches of rain a year. Nobody except "Ripley's Believe It or Not" quite knows what to make of this, although scientists suspect the lake is replenished by snow melt and permafrost from submerged lava tubes. You can't see the lake from Summit Road; you must take a brief, high-altitude hike. But it's easy: On the final approach to the summit area, upon regaining the blacktop road, go about 200 yards to the major switchback, and make a hard right turn. Park on the shoulder of the road (which, if you brought your altimeter, is at 13,200 ft.). No sign points the way, but there's an obvious half-mile trail that goes down to the lake about 200 feet across the lava. Follow the base of the big cinder cone on your left; you should have the summit of Mauna Loa in view directly ahead as you walk.

THE HAMAKUA COAST

A SELF-GUIDED DRIVING TOUR OF THE HAMAKUA
COAST The rich history of 117 years of the sugar industry, along the scenic 45-mile coastline from Hilo to Hamakua, comes alive in the interpretive "Hilo-Hamakua Heritage Coast" drive guide, produced by the **Hawaii Island Economic Development Board,** 200 Kanoelehua Ave., Suite 103, Hilo, HI 96720, ☎ **808/966-5416** or fax 808/966-6792.

The free drive guide not only points out the historical sites and museums, scenic photo opportunities, restaurants and stores, and even rest rooms along the Hawaii Belt Road (Hwy. 19), but also has corresponding brown-and-white points-of-interest signs on the highway. Visitor information centers anchored at either end in Hilo and in Hamakua have additional travel information on the area.

NATURAL WONDERS ALONG THE COAST

Akaka Falls. On Hwy. 19, Honomu (8 miles north of Hilo). Turn left at Honomu and head 3.6 miles inland on Akaka Falls Rd. (Hwy. 220).

One of Hawaii's most scenic waterfalls is an easy, 1-mile paved loop through a rain forest, past bamboo and ginger and down to an observation point, where you'll have a perfect view of 442-foot Akaka and nearby Kahuna Falls, which is a mere 100-footer. Keep your eyes peeled for rainbows.

Hawaii Tropical Botanical Garden. Off Hwy. 19 on the 4-mile Scenic Route, Onomea Bay (8 miles north of Hilo). ☎ **808/964-5233.** www.htbg.com. Admission $15 adults, $5 children 6–16. Daily 8:30am–4:30pm.

More than 1,800 species of tropical plants thrive in this little-known Eden by the sea. The 40-acre garden, nestled between the crashing surf and a thundering waterfall, has the world's largest selection of tropical plants growing in a natural environment, including a torch ginger forest, a banyan canyon, an orchid garden, a banana grove, a bromeliad hill, and a golden bamboo grove, which rattles like a jungle drum in the trade winds. The torch gingers tower on 12-foot stalks. Each spectacular specimen is named by genus and species, and caretakers point out new or rare buds in bloom. Some endangered Hawaiian specimens, like the rare Gardenia remyi, are flourishing in this habitat.

The gardens are seldom crowded; you can wander around by yourself all day, taking pictures, writing in your journal, or just soaking up the peace and quiet.

Laupahoehoe Beach Park. Laupahoehoe Point exit off Hwy. 19.

This idyllic place holds a grim reminder of nature's fury. In 1946, a tidal wave swept across the village that once stood on this lava-leaf (that's what *laupahoehoe* means) peninsula and claimed the lives of 20 students and four teachers. A memorial in this pretty little park recalls the tragedy. The land here ends in black sea stacks that resemble tombstones. It's not a place for swimming, but the views are spectacular.

HONOKAA

Honokaa is worth a visit to see the remnants of plantation life when sugar was king. This is a real place that hasn't yet been boutiqued into a shopping mall; it looks as if someone had kept it in a bell jar since 1920. There's a real barber shop, a real Filipino store, some really good shopping (see "Shops & Galleries," below), and a hotel with creaky floorboards that serves real, hearty food. The town also serves as the gateway to spectacular Waipio Valley (below).

Honokaa has no attractions, per se, but you might want to check out the **Katsu Goto Memorial,** next to the library at the Hilo end of town. Katsu Goto, one of the first indentured Japanese immigrants, arrived in Honokaa in the late 1800s to work on the sugar plantations. He learned English, quit the plantation, and aided his fellow immigrants in labor disputes with American planters. On Oct. 23, 1889, he was hanged from a lamppost in Honokaa, a victim of local-style justice. Today, a memorial recalls Goto's heroic human-rights struggle.

THE END OF THE ROAD: WAIPIO VALLEY

Long ago, this lush, tropical place was the valley of kings, who called it the valley of "curving water" (which is what *Waipio* means). From the black-sand bay at its mouth, Waipio sweeps back 6 miles between sheer, cathedral-like walls that reach almost a mile high. Here, 40,000 Hawaiians lived in a garden of Eden etched by streams and waterfalls amid evergreen taro, red bananas, and wild guavas. Only about 50 Hawaiians live in the valley today, tending taro, fishing, and soaking up the ambiance of this old Hawaiian place.

Many of the ancient royals are buried in Wapio's hidden crevices; some believe they rise up to become Marchers of the Night, whose chants reverberate through the valley. It's here that the caskets of Hawaiian chiefs Liloa and Lono Ika Makahiki, recently stolen from Bishop Museum, are believed to have been returned by Hawaiians. The sacred valley is steeped in myth and legend, some of which you may hear, usually after dark in the company of Hawaiian elders. Sometimes they talk of Nenewe the Shark Man, who lives in a pool, and of the ghost of the underworld, who periodically rises to the surface through a tunnel by the sea.

To get to Waipio Valley, take Hwy. 19 from Hilo to Honokaa, then Hwy. 240 to ✪ **Waipio Valley Lookout,** a grassy park on the edge of Waipio Valley's sheer cliffs with splendid views of the wild oasis below. This is a great place for a picnic; you can sit at old redwood picnic tables and watch the white combers race upon the black-sand beach at the mouth of Waipio Valley.

From the lookout, you can hike down into the valley (see "Hiking & Camping," in chapter 6). Do not, repeat *do not,* attempt to drive your rental car down into the valley (even if you see someone else doing it). The problem is not so much going down as coming back up. Every day, rental cars have to be "rescued" and towed back up to the top, at great expense to the driver. Don't try it. Instead, take the **Waipio Valley Shuttle** (☎ **808/775-7121**) on a 90-minute guided tour. The shuttle runs Monday to Saturday from 9am to 4pm; tickets are $36.40 for adults, $15 for kids ages 3 to 11. Get your tickets at **Waipio Valley Art Works,** on Hwy. 240, 2 miles from the lookout (☎ **808/775-0958**).

You can also explore the valley on a **Waipio Valley Wagon Tour** (☎ **808/775-9518;** fax 808/775-9318), a mule-drawn surrey that takes you on a narrated 90-minute historical tour of the valley. Tours are offered Monday to Saturday at 9:30am, 11:30am,

1:30pm, and 3:30pm. They're $40 for adults, $20 for children ages 3 to 12; call for reservations.

If you want to spend more than a day in the valley, plan ahead. A few simple B&Bs are situated on the ridge overlooking the valley and require advance reservations. While it's possible to camp (see "Hiking & Camping," in chapter 6), it does put a strain on the natural environment here.

HILO

A SELF-GUIDED WALKING TOUR Contact or stop by the **Hilo Main Street Program,** 252 Kamehameha Ave., Hilo, HI 96720 (☎ **808/935-8850**) for a copy of their very informative self-guided walking tour of 18 historic sites in Hilo, focusing on various sites from the 1870s to the present.

ON THE WATERFRONT

Old banyan trees shade **Banyan Drive,** the lane that curves along the waterfront to the Hilo Bay hotels. Most of the trees were planted in the mid-1930s by memorable visitors like Cecil B. DeMille (who was here in 1933 filming *Four Frightened People*), Babe Ruth (his tree's in front of Hilo Hawaiian Hotel), King George V, and Amelia Earhart, but many were planted by celebrities whose fleeting fame didn't last as long as the trees themselves.

It's worth a stop along Banyan Drive—especially if the coast is clear and the summit of Mauna Kea is free of clouds—to make the short walk across the concrete-arch bridge in front of the Naniloa Hotel to **Coconut Island,** if only to gain a panoramic sense of the place.

Also along Banyan Drive is ✪ **Liliuokalani Gardens,** the largest formal Japanese garden this side of Tokyo. This 30-acre park, named for Hawaii's last monarch, Queen Liliuokalani, is as pretty as a postcard from the Orient, with bonsai, carp ponds, pagodas, and a moon-gate bridge. Free admission; open 24 hours.

Since 1914, Hilo fishermen have delivered the catch of the day—fresh ahi, mahimahi, and opakapaka—to **Suisan Fish Auction** (☎ **808/935-8051**), at Kamehameha Avenue and Banyan Drive. The boats return to harbor just at sunrise after fishing all night. The auction is conducted in three lingoes, including Hawaii's own pidgin, and can last an hour if the catch has been good. It begins at 7:30am Monday through Saturday, so arrive at 6:30am to get a good look as the fishers unload the boats. The **Suisan Fish Market** (☎ **808/935-9349;** Monday to Friday 8am to 5pm, Saturday 8am to 4pm) is next door if you miss the early-morning action.

OTHER HILO SIGHTS

Lyman Museum & Mission House. 276 Haili St. (at Kapiolani St.), Hilo. ☎ 808/935-5021. Fax 808/969-7685. E-mail lymanwks@interpac.net. Admission $7 adults, $5 seniors over 60, $3 children under 18, and $15 family. Mon–Sat 9am–4:30pm.

The oldest wood-frame house on the island was built in 1839 by David and Sarah Lyman, a missionary couple who arrived from New England in 1832. This hybrid combined New England– and Hawaiian-style architecture with a pitched thatch roof. Built of hand-hewn koa planks and timbers, it's crowned by Hawaii's first corrugated zinc roof, imported from England in 1856. Here, the Lymans served as the spiritual center of Hilo, receiving such guests as Mark Twain, Robert Louis Stevenson, and Hawaii's own monarchs. The well-preserved house is the best example of missionary life and times in Hawaii. You'll find lots of artifacts from the last century, including furniture and clothing from the Lymans and one of the first mirrors in Hawaii. The 21st century has also entered the museum, which offers online computers and interactive, high-tech exhibits.

The **Earth Heritage Gallery** next door continues the story of the islands with geology and astronomy exhibits, a mineral rock collection that's rated as one of the top 10 in the country, and a section on local flora and fauna. Upstairs is the **Island Heritage Gallery,** which features displays on native Hawaiian culture, including a replica of a grass hut, as well as on other cultures that were transplanted to Hawaii's shores.

Maunaloa Macadamia Nut Factory. Macadamia Nut Rd. (8 miles from Hilo, off Hwy. 11), Hilo. ☎ 808/966-8618. Free admission, self-guided factory tours. Orchard tours every hour 10am–4pm; $5 adults, $3 children. Daily 9am–4pm. From Hwy. 11, turn on Macadamia Nut Road; go 3 miles down the road to the factory.

Explore this unique factory and learn how Hawaii's favorite nut is grown and processed. The 1-hour guided van tour even takes you through the macadamia orchard. And, of course, you'll want to sample the tasty mac nuts, too.

Naha Stone. In front of Hilo Public Library, 300 Waianuenue Ave.

This $2\frac{1}{2}$-ton stone was used as a test of royal strength: Ancient legend says that whoever could move the stone would conquer and unite the islands. As a 14-year-old boy, King Kamehameha the Great moved the stone—later he fulfilled his destiny. The **Pinao stone,** next to it, once guarded an ancient temple.

Hilo

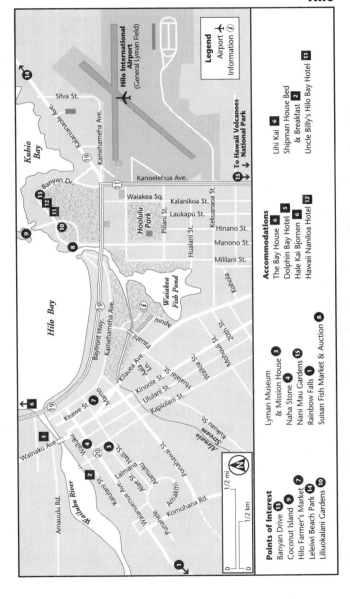

Legend

✈ Airport
ⓘ Information

Hilo International Airport (General Lyman Field)

→ To Hawaii Volcanoes National Park

Points of Interest

Banyan Drive ⑬
Coconut Island ⑨
Hilo Farmer's Market ⑦
Leleiwi Beach Park ⑭
Liliuokalani Gardens ⑩

Lyman Museum & Mission House ③
Naha Stone ③
Nani Mau Gardens ⑮
Rainbow Falls ①
Suisan Fish Market & Auction ⑧

Accommodations

The Bay House ⑥
Dolphin Bay Hotel ⑤
Hale Kai Bjornen ⑥
Hawaii Naniloa Hotel ⑫

Lihi Kai ⑥
Shipman House Bed & Breakfast ②
Uncle Billy's Hilo Bay Hotel ⑪

Nani Mau Gardens. 421 Makalika St. (3 miles south of Hilo Airport on Hwy. 11, turn on Makalika St., go ³/₄ mile), Hilo. ☎ **808/959-3541.** Fax 808/959-3152. www.nanimau.com. Admission $7.50 adults, $6 seniors, $4.50 children 6–18. Tram tours $5 extra. Daily 8am–5pm.

Just outside Hilo is Nani Mau ("forever beautiful") Gardens, where Makato Nitahara, who turned a 20-acre papaya patch into a tropical garden, claims to have every flowering plant in Hawaii. His collection includes more than 2,000 varieties, from fragile hibiscus, whose bloom lasts only a day, to durable red anthuriums imported from South America. There are also Japanese gardens, an orchid walkway, a botanical museum, and a restaurant, open for lunch and dinner.

Panaewa Rainforest Zoo. Stainback Highway (off Hwy. 11), Hilo. ☎ **808/ 959-7224.** Fax 808/961-8411. Admission free. Daily 9am–4pm.

This 12-acre zoo, nestled in the heart of the Panaewa Forest Reserve south of Hilo, is the only outdoor rain forest zoo in the U.S. Some 50 species of animals from rain forests around the globe call Panaewa home—including several endangered Hawaiian birds. All of them are exhibited in a natural setting. This is one of the few zoos where you can observe Sumatran tigers, Brazilian tapirs, and the rare pygmy hippopotamus, an endangered "minihippo" found in Western Africa.

✪ **Rainbow Falls.** West on Waianuenue Ave., past Kaumana Dr.

Go in the morning, around 9 or 10am, just as the sun comes over the mango trees, to see Rainbow Falls at its best. The 80-foot falls spill into a big round natural pool surrounded by wild ginger. If you like legends, try this: Hina, the mother of Maui, lives in the cave behind the falls. In the old days, before liability suits and lawyers, people swam in the pool, but it's now prohibited.

ON THE ROAD TO THE VOLCANO
VOLCANO VILLAGE: GATEWAY TO HAWAII VOLCANOES NATIONAL PARK

In the 19th century, before tourism became Hawaii's middle name, the islands' singular attraction for world travelers wasn't the beach, but the volcano. From the world over, curious spectators gathered on the rim of Kilauea's Halemaumau crater to see one of the greatest wonders of the globe. Those who came to stand in awe took shelter after sundown in a large grass hut perched on the rim of Kilauea—Hawaii's first tourist hotel, which became **Volcano House.**

Since Kilauea and environs were officially designated Hawaii Volcanoes National Park in 1916, a village has popped up at its front door. Volcano isn't a town so much as a wide spot in Old

Volcano Road: a 10-block area with two general stores, a couple of restaurants, a post office, a coffee shop, a new firehouse (built in one weekend by volunteers), and the only ATM between Keeau and Ocean View. Volcano has no stoplights or jail, and not even a church or a cemetery, though it does have a winery. There's no baseball diamond either, which is probably just as well, since it rains a lot in Volcano—100 inches a year—which makes everything grow Jack-and-the-Beanstalk style. If Volcano didn't have a real volcano in its backyard, it would probably be called Rain Forest.

Geographically speaking, Volcano isn't actually the gateway to Hawaii Volcanoes National Park; it's really a little off to the side and north. Highway 11, the Hawaii Belt Road, which leads directly to the park, bypasses Volcano Village. But if you're going to see the volcano, Volcano is a great place to spend a few days—in fact, it's the only place.

Even if you're just visiting the park for the day, it's worth turning off to stop for gas at **Volcano General Store,** on Haunani Road, where kindly clerks give directions and sell fresh orchid sprays, local poha berry jam, and bowls of chili rice, a local favorite.

Volcano Winery, Pii Mauna Dr., off Hwy. 11 at the 30-mile marker (go all the way to the end; ☎ **808/967-7479;** www. volcanowinery.com), is worth a stop to taste the local wines, made from tropical honey (no grapes) and tropical fruit blends (half-grape and half-fruit). Lift a glass of Volcano Blush or Macadamia Nut Honey and toast Madame Pele at this boutique winery, open daily from 10am to 5:30pm; tastings are free.

APPROACHING THE PARK FROM THE SOUTH: CROSSING THE KAU DESERT

Hot, scorched, quake-shaken, bubbling-up, new/dead land: This is the great Kau Desert, layer upon layer of lava flows and fine ash and fallout. Only those eruptions in recent history have been recorded— 1790, 1880, 1920, 1926, 1950, 1969, 1971, 1974. As you traverse the desert, you cross the Great Crack and the Southwest Rift Zone, a major fault zone that looks like a giant groove in the earth, before you reach Kilauea Volcano.

✪ HAWAII VOLCANOES NATIONAL PARK

Yellowstone, Yosemite, and other national parks are spectacular, no doubt about it. But in my opinion they're all ho-hum compared to this one: Here, nothing less than the miracle of creation is the daily attraction.

Founded in 1916, Hawaii Volcanoes National Park is Hawaii's premier natural attraction. Visiting the park is a yin/yang experience. It's the only rain forest in the U.S. National Park system—and the only park that's home to an active volcano. Most people drive through the park (it has 50 miles of good roads, some of them often covered by lava flows) and call it a day. But it takes at least 3 days to explore the whole park, including such oddities as **Halemaumau Crater,** a still-fuming pit of steam and sulfur; the intestinal-looking **Thurston Lava Tube; Devastation Trail,** a short hike through a desolated area destroyed by lava, right next to an Eden-like rain forest; and finally, the end of **Chain of Craters Road,** where lava regularly spills across the man-made two-lane blacktop to create its own red-hot freeway to the sea. In addition to some of the world's weirdest landscape, the park also has hiking trails, rain forests, campgrounds, a historic old hotel on a crater's rim, and that spectacular, still-erupting volcano.

NOTES ON THE ERUPTING VOLCANO   In Hawaii, volcanoes aren't violent killers like Mount Pinatubo in the Philippines or even Mt. St. Helens in Oregon. Vulcanologists refer to Hawaii's volcanic eruptions as "quiet" eruptions, since gases escape slowly instead of building up and exploding violently all at once. Hawaii's eruptions produce slow-moving, oozing lava that provides excellent, safe viewing most of the time. In Hawaii, people run to volcanoes instead of fleeing from them.

Since the current eruption of Kilauea began on January 3, 1983, lava has covered some 16,000 acres of lowland and rain forest, threatening rare hawks, honeycreeper birds, spiders, and bats, while destroying power and telephone lines and eliminating water service possibly forever. Some areas have been mantled repeatedly and are now buried underneath 80 feet of lava.

Even though people haven't had to run fleeing from this flow, it has still caused its share of destruction. At last count, the lava flow had destroyed nearly 200 homes and businesses, wiped out Kaimu Black Sand Beach (once Hawaii's most photographed beach) and Queen's Bath, obliterated entire towns and subdivisions (Kalapana, Royal Gardens and Kalapana Gardens subdivisions, and Kapaahu Homesteads), and buried natural and historic landmarks (a 12th-century heiau, the century-old Kalapana Mauna Kea Church, Wahaulu Visitors Center, and thousands of archaeological artifacts and sites). The cost of the destruction of the eruption—so far—is estimated at $100 million. But how do you price the destruction of a 700-year old temple or a 100-year-old church?

Hawaii Volcanoes National[

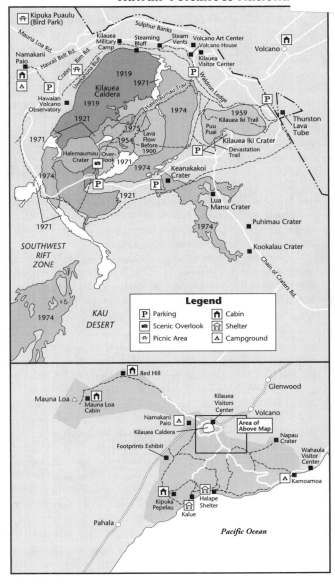

Legend

P	Parking	🏠	Cabin
📷	Scenic Overlook	🏠	Shelter
🎋	Picnic Area	△	Campground

Kipuka Puaulu (Bird Park)

Mauna Loa Rd.

Namakani Paio

Hawaii Belt Rd.

Crater Rim Rd.

Uwekahuna Bluff

Kilauea Military Camp

Steaming Bluff

Sulphur Banks

Steam Vents

Volcano Art Center
Volcano House

Kilauea Visitor Center

Volcano

1919

1971

Kilauea Caldera

1919

Hawaiian Volcano Observatory

1921

1975

1954

Lava Flow Before 1900

Halemaumau Trail

1974

1959

Kilauea Iki Trail

Puu Puai

Waldron Ledge

Thurston Lava Tube

Halemaumau Crater

Overlook

1971

1971

Devastation Trail

Kilauea Iki Crater

1974

Keanakakoi Crater

1974

1921

Lua Manu Crater

Puhimau Crater

1971

1974

Kookalau Crater

SOUTHWEST RIFT ZONE

1974

KAU DESERT

Chain of Craters Rd.

Red Hill

Glenwood

Mauna Loa △

Mauna Loa Cabin

Kilauea Visitors Center

Namakani Paio

Kilauea Caldera

Volcano

Area of Above Map

Footprints Exhibit

Napau Crater

Wahaula Visitor Center

Kipuka Pepelau

Halape Shelter

Kalue

Kamoamoa

Pahala

Pacific Ocean

163

But the volcano has not only destroyed, it has also added—more than 560 acres of new land to the island by the beginning of 1998. The volume of erupted lava over the last $1^1/2$ decades measures nearly two billion cubic yards—that's enough new rock to pave a two-lane highway 1.2 million miles long, circling the earth some 50 times. Or, as a spokesperson for the park puts it: "Every five days, there is enough lava coming out of Kilauea volcano's eruption to place a thin veneer over Washington D.C.—all 63 square miles."

The most prominent vent of the eruption has been Puu Oo, a 760-foot-high cinder-and-spatter cone. The most recent flow—the one you'll be able to see, if you're lucky—follows a 7-mile-long tube from the Puu Oo vent area to the sea. This lava flow has extended the Big Island's shoreline seaward and added hundreds of acres of new land along the steep southern slopes. Periodically, the new land proves unstable, falls under its own weight, and slides into the ocean. (These areas of ground gained and lost are not included in the tally of new acreage—only the land that sticks counts.)

Scientists are also keeping an eye on Mauna Loa, which has been swelling since its last eruption in 1983. If there's a new eruption, they predict that there could be a fast-moving flow down the southwest side of the island, possibly into South Kona or Kau.

What You're Likely to See Hopefully, the eruption will still be going on when you visit the park. As this book went to press, vulcanologists predicted that the eruption would continue unabated, with no end in sight. Scientists are perplexed by Kilauea's continuing eruption, as major eruptions in the past have ended abruptly after only several months. A continuous eruption of more than a decade and a half is setting new ground, so to speak.

But neither Mother Nature nor Madame Pele (the volcano goddess) runs on a schedule. The volcano could be shooting fountains of lava hundreds of feet into the air on the day you arrive, or it could be completely quiet—there are no guarantees with nature. On many days, the lava flows right by accessible roads, and you can get as close as the heat will allow; sometimes, however, the lava flow is miles away from the nearest access point, visible only in the distance or in underground tubes where you can't see it.

VOLCANO VOCABULARY The volcano has its own unique, poetic vocabulary that describes in Hawaiian what cannot be said so well in English. The lava that looks like swirls of chocolate cake frosting is called **pahoehoe;** it results from a fast-moving flow that curls artistically as it flows. The big, blocky, jumbled lava that looks like a chopped-up parking lot is called **aa;** it's caused by lava that moves slowly, pulling apart as it overruns itself.

Newer words include **Vog,** which is volcanic smog made of volcanic gases and smoke from forests set on fire by aa and pahoehoe. **Laze** results when sulfuric acid hits the water and vaporizes and mixes with chlorine to become, as any chemistry student knows, hydrochloric acid. Both vog and laze sting your eyes and can cause respiratory illness; don't expose yourself to either for too long. Anyone with heart or breathing trouble, or women who are pregnant, should avoid both vog and laze.

JUST THE FACTS

WHEN TO GO   The best time to go is when Kilauea is really pumping. If you're lucky, you'll be in the park when the volcano is really active and fountaining; mostly, the lava runs like a red river downslope into the sea. If you're on another island and hear a TV news bulletin that the volcano is acting up, catch the next flight to Hilo to see the spectacle. You won't be sorry—and your favorite beach will still be there when you get back. Also see "Notes on the Erupting Volcano," above.

ACCESS POINTS   Hawaii Volcanoes National Park is 29 miles from Hilo, on Hawaii Belt Road (Hwy. 11). If you're staying in Kailua-Kona, it's 100 miles, or about a 2¹/₂-hour drive, to the park. Admission is $10 per vehicle; you can come and go as often as you want for 7 days. Hikers and bicyclists pay $5; bikes are allowed only on roads and paved trails.

INFORMATION & VISITOR CENTERS   For information before you go, contact **Hawaii Volcanoes National Park,** P.O. Box 52, Hawaii Volcanoes National Park, HI 96718 (☎ **808/ 985-6000;** www.nps.gov/havo). **Kilauea Visitor Center** is at the entrance of the park, just off Hwy. 11; it's open daily from 7:45am to 5pm.

For the latest **eruption update** and information on volcanic activity in the park, call the park's 24-hour hotline at ☎ **808/ 985-6000.** Updates on volcanic activity are also posted daily on the bulletin board at the visitor center.

FOLLOWING THE ERUPTION ON THE INTERNET   Everything you wanted to know about Hawaii's volcanoes, from what's going on with the current eruptions to where the next eruption is likely to be, is now available on the Hawaiian Volcano Observatory's new web site, http://hvo.wr.usgs.gov.

The site is divided into areas of information about Kilauea (the currently erupting volcano), Mauna Loa (which last erupted in 1984), and Hawaii's other volcanoes (including Lo'ihi, the submerged volcano off the coast of the Big Island). Each site has photos, maps, eruption summaries, and historical information.

HIKING & CAMPING IN THE PARK   Hawaii Volcanoes National Park offers a wealth of hiking and camping possibilities. See "Hiking & Camping," in chapter 6, for details.

ACCOMMODATIONS IN & AROUND THE PARK   If camping isn't your thing, don't worry. In addition to historic Volcano House, on the rim of Halemaumau Crater, adjacent Volcano Village has plenty of comfortable and convenient places to stay.

EMERGENCIES   Call ☎ **911** if you have an emergency in the park.

SEEING THE HIGHLIGHTS

Your first stop should be **Kilauea Visitor Center,** a rustic structure in a shady grove of trees just inside the entrance to the park. Here, you can get up-to-the-minute reports on the volcano's activity, learn how volcanoes work, see a film showing blasts from the past, get information on hiking and camping, and pick up the obligatory postcards.

Filled with a new understanding of vulcanology and the volcano goddess, Pele, you should then walk across the street to **Volcano House;** go through the lobby and out the other side, where you can have a good look at **Kilauea Caldera,** a 2^1/$_2$-mile-wide, 500-foot-deep pit. The caldera used to be a bubbling pit of fountaining lava; today you can still see wisps of steam that could, while you're standing there, turn into something more.

Now get out on the highway and drive by the **Sulphur Banks,** which smell like rotten eggs, and the **Steam Vents,** where trails of smoke, once molten lava, rise from within the inner reaches of the earth. This is one of the few places where you feel that the volcano is really alive. Stop at the **Thomas A. Jaggar Museum** (open daily 8:30am to 5pm; free admission) for a good look at Halemaumau Crater, which is a half-mile across and 1,000 feet deep, and (maybe) Mauna Loa, 20 miles to the west. The museum shows eruption videos, explains the Pele legend in murals, and monitors earthquakes (a precursor of eruptions) on a seismograph, recording every twitch in the earth.

Once you've seen the museum, drive around the caldera to the other side, park, and take the short walk to Halemaumau Crater's

---

Travel Tip

Remember: Thanks to its higher elevation and windward (rainier) location, this neck of the woods is always colder than it is at the beach. If you're coming from the Kona side of the island in the summer, expect it to be at least 10 to 20°F cooler at the volcano, so bring a sweater or light jacket. In the winter months, expect temperatures to be in the 40s or 50s, and dress accordingly. Always have rain gear on hand, especially in winter.

---

edge, past stinky sulfur banks and steam vents, to stand at the overlook and stare in awe at this once-fuming and bubbling old firepit, which still generates ferocious heat out of vestigial vents.

If you feel the need to cool off now, go to the **Thurston Lava Tube,** the coolest place in the park. You'll hike down into a natural bowl in the earth, a forest preserve the lava didn't touch—full of native bird songs and giant tree ferns. Then you'll see a black hole in the earth; step in. It's all drippy and cool here, with bare roots hanging down. You can either resurface into the bright daylight or, if you have a flashlight, poke on deeper into the tube, which goes for another quarter-mile or so.

If you're still game for a good hike, try **Kilauea Iki Crater,** a 4-mile, 2-hour hike across the floor of the crater, which became a bubbling pool of lava in 1959 and sent fountains of lava 1,900 feet in the air, completely devastating a nearby ohia forest and leaving another popular hike, ominously known as **Devastation Trail.** This half-mile walk is a startling look at the powers of a volcanic eruption on the environment. (See chapter 6 for details on these and other park hikes.)

For a glimpse of ancient Hawaiian art, check out the **Puu Loa Petroglyphs,** around the 15-mile marker on Chain of Craters Road. Look for the stack of rocks on the road to park. A brief, half-mile walk from the road will bring you to a circular boardwalk where you can see the thousands of mysterious Hawaiian petroglyphs, carved in stone. This area, Puu Loa, was a sacred place for generations; fathers came here to bury their newborn's umbilical cord in the numerous small holes in the lava, thus ensuring a long life for the child. *A word of warning:* It's very easy to destroy these ancient works of art. Do not leave the boardwalk, and don't walk on or around the petroglyphs. Rubbings of petroglyphs will destroy them; the best way to capture the petroglyphs is with a photo.

THE VOLCANO AFTER DARK   If the volcano is still erupting, be sure to see it after dark as the lava snakes down the side of the mountain and pours into the sea. About an hour before sunset, head back into the park, 23 miles down **Chain of Craters Road.** Get ready to see the red—it's a vivid display you'll never forget. If conditions are good and the flow is accessible when you're there—sometimes it's too far from the road to hike to, so you'll have to be content with seeing it from a distance—park rangers positioned at the barricades will tell you how to get to the current lava flow. *Be sure to heed the ranger:* In the past, a handful of hikers who ignored these directions died en route; new lava can be unstable and break off without warning. Take water, a flashlight, and your camera, and wear sturdy shoes.

VIEWING THE VOLCANO FROM THE AIR   The best way to see the volcano is from on high, in a helicopter. This bird's-eye view puts the enormity of it all into perspective. No two ways about it—this is an extraordinary way to see the red. The best helicopter firm is ✪ **Blue Hawaiian Helicopter** (☎ **800/745-BLUE** or 808/886-1768; www.bluehawaiian.com), the Cadillac of helicopter tour companies. This professionally run, locally based company has an excellent safety record, comfortable, top-of-the-line 'copters, and pilots who are extremely knowledgeable about everything from vulcanology to Hawaii lore. The company flies out of both Hilo and Waikoloa (Hilo is cheaper because it's closer). The **Circle of Fire/ Waterfalls** 50-minute flight from Hilo takes you to the volcano and past waterfalls, valleys, and remote beaches for $130 per person; the 70-minute **East Island Epic,** a tour of rain forests, waterfalls, and the volcano, is $175 per person. From Waikoloa, there's the **Kohala Coast Adventure,** a 50-minute flight over the Kohala Mountains and remote valleys for $135 per person (volcano not included); or— my favorite—the 2-hour **Big Island Spectacular,** starring the volcano, tropical valleys, Hamakua Coast waterfalls, and the Kohala Mountains, for $290 (worth every penny).

If you'd prefer a fixed-wing aircraft, try **Big Island Air** (☎ **808/ 329-4868**), which offers 1-hour volcano tours from Kona Airport in a twin-engine, air-conditioned airplane for $135 per person. **Classic Aviation** (☎ **800/695-8100** or 808/329-8687) offers flights to the volcano from Hilo Airport in a new edition of the classic 1935 Waco biplane for $99 each. Two passengers, seated side by side in the open cockpit of this propeller plane, get cloth helmets, goggles, and white silk scarves to wear on their classic flight over the volcano ("Curse you, Red Baron!").

SOUTH POINT: LAND'S END

The history of Hawaii is condensed here, at the end of 11 miles of bad road that peters out at Kaulana Bay, in the lee of a jagged, black-lava point—the tail end of the United States. No historic marker marks the spot or gives any clue as to the geographical significance of the place. If you walk out to the very tip, beware of the big waves that lash the shore. The nearest continental landfall is Antarctica, 7,500 miles away.

It's a 2¹/₂-mile four-wheel–drive trip and a hike down a cliff from South Point to the anomaly known as **Green Sand Beach** (see "Beaches," in chapter 6).

Back on the Mamalahoa Highway (Hwy. 11), about 20 miles east is the small town of Pahoa; turn off the highway and travel about 5 miles through this once-thriving sugar plantation and beyond to the **Wood Valley Temple and Retreat Center** (☎ 808/928-8539), also known as *Nechung Drayang Ling* ("Island of Melodious Sound"). It's an oasis of tranquillity tucked into the rain forest. Built by Japanese sugarcane workers, the temple, retreat center, and surrounding gardens were rededicated by the Dalai Lama in 1980 to serve as a spiritual center for Tibetan Buddhism. You can walk the beautiful grounds, attend morning or evening services, and breathe in the quiet mindfulness of this serene area.

2 Shops & Galleries

by Jocelyn Fujii

While chefs and farmers tout this island as fertile ground for crops and food, artists point to its primal, volcanic energy as a boost to their creative endeavors, too. Arts communities and galleries are sprinkled across the Big Island, in villages like Holualoa and Volcano, where fine works in pottery, wood-turning, handmade glass, and other two- and three-dimensional media are sold in serene settings.

Although the visual arts are flourishing on this island, the line between shop and gallery can often be too fine to define, or even to approach. Too many self-proclaimed "galleries" purvey schlock or a mixture of arts, crafts, and tacky souvenirs. T-shirts and Kona coffee mugs are a souvenir staple in many galleries.

The galleries and shops below offer a broad mix in many media. Items for the home, jewelry and accessories, vintage Hawaiiana, and accoutrements at various prices and for various tastes can make great gifts to go, as can locally made food products like preserves, cookies, flowers, Kona coffee, and macadamia nuts. You'll find that bowls made of rare native woods such as koa are especially abundant on this island. This is an area in which politics and art intersect: Although reforestation efforts are underway to plant new koa trees, the decline of old-growth forests is causing many artists to turn to equally beautiful, and more environmentally correct, alternative woods.

THE KONA COAST
IN & AROUND KAILUA-KONA

Kailua-Kona's shopping prospects pour out into the streets in a festival atmosphere of T-shirts, trinkets, and dime-a-dozen souvenirs, with Alii Drive at the center of this activity. But a hot newcomer is changing that image: the **Coconut Grove** on Alii Drive, across the street from the seawall, where some great new shops and restaurants have recently opened. The **Rift Zone** gallery ☎ 808/331-1100) pulled up its Hilo stakes and moved to this prime location with a large selection of ceramics and crafts by 150 Island artists, including gallery owners Robert and Kathy Joiner, whose own work in ceramics is liberally displayed. Oil paintings, Niihau shells, etched and blown glass, slumped glass, koa furniture (dining room tables to beds, coffee, and end tables), Avi Kiriaty oils, Ed Kayton originals, Brad Lewis photography, Mike Felig's koa furniture, and Judy St. Croix's bronze sculptures are among the works represented. Also in Coconut Grove, **Kane Coconut Grove** (☎ 808/334-1717) is a good source of aloha wear for men and women, mostly made by local manufacturer Malia. And who can resist the lighthearted appeal of **Giggles** (☎ 808/329-7763) ("fun and fancy fashions for kids"), also in the Grove, with a collection of children's treasures that will have you reeling—and reaching for your pocketbook. Next door in the Alii Sunset Plaza, next to Hard Rock Café, beaders can make a beeline for **Mana Beads** (☎ 808/331-2161) and peruse a dizzying—and handsome—collection of beads from all over the world.

Shopping stalwarts in Kona, in more familiar shopping territory, are the **Kona Square,** across from **King Kamehameha's Kona Beach Hotel;** the hotel's shopping mall, with close to two dozen shops, including a Liberty House; and **the Kona Inn Shopping Village** on Alii Drive. All include a plethora of shops for vacationers' needs, but be forewarned: The going can be rocky for those with refined tastes. In Kailua-Kona, tacky is king—so set your expectations accordingly.

Alapaki's Hawaiian Gifts. In the Keauhou Shopping Village, Alii Dr. ☎ **808/ 322-2007.**

Lovers of Hawaiian crafts will appreciate this attractive selection of gift items, made by more than 120 artists from Hawaii's islands, with a small percentage of the inventory from Fiji, Samoa, Marquesas, and other Polynesian islands. Alapaki's includes bookmarks with pressed island flowers, Molokai lauhala (woven pandanus leaves), made-in-Kona Hawaiian Girl soaps, native-wood utensils and bowls, jewelry, kukui nut leis, original paintings, and handblown glass by the noted Holualoa artist Wilfred Yamazawa. The owners clearly make an effort to showcase quality local works and are active in fundraising activities for Big Island hula schools, canoe projects, and other Hawaiian efforts.

Honolua Surf Company. In the Kona Inn Shopping Village, Alii Dr. ☎ **808/329-1001.**

This shop targets the surf-and-sun enthusiast with good things for good times: towels, flip-flops, body boards, sunglasses, swimsuits, and everything else you need for ocean and shore action. Quiksilver, Tommy Bahama, Roxy, Billabong, and Kahala are among the top menswear labels here, but we also like the quirky, colorful Toes on the Nose. Also popular is the full line of products with the Honolua Surf Co. label, including T-shirts, hats, bags, dresses, sweatshirts, aloha shirts, and swimwear.

✪ **Hula Heaven.** In the Kona Inn Shopping Village, Alii Dr. (next to Hulihee Palace). ☎ **808/329-7885.**

Of course it's heavenly, but there's a good dose of kitsch here as well. There's no such thing as "dropping in" at Hula Heaven. Neighbor islanders have been known to make special trips to Kona to shop here. Gwen and Evan Olins have made their treasure-laden shop the nexus of Hawaiian collectibles for serious and casual collectors, or anyone with an eye for island-style treasures. And their new Hula Heaven Hawaiian Shirt Museum, temporarily located a few doors away in the Kona Inn Shopping Village, is worth a special trip. Give yourself time to linger among the vintage aloha shirts, nodding hula-girl dolls, out-of-print books, lauhala bags, Mundorff prints, Matson liner menus, vintage ukuleles and guitars, Don Blanding dinnerware, koa perfume bottles, Ming's jewelry (the *ne plus ultra* of vintage jewelry), and accessories made of authentic vintage bark cloth. Gwen's fondness for textiles is reflected in the window displays, often featuring one-of-a-kind 1940s fabrics, and on the racks, where traditional tea-timer tops and muumuus in spirited old prints mingle with new clothing in faithfully reproduced fabrics. What isn't vintage—and 50% of the store is—is vintage-looking, exuding nostalgia, color, and a high-spirited style.

Just Looking

The finest art on the Kona Coast hangs, of all places, in a bank. Award-winning **First Hawaiian Bank,** 74-5593 Palani Rd. (☎ **808/ 329-2461**), has art lovers making special trips to view Hiroki Morinoue's mural, John Buck's prints, Chiu Leong's ceramic sculpture, Franco Salmoiraghi's photographs, Setsuko Morinoue's abstract fiber wallpiece, and other works that were incorporated as part of the bank's design, rather than added on as an afterthought. Artists Yvonne Cheng and Sharon Carter Smith, whose works are included, assembled this exhibition, a sterling example of corporate sponsorship of the arts.

Island Salsa. In the Kona Inn Shopping Village, Alii Dr. ☎ **808/329-9279.**

There's no food involved here, but the sportswear does sizzle. The tiny boutique is lined with excellent, high-quality sportswear and accessories: slouchy linens by Flax, top-of-the-line City Lights active wear, an excellent selection of Tommy Bahama aloha shirts, leather bags by Fossil, and the obscure and wonderful Sven Design.

Kailua Village Artists Gallery. King Kamehameha's Kona Beach Hotel, 75-5660 Palani Rd. ☎ **808/329-6653.**

A co-op of 40 Hawaii island artists, plus a few guest artists, display their works here in various media: watercolors, paintings, prints, handblown and blasted glass, and photography. Books, pottery, and an attractive assortment of greeting cards are among the lower-priced items.

MiddleEarth Bookshoppe. In Kona Plaza, 75-5719 Alii Dr. ☎ **808/ 329-2123.**

Every square inch is occupied with bestsellers, cookbooks, literary fiction, travel guides, metaphysical books, health books, and offbeat titles. With its strong selection of Hawaii-themed publications and piles of discounted books, MiddleEarth is a staple for residents and a pleasant surprise for visitors, appreciated more for its longevity than for its sometimes unsmiling service.

Once in a Blue Moon. 74-5598 Luhia St. ☎ **808/334-0022.**

Tuck in your elbows and hang on to your backpack, lest you topple a crystal vase or piece of estate china packed into this showroom in Kailua's industrial area. This antiques/secondhand store is chockablock with vintage Hawaiian items, estate jewelry, handwoven throws and linens, and an entire floor of furniture (some koa pieces, which disappear quickly). Among the treasures, if your timing is right: fine, high-thread-count vintage sheets in excellent condition, mint-condition Japanese dolls, and vintage koa bowls.

Pacific Vibrations. 75-5702 Alii Drive. ☎ **808/329-4140.**

Located across from Hulihee Palace, next to the free county parking lot, this retail sports shop sells surfwear, bikinis, and sunglasses. You don't have to be a triathlete to love this place (although many triathletes do), because the owners are generous with information about Kona's abundant outdoor activities. They'll keep you up to date on local sports events, races, surfing, biking, swimming, and diving spots.

Paradise Found. In the Keauhou Shopping Village, Alii Dr. ☎ **808/ 329-2221.**

Paradise Found appeals to women who like to make a grand entrance with sequined, retro-style camp shirts, stylish T-shirts, and drapey, Harlow-esque dresses. There are practical accessories and sports and resort wear to bolster the bold clothing selection.

Te-Noe, Inc. Phone orders only. ☎ **800/322-3579.**

Noelani Whittington's grandfather planted the coffee trees on their farm when he was 85 years old. He's well past 90 now, but the trees are yielding tasty coffee beans that Noelani and her husband, Rick, sell wholesale and retail in 2-ounce, 3-ounce, and 1-pound bags. The 100% Kona coffee is available by phone order or at various outlets in Kailua-Kona. The beans are hand-roasted—only 15 pounds at a time—and packed with lots of TLC. You can also order the seasonally available pincushion and miniature king protea, and the dazzling Telopa protea, which resemble torch gingers in all red and all white. Protea are sturdy, showy flowers with a long afterlife—they dry beautifully. The selection varies, depending on the time of year, so there are always surprises. (See also Kailua Candy Company, below.)

Edibles & Everyday Things

The Big Island's **greenmarkets** are notable for the quality of produce and the abundance of island specialties at better-than-usual prices. From 7am to 3pm on Wednesday and Saturday, look for the loosely assembled tarps of the **Kona Farmers Market,** in the Kona Inn parking lot on Alii Drive. (Go as early as possible to avoid the heat.) Local farmers sell organic produce, unsprayed Waimea corn, anthuriums of every hue, star fruit, breadfruit, papayas, sugarcane, Ka'u oranges, vine-ripened tomatoes, locally made crafts, and macadamia nuts. It's a great way to sample the region's specialties, some of which also make affordable souvenirs.

Java junkies are jump-starting their day at **Island Lava Java** (☎ **808/327-2161**), the hot new magnet for coffee lovers at the Coconut Grove marketplace on Alii Drive. At the other end of Kailua-Kona, the hand-made, hand-dipped candies of **Kailua Candy Company** (☎ **808/329-2522**; 800/622-2462 for mail-order) also beckon, especially the macadamia nut clusters with ground ginger or the legendary macadamia nut *honu* (turtle). Other products include a large selection of white, milk, and dark chocolate, truffles, and fresh Kona products, including pure Kona coffee, shortbread cookies, toffee, and dry roasted macadamia nuts. The selection also includes T-shirts, mugs, mustards, and other gift and souvenir items. In addition, Kailua Candy Co. sells products by **NoeLani Farms** in Holualoa (☎ **877/322-8579** toll-free, or 808/ 322-3579). You can also order directly from NoeLani Farms, which has its own extensive mail-order business in proteas, protea wreaths, kava, and private-label Kona coffee grown at the farm, which is 1,400 feet in elevation.

Good news for wine lovers: **Kona Wine Market** (☎ **808/ 329-9400**) in the King Kamehameha Mall has a noteworthy wine selection, including some esoteric vintages, at prices you will love. This is a wine lover's store, with selections from California, Europe, and points beyond, as well as gift baskets, cheeses, cigars, oils and vinegars, specialty pastas and condiments, coffee, Riedel glassware, and friendly, knowledgeable service.

For ice cream lovers, **Big Island Ice Cream** (formerly Great Pacific) in Keauhou Shopping Center (corner of Kam III Highway and Alii Drive, with an additional store scheduled for Crossroads Center) offers award-winning gourmet flavors: Toasted Coconut, Extreme Ginger, Volcano (fresh banana with strawberry swirl and Oreo cookies), Kealakekua Krunch (Kona coffee ice cream with a coffee swirl and coffee cinnamon brittle), and dozens of others. The classics (mac nut, Kona coffee, sorbets) remain as well.

For everyday grocery needs, **KTA Stores** (in the Kona Coast Shopping Center, at Palani Road and the Queen Kaahumanu Highway, and in the Keauhou Shopping Village on Alii Drive) are always our first choice. Through its Mountain Apple brand, KTA sells hundreds of top-notch local products—from Kona smoked marlin and Hilo-grown rainbow trout to cookies, breads, jams and jellies, taro chips, and *kulolo,* the decadently dense taro-coconut steamed pudding—by dozens of local vendors. The fresh-fish department is always an adventure; if anything esoteric or rare is running, such as the flashy red aweoweo, it's sure to be on KTA's counters, along with a large spread of prepared foods for sunset picnics and barbecues. Our other favorite is **Kona Natural Foods** (☎ 808/329-2296) in the Crossroads Center. It's been upgraded from a petite *boite* of a health-food store to a full-on healthy supermarket. And it's the only full-service health-food store for miles, selling bulk grains and cereals, vitamins, snacks, fresh-fruit smoothies, and sandwiches and salads from its takeout deli. Organic greens, grown with special cachet in the South Kona area, are a small but strong feature of the organic produce section.

For produce and flowers straight from the farm, go to the **Farmers Market in Kaiwi Square,** in Kona's old industrial area (follow the sign on the Queen Kaahumanu Highway). Open on Saturday from 7am to 1pm, it teems with dedicated vendors and eager shoppers. You'll find live catfish, taro, organic vine-ripened tomatoes, fresh Kamuela string beans, lettuces, potatoes, and just-picked blooms, such as anthuriums and feathery, sturdy protea, at friendly prices.

UPCOUNTRY KONA: HOLUALOA

Charming Holualoa, 1,400 feet and 10 minutes above Kailua-Kona at the top of Hualalai Road, is a place for strong espresso, leisurely gallery hopping, and nostalgic explorations across several cultural and time zones. One narrow road takes you across generations and cultures.

Paul's Place is Holualoa's only all-purpose general store, a time warp tucked between frame shops, galleries, and studios. Prominent Holualoa artists include the jewelry maker/sculptor Sam Rosen, who years ago set the pace for found-object art; the furniture maker and wood sculptor Gerald Ben; the printmaker Nora Yamanoha; the glass artist Wilfred Yamazawa; the sculptor Cal Hashimoto; and Hiroki and Setsuko Morinoue of Studio 7 gallery. All galleries listed are on the main street, Mamalahoa Highway, and all are within walking distance of each other.

Chestnut & Co. Mamalahoa Hwy. ☎ 808/324-1446.

This place is worth a special trip to Holualoa. Look for the Hawaiian flag and the quaint architecture of an old post office, across from the Kona Arts Center. Chestnut is a gallery of great things, inside and out. Artists Peggy Chestnut and Sam Rosen took the old Holualoa Post Office (which closed in 1961) and turned it into a top-notch gallery of works by Big Island artists. Rosen's studio within Chestnut & Co., Hale O Kula Gallery, displays the jewelry and ceramic/copper/bronze sculptures and vessels that have made him a top name in Big Island Art. The eclectic selection includes Chestnut's handwoven table runners, tansus, Asian and South American furniture, hand-turned bowls by Renee Fukumoto Ben and furniture and bowls by her husband, Gerald, handmade dolls by Linda Wolfsberg, journals by Ira Ono, boxes, fiber art, and more jewelry ranging from $2 into the thousands.

Cinderella Unlimited. Mamalahoa Hwy. ☎ **808/322-2474.**

Most of the treasures here are tucked away, so don't be shy about asking the owner, Cindi Nespor, where she keeps her prized antique engravings or her cache of out-of-print naturalists' books of handpainted engravings. Many of the items here come from the estate of a reclusive couture model who retired in Kona and died there, after a prolific career sitting for Picasso, Cecil Beaton, and the world's most prominent photographers. There are engravings of old Hawaii, rare prints and vases, kimono, lamps, and home accessories. The rare books will quicken a book-lover's heart, and the estate jewelry, vintage linens, rattan furniture, and hats make this a brilliant browse. Call ahead, though; the owner keeps *really* flexible hours.

Country Frame Shop & Gallery. Mamalahoa Hwy. ☎ **808/324-1590.**

Darryl Hill's acrylics and small plein-air watercolors are framed in koa and bamboo and hung in this eclectic gallery. His other creations here include wood vessels, boxes, small accessories, fantastic chairs made of old moldings, pieces of framing, and other found objects.

Holualoa Gallery. 76-5921 Mamalahoa Hwy. ☎ **808/322-8484.**

Owners Matthew and Mary Lovein show their own work as well the work of selected Hawaii artists in this roadside gallery in Holualoa. Sculptures, paintings, koa furniture, fused-glass bowls, and creations in paper, bronze, metal, and glass are among the gallery's offerings.

Kimura Lauhala Shop. At Mamalahoa Hwy. and Hualalai Rd. ☎ **808/ 324-0053.**

Tsuruyo Kimura, looking 2 decades younger than her 90 years, presides over a labor-intensive legacy (lauhala) that's increasingly difficult to maintain. All the better, because everyone loves Kimura's and the masterpieces of weaving that spill out of the tiny shop. It's lined with lauhala, from rolled-up mats and wide-brimmed hats to tote bags, coasters and coin purses. The fragrant, resilient fiber, woven from the spiny leaves of the *hala* (pandanus) tree, is smooth to the touch and becomes softer with use. Lauhala also varies in color (terra-cotta to beige) according to region and growing conditions. Although Kimura employs a covey of local weavers who use the renowned hala leaves of Kona, some South Pacific imports bolster the supply.

Kona Arts Center. Mamalahoa Hwy. (P.O. Box 272), Holualoa, HI 96725.

Because this not-for-profit center has never had a phone, anyone interested in the pottery, tie-dye, weaving, painting, and other arts-and-crafts workshops here, in a ramshackle tin-roofed former coffee mill, has to write or drop in. Carol Rogers is the director of the program, a mainstay of the local arts community since 1965.

Studio 7. Mamalahoa Hwy. ☎ **808/324-1335.**

Some of Hawaii's most respected artists, among them gallery owners Setsuko and Hiroki Morinoue, exhibit their works in this serenely beautiful studio. Smooth pebbles, stark woods, and a garden setting provide the backdrop for Hiroki's paintings and prints and Setsuko's pottery, paper collages, and wallpieces. The Main Gallery houses multimedia art, the Print Gallery houses sculptural pieces and two-dimensional works, and the Ceramic Gallery showcases the works of Clayton Amemiya, Chiu Leong, and Gerald Ben, whose mixed-media sculptures made of ceramic raku with wood continue to be a pleasing attraction. With the Morinoues at the helm of the volunteer-driven Holualoa Foundation for Culture and the Arts, this is the hub of the Holualoa art community; activities include workshops, classes, and special events by visiting artists.

White Garden Gallery. Mamalahoa Hwy. ☎ **808/322-7733.**

Shelly Maudsley White's original paintings, limited editions, and prints are available in her studio and gallery on Holualoa's main street. Her subjects include cows, bird-of-paradise, gingers, and exotic blooms.

SOUTH KONA

Aloha Store. Hwy. 11, Kainaliu. ☎ **808/322-1717.**

This is a good stop for gifts and clothing, with a small but attractive selection of aloha shirts, dresses, and home accessories. Located on the main road leading through town, next to the Aloha Café, it carries beeswax candles handmade on the slopes of Hualalai, Tommy Bahama duffelbags, bark-cloth cushions with a vintage look, home accessories, easy-care clothing, and a strong selection of books.

The Grass Shack. Hwy. 11, Kealakekua. ☎ **808/323-2877.**

Grass Shack has been here for three decades with its large selection of local woodcrafts, Niihau shell and wiliwili-seed leis, packaged coffee, pahu drums, nose flutes, and *lauhala* (woven pandanus leaves) in every form. Bowls, boxes, and accessories of Norfolk pine, the rare kou, and other local woods also take up a sizable portion of the shop. Lauhala baskets, made of fiber from the region and the Hamakua Coast, are among the Shack's finest, as are the custom ukuleles and feather gourds for hula dancing.

Kimura Store. Hwy. 11, Kainaliu. ☎ **808/322-3771.**

This old-fashioned general store is one of those places you'll be glad you found—a store with spirit and character, and everything you need and don't need. You'll find Hawaii's finest selection of yardage, enough cookware for a multicourse dinner, aspirin, Shiseido cosmetics, and an eye-popping assortment of buttons, zippers, and quilting materials. Irene Kimura, whose store has been here for nearly 60 years, says she quit counting the fabric bolts at 8,000 but knows she has more than 10,000. Kimura's is the spot for pareu and Hawaiian fabrics, brocades, silks, and offbeat gift items, such as Japanese china and *tabi,* the comfortable cloth footwear.

The Rainbow Path. Hwy. 11, Kainaliu. ☎ **808/322-0651.**

This shop specializes in products for healing and well-being, such as New Age crystals and gems, metaphysical books and accessories, aromatherapy oils, jewelry, flaxseed eye pillows (don't knock 'em till you've tried 'em!), tapes and CDs, candles, cards, art books, and Ayurvedic self-care health products. The made-on-Oahu Paradise essential oils are pure and popular, and when the owner's fruit trees are bearing, he shares the bounty. Adjoining the store is the newly opened **Rainbow Cafe,** serving soups, salads, sandwiches, smoothies, shaved ice, and ice cream.

Edibles

In Kealakekua, the **Kamigaki Market** on Highway 11 is a reliable source for food items, especially for regional specialties such as macadamia nuts and Kona coffee. In Honaunau, farther south, keep an eye out for the **Bong Brothers Store** on Highway 11 and its eye-catching selections of fresh local fruit—from chirimoya (in season) to star fruit and white **Sugarloaf pineapples.** The Bongs are known for their Kona coffee and deli items, but we think their black, very hip Bong Brothers T-shirts are the find of the region and season.

THE KOHALA COAST

Shops on the Kohala Coast are concentrated in the resorts.

HILTON WAIKOLOA VILLAGE   Among the hotel's shops, **Sandal Tree** carries footwear with style and kick: Italian sandals at non-Italian prices, designer pumps, and other footwear to carry you from sailing deck to dance floor.

KING'S SHOPS   These stores are located near the Hilton. A recent find here—and a life-saving one!—is **Paradise Walking Company.** This is a striking concept for anyone exploring the harsh lava terrain of this island or the pedestrian culture of Kailua's Alii Drive with its many shops and restaurants. The footwear—much of it made in France (Mephisto, Arche)—can be expensive, but it's worthwhile for those seeking comfort without sacrificing style. Toward the mauka (mountainside) end is **Noa's Ark** for children, a tot-sized space filled with tropical cottons, pricey but colorful minimuumuus, pint-sized aloha shirts, and sophisticated linens and jerseys in cradle-to-teen sizes. Its sibling store for adults, **Noa Noa,** several doors away, is filled with exotic artifacts from Java and Borneo and tropical clothing for easygoing life in the Pacific Rim. **Kunah's** offers Kahala, Kamehameha, and other hip aloha shirts, as well as baseball caps, flip-flops, swim shorts, and colorful tropical-print canvas bags. For snacks, ice, sunscreen, wine, postcards, news-papers, and everyday essentials, there's the **Whalers General Store.**

HUALALAI RESORT   **Ka'upulehu Store** in Hualalai Resort's Four Seasons hotel is a perfect blend of high quality and cultural integrity. Located within the award-winning Ka'upulehu Cultural Center, the store carries only items made in Hawaii: handmade paper, hand-painted silks, seed lei, Niihau shell lei, greeting cards, koa bowls, wreaths, John Kelly prints, and a selection of Hawaii-themed books. **Hualalai Sports Club and Spa,** in the same resort, has a winning retail section of beauty, aromatherapy, and treatment products, including Hana Nai'a Aromatherapy Products by Maryanne Rose of Pa'auilo. The products include mango and jasmine perfumes, Bulgarian rose water, and herbal lotions and potions.

NORTH KOHALA

Ackerman Gallery. Hwy. 270 (across from the Kamehameha statue; also 3 blocks away, on the opposite side of the street), Kapaau. ☎ **808/889-5971.**

Crafts and fine arts are housed in two separate galleries a few blocks apart. The craft and gift gallery across from the King Kamehameha

Just Looking

The **Mauna Kea Beach Hotel,** 62-100 Mauna Kea Beach Dr. (☎ 808/882-7222), is home to one of the world's most impressive collections of Asian and Oceanic art. It's displayed unpretentiously, in public and private spaces. Laurance Rockefeller planned his resort so the art would be totally integrated into the environment: indoors, outdoors, in hallways, lounges, and alcoves. The result is a spiritually and aesthetically uplifting view in every direction. A 7th-century granite Buddha is the oldest work in a collection that includes art from China, Japan, India, Southeast Asia, Melanesia, and Polynesia, including Hawaii. The Lloyd Sexton Gallery and John Young paintings throughout the hotel reflect Rockefeller's commitment to the finest.

---

statue has doubled in size recently; it features gift ideas in all media and price ranges. Artist Gary Ackerman and his wife, Yesan, display gifts, crafts, and the works of award-winning Big Island artists, including Ackerman's own impressionistic paintings. There are Kelly Dunn's hand-turned Norfolk pine bowls, Jer Houston's heirloom-quality koa-and-ebony desks, jewelry, and Wilfred Yamazawa's handblown-glass perfume bottles and sculptures. Primitive artifacts, Asian antiques, and Cal Hashimoto's bamboo sculptures are also among the discoveries here.

Kohala Book Shop. Hwy. 270, Kapaau. ☎ **808/889-6732.**

Jan and Frank Morgan were just setting up their new store in the town's historic Hotel Nanbu building, one block from the Kamehameha Statue, when we were going to press. The Morgans bought out two significant book collections for their new endeavor, those of the Tusitala book store on Oahu and of the Upcountry Booksellers in Waimea. With this impressive inventory and their own collection of rare, used, and out-of-print books as well as popular fiction, their store should be a find. Kohala Book Shop will specialize in books of Hawaii, Oceania, and vintage editions; at last count the inventory was 20,000 and climbing.

Kohala Kollection. In the Kawaihae Shopping Center, Hwy. 270. ☎ **808/882-1510.**

This two-story gallery, the biggest draw next to the Cafe Pesto in this industrial harbor area, features Pegge Hopper originals and prints, Frances Dennis' painted island scenes on canvas and ceramics, bright tropical paintings by the internationally known Zhou Ling, and other works by more than 150 artists, primarily from the Big Island. The range is vast—from jewelry to basketry to heirloom-quality koa furniture—and the works are tastefully displayed on two floors. Upstairs, you'll find a large selection of fine-art prints; downstairs are bowls, boxes, jewelry, and bronze and wood sculptures, ranging from a few dollars to the high prices expected of original fine art.

WAIMEA

Shops here range from the small roadside storefronts lining Highway 19 and Highway 190, which intersect in the middle of town, to complexes such as **Parker Square** and **Waimea Center,** where you'll find the trusty old **KTA Super Store,** the one-stop shop for all your basic necessities, plus a glorious profusion of interesting local foods. At **Parker Ranch Shopping Center** across the street is **Big Island Coffee Co.** and a smattering of shops and casual eateries, including the ever popular **Reyn's,** but generally this complex is unremarkable. The petite but satisfying **Opelo Plaza,** the historic **Spencer House,** and **Parker Square** will likely be your most rewarding stops.

Hilo's wonderful **Dan De Luz Woods** (see below) has a branch at 64-1013 Mamamlahoa Hwy., in front of the True-Value hardware store.

Bentley's Home & Garden Collection. In Parker Square, Hwy. 19. ☎ **808/ 885-5565.**

To its lavish list of glassware, linens, chenille throws, home fragrances, stuffed animals, and Wild West giftwraps, Bentley's has added casual country clothing in linens and cottons. Dresses, sweaters, raffia hats, top-drawer Western shirts, handbags, woven shoes, and all things Martha Stewart adorn this fragrant, gardenesque shop. This is for people who like to raise flowers and herbs, cook with them, breathe potpourried air, take relaxing baths (with expensive designer soaps), and look good.

Cook's Discoveries. At the Historic Spencer House, in front of Waimea Center, Hwy. 190. ☎ **808/885-3633.**

It's a heady mix: Hawaii-themed wearables, fine collectibles, locally made crafts, books, Hawaiian quilts, and ranching memorabilia. You could start with Waipio poi hotcakes at **Maha's Cafe** in one part of the tiny shop; then select a lei by Alice Humbert from her veranda flower shop, **Made in a Hawaiian Garden;** and then dive into the nooks and crannies of **Cook's Discoveries.** Treasures you'll find:

palaka nightshirts and napkins, kupe'e shell necklaces by Patrick Horimoto, the rare miniature kukui-nut lei, locally designed pareus, lauhala baskets, T-shirts, Doug Tolentino originals and prints, and hundreds of other surprises. The rare ivory and silver Ming jewelry has collectors salivating over the counter, while foodies throng to the Hamakua coffee, mango chutney, and the new line of condiments and seasonings by renowned chef Amy Ferguson Ota. The Cooks' own triple-chocolate-chunk or oatmeal cookies should claim a fair share of the shopping basket. Another special touch: Alice Humbert sells hand creams, sea salts, and potpourris she makes from the harvests of her own garden. The old-fashioned tea cups filled with potted narcissuses and tea roses make superb gifts, as do the Hawaiian lomi lomi massage oil, gardener's hand cream, and made-from-scratch perfumes.

Gallery of Great Things. In Parker Square, Hwy. 19. ☎ **808/885-7706.**

Here's an eye-popping assemblage of local art and Pacific Rim artifacts. Browse under the watchful gaze of an antique Tongan war club (not for sale) and authentic rhinoceros- and deer-horn blowguns from Borneo among the plethora of treasures from Polynesia, Micronesia, and Indonesia. You'll find jewelry, glassware, photographs, greeting cards, fiber baskets, and hand-turned bowls of beautifully grained woods. There are a few pieces of etched glass and vintage clothing, too.

Imagination. In Parker Square, Hwy. 19. ☎ **808/885-0430.**

This children's shop is stacked high with upscale toys, dolls, books, games, and other upper-end diversions. The selection includes a first-rate selection of educational toys and European and Asian imports.

Kamuela Hat Company. In Waimea Center, Hwy. 190. ☎ **808/885-8875.**

The requisite hats of the paniolo life appear here in spades. Choose from among Kona lauhala, Stetsons, Panamas, Italian straw, white coconut, and more. You'll also find other accoutrements for a life astride: belts, macho buckles, Western jewelry, and oilskin jackets à la J. Peterman, plus cowboy boots at non-Dallas prices. A personal favorite are the slippers made of palaka, the two-color plaid that has come to symbolize the rugged ranching and plantation eras of Hawaii. Styled into thongs, they're a hit.

✪ Silk Road Gallery. In Parker Square, Hwy. 19. ☎ **808/885-7474.**

It's worth a special stop if you love Asian antiques: porcelain tea cups, jade cups, kimono, lacquerware, Buddhas, tansus, bronze bells and chimes, Indonesian woven baskets, and all manner of delights for elevated living. You can part with $15 for a bronze bell, thousands for an antique tansu, or something in between.

Sweet Wind. In Parker Square, Hwy. 19. ☎ **808/885-0562.**

Because the owner loves beauty and harmonious things, you'll find chimes, carved dolphins, crystals, geodes, incense, beads, essential oils, and thoughtfully selected books worth more than a casual glance. The books cover self-help, health, metaphysics, Hawaiian spirituality, yoga, meditation, and other topics for wholesome living.

✪ Upcountry Connection. At the Mauna Kea Center, Hwy. 19 and Hwy. 190. ☎ **808/885-0623.**

This warm, gleaming gallery and gift shop offers an even mix of fine art, antiques, and crafts, all of impeccable taste, and a recently expanded collection of home accessories, gifts, and decorative pieces. You may not be looking for a koa chest, but it's here, along with antique koa mirrors, Ed Kayton originals, fine crocheted linens, jewelry boxes, and all manner of collectibles and contemporary art. One-of-a-kind finds for bountiful budgets have included a $1,200 coconut-wood Polynesian drum, Hawaiian musical instruments of feathers and coconut shells, Jerry Kotz's hand-turned Norfolk pine bowls, and raku-fired ceramic vases for under $100. Other great finds: the original oils, limited prints, cards, and books of Herb Kawainui Kane, a living treasure of Hawaii; and the vibrant paintings of Harry Wishard and James Hutchinson. A show-stopper recently was an antique mirror with carved jade, a collector's item; and an old mahogany bureau with carved bed posts and a matching foot board.

Waimea General Store. In Parker Square, Hwy. 19. ☎ **808/885-4479.**

This charming, unpretentious country store has always offered a superb assortment of Hawaii-themed books, soaps and toiletries, cookbooks and kitchen accessories, candles and linens, greeting cards and dolls, Japanese hapi coats and island teas, rare kiawe honey, preserves, and countless gift items from the practical to the whimsical. This is a great stop for Crabtree and Evelyn soaps, fragrances, and cookies—and a thousand other delights.

FARMER'S MARKETS

Small and sublime, with only about five booths, the ✪ **Waimea Farmers Market,** Highway 19, at mile marker 55 on the Hamakua side of Waimea town (on the lawn in front of the Department of Hawaiian Home Lands, West Hawaii office), draws a loyal crowd from 7am to noon on Saturday mornings. Waimea is lei country and the island's breadbasket, so look for protea, vegetables, vine-ripened tomatoes, and tuberose stalks here at reasonable prices. Mainstays include **Honopua Farm** and **Hufford's Farm,** side by side selling flowers and organic vegetables: a dozen different lettuces, three different types of kale, and many other finds you'd never encounter in a supermarket. And the flowers: freesias, irises, heather, stars-of-Bethlehem, Australian teas, and cleomes, all freshly clipped. The colors and fragrances change with the season. You'll find **Marie McDonald** at the booth, one of Hawaii's premier lei-makers. (If you want one of her designer Waimea leis, you have to order ahead; call ☎ 808/885-4148.) Also here is **Bernice Berdon,** considered the best maker of akulikuli leis, a Waimea signature that comes in yellows, oranges, and fuchsias. Ask about her bat-face kika, the cigar-flower lei with bat-faced blossoms. If you're here around Christmas, the protea wreaths are phenomenal.

At the other end of Waimea, the **Parker School Farmers Market** is smaller and more subdued, but with choice items as well. The Kalopa macadamia nuts are the sweetest and tastiest we've ever had, and Lokelani Gardens' fabulous herbal vinegars and luxuriant herb topiaries are worth a special trip.

THE HAMAKUA COAST

Waipio Valley Artworks. Kukuihaele. ☎ 808/775-0958.

Housed in an old wooden building at the end of the road before the Waipio Valley, this gallery/boutique offers treasures for the home. The focus here is strictly local, with a strong emphasis on wood works—one of the largest selections, if not the largest, in the state. A recent expansion has brought more chests and tables and gift items by Big Island artists. All the luminaries of wood-turning have works here: Jack Straka, Robert Butts, Scott Hare, Kevin Parks. Their bowls, rocking chairs, and jewelry boxes exhibit flawless craftsmanship and richly burnished grains. More affordable are the pens and hair accessories, and the deli sandwiches and Tropical Dreams ice cream served in the expanded cafe section.

HONOKAA

Mamane Street Bakery on the main drag will fill all your coffee-shop needs. Fresh-baked breads, pies, and pastries (including melt-in-your-mouth danishes) are served with good coffee in a tiny cafe lined with old photographs. Every Saturday morning from 7am, about a dozen local farmers and vendors set up their wares at the

Honokaa Farmers Market in front of the Botelho Building. No crafts or arts here—just edibles, good and fresh. Vendors bring their home-baked breads and pastries, bananas, papayas, and bushels of freshly picked garden vegetables—and they're all available at unbeatable prices.

Decorative Arts by Joe Rivera. Mamane St. ☎ **808/775-9090.**

The 10 local artists of this cooperative display their notable works here. You'll find Susan Sanders' curly koa, Georgia Russell's watercolors on handmade paper, and Joe Rivera's stained glass. We loved the monkeypod pig board ($180), a curly tiger-koa jewelry box ($440), koa corner tables with wenge wraps, etched glass, wood hair clips, and palaka house slippers. The hand-turned wooden bowls and milo bracelets, koa and mango wood chests, and lamps of hammered copper are also among the fine works we remember.

Honokaa Market Place. 45-3321 Mamane St. ☎ **808/775-8255.**

This shop is gaining recognition for its old and new Hawaiiana. Antiques and imports mingle freely in this eclectic selection of Hawaiian, Asian, and Indonesian handicrafts. There's a large selection of wood bowls (koa, mango, hau, kou, ohia, kamani, Norfolk pine). Hawaiian quilts come in several forms and sizes, from wall hangings and pillows to the full-sized quilts. Hawaiian prints and lithographs, a few Oriental antiques, and a profusion of beads attract shoppers, collectors, and jewelry makers.

Honokaa Trading Company. Mamane St. ☎ **808/775-0808.**

"Rustic, tacky, rare—there's something for everyone," says owner Grace Walker. Every inch of the labyrinthine, 2,200-square-foot bazaar is occupied by antiques and collectibles, new and used goods, and countless treasures—all of it plantation memorabilia or Hawaiiana. Bark-cloth fabrics from the 1940s, rhinestone jewelry and rattan furniture from the 1930s, vintage ukuleles, Depression glass, dinnerware from Honolulu's landmark Willows restaurant, koa lamps, Francis Oda airbrush paintings—it's an unbelievable conglomeration, with surprises in every corner. Vigilant collectors make regular forays here to scoop up the 1950s ivory jewelry and John Kelly prints.

Kamaaina Woods. Lehua St. (down the hill from the post office). ☎ **808/775-7722.**

The showroom is adjacent to the workshop, so visitors can watch the craftspeople at work on the other side of the glass panel. Local woods are the specialty here, with a strong emphasis on koa and milo bowls.

Boxes, carvings, albums, and smaller accessories are also included in the mix, but bowl-turning is clearly the focus. Prices begin at about $10.

S. Hasegawa, Ltd. Mamane St. ☎ **808/775-0668.**

Here's a sampling of what you'll find in the narrow aisles of this 70-year-old country store: playing cards, shoes, Shiseido cosmetics, totebags, stuffed animals, dishes, baby dresses, stockings, zippers, and fabrics (including pareu—a big plus), plus hardware and cable cord for the industrial-minded.

Seconds to Go. Mamane St. ☎ **808/775-9212.**

Elaine Carlsmith spends a lot of time collecting vintage pottery, glassware, kimono, fabrics, and other treasures, only to release them to eager seekers of nostalgia. Many beautiful things have passed through her doors, including antique koa furniture sets, old maps, music sheets, rare and out-of-print books, and reams of ephemera. The vintage ivory jewelry and Don Blanding dinnerware is grabbed up quickly. The main store is a few doors away from the warehouse, where furniture and larger pieces are displayed.

Starseed. Mamane St. ☎ **808/775-9344.**

Shop here for offbeat holographic bumper stickers, jewelry, beads, incense, and New-Age amulets. The selection of beads and crystals is impressive. The owner has a special camera that purportedly photographs people's auras, or electromagnetic fields. Find out what your colors are, or look for them in the hundreds of boxes of beads, some of them rare European and Asian imports.

Taro Patch Gifts. In the Andrade Building, Mamane St. ☎ **808/776-1602.**

Taro Patch carries an eclectic assortment of Hawaiian music tapes and CDs, switchplates printed with Hawaiian labels, Ka'u coffee, local jams and jellies, soaps, and sportswear. The Hawaiian seed lei selection is the best in town: kamani, blue marble, wiliwili, double sheep eye, betel nut, and several other attractive native species.

HONOMU

An artists' colony has sprouted in Honomu, near Akaka Falls on the outskirts of Hilo. In recent years, artists and entrepreneurs have spruced up old storefronts and breathed new life into the area. Start your jaunt with a lilikoi shaved ice, smoked-turkey plate lunch, or an opihi miso soup at **Aloha Akaka,** a local-style diner that's been there since 1936—lots of home-style noodles, wooden school chairs and concrete floors, and an ancient counter with an antique shaved-ice machine.

A few doors down, the **Woodshop Gallery** sells Island-made crafts and gift items, koa bowls, furniture, pottery, and a noteworthy selection of gallery and gift items. The fine works we saw there included Peter McLaren's purple-heart table ($1,400); Jack Straka koa bowls; Kevin Keller's Norfolk pine bowls; Ira Ono's garden goddesses; and other works by leading island artists. Next door is **Tropical Grinds,** selling delectable scoops of Hilo Homemade and Big Island ice creams in a rainbow of flavors. Nearby (heading inland) at the **Akaka Falls Inn and Gift Gallery** (housed in a 1923 building, the old Akita Store), you can browse among tea sets, dinnerware, koa and lacquer bowls, cookbooks, shell and seed leis, koa accessories, candles, lauhala bags, and household accents. This is also the new franchise for **Rainbow Moon Gourmet Pizza,** the universally loved pizza from Volcano, with 9-spice herbal blends, smoked marlin (Pele's Pizza), and striking combinations of vine-ripened tomatoes, artichoke hearts, local peppers, balsamic marinated garlic, and many other delights.

At the two-story **Ohana Gallery,** Nara and Clifford Chow have assembled an attractive collection of precious wood sculptures, paintings, koa gift items, jewelry, clothing (including the eminently practical hemp fashions), and other works by local artists. Avi Kiriaty oils, Niihau shell leis, Norfolk pine vessels by Uve Dost, and a Tom Barboza curly koa platter were among the treasures we last saw there. A few feet away, a new bookstore, **Play on Words,** has brought the joys of storytelling to Honomu's main drag with its Saturday afternoon story hour for children and adults. The charming bookstore has hardwood floors, a small veranda, and new and used books at reasonable prices. From nearby **Panua Collections** come imports from Papua New Guinea.

HILO

Shopping in Hilo is centered around the **Kaiko'o Hilo Mall** at 777 Kilauea Ave., near the state and county buildings; the **Prince Kuhio Shopping Plaza,** at 111 E. Puainako, just off Highway 11 on the road north to Volcano, where you'll find a supermarket, drugstore, Liberty House, and other standards; the **Bayfront area** downtown, where the hippest new businesses have taken up residence in the historic buildings lining Kamehameha Avenue; and the new **Waiakea Plaza,** where the big-box retailers (Ross, Office Max, Borders, Wal-Mart) have taken up residence. For practical needs, there's a **KTA Super Store** at 323 Keawe St. and another at 50 E. Puainako, and a Sure Save supermarket at 1990 Kinoole St. Also see "Edibles," below.

Basically Books. 160 Kamehameha Ave. ☎ **808/961-0144.**

We're happy to see our favorite Hilo bookstore in larger, more convenient digs in the bayfront area, next to the historic Kress Building. Affectionately called "the map shop," this is a sanctuary for lovers of books, maps, and the environment, with an engaging selection of printed materials in geology, history, topography, botany, mythology, and more. Get your bearings by browsing among the nautical charts, U.S. Geological Survey maps (the authoritative word in cartography), street maps, raised relief maps, atlases, and compasses, and countless books on travel, natural history, music, spirituality, and countless other topics. Specializing in Hawaii and the Pacific, this is a bountiful source of information that will enhance any visit. Even the most knowledgeable residents stop by here to keep current and conscious.

Dan De Luz Woods. Hwy. 11, Kurtistown. ☎ **808/935-5587.**

The unstoppable Dan De Luz has been turning bowls for more than 30 years. His new location, on the highway on the way to Volcano, is a larger, more stunning showcase than his previous location in Hilo. He turns koa, milo, mango, kamani, kou, sandalwood, hau, and other island woods, some very rare, into bowls, trays, and accessories of all shapes and sizes. You can find bookmarks, rice and stir-fry paddles, letter openers, and calabashes, priced from $3 to $1,000.

Dragon Mama. 266 Kamehameha Ave. ☎ **808/934-9081.**

For a dreamy stop in Hilo, head for this haven of all-natural comforters, cushions, futons, meditation pillows, hemp yarns and shirts, antique kimono and obi, tatami mats sold by the panel, and all manner of comforts in the elegantly spare Japanese esthetic. The bolts of lavish silks and pure, crisp cottons, sold by the yard, can be used in clothing or interior decorating. Dragon Mama also offers custom sewing, and you know she's good: She sewed the futon and bedding for the Dalai Lama when he visited the island a few years ago.

Ets'ko. 35 Waianuenue Ave. ☎ **808/961-3778.**

Shop and be entertained by the dizzying selection of loungewear, porcelains, teapots, home accessories, purses, and miscellaneous good things the owner collects from the design centers of the world. Futuristic wine racks, minimalist jewelry, handblown-glass pens, Japanese furniture and accessories, and ultra-luxe candles are included in the glittering assortment.

Hana Hou. 164 Kamehameha Ave. ☎ **808/935-4555**.

Michele Zane-Faridi has done a superlative job of assembling, designing, and collecting things of beauty that evoke old and new Hawaii. Impeccable taste and good fortune in collecting have made this a prime stop in Hilo for all kinds of treasures. Vintage shirts, china, books, furniture, lamps, jewelry, handbags, accessories, and fabrics are displayed in surprising corners. The bark-cloth lampshades and collector's dreams—such as vintage silver and ivory jewelry by Ming's—disappear quickly. Mundorff prints, 1940s sheet music, and the nicest dressing room on the island (with a mango-wood bench made from the same tree as the desk), are more reasons for a standing ovation.

Hawaiian Force. 140 Kilauea Ave. ☎ **808/934-7171**.

Artist Craig Neff and his wife, Luana, set out their shingle in the original location of Sig Zane Designs (good karma), where they sell bold, wonderful T-shirt dresses, mamaki tea they gather themselves, lauhala fans and trivets, surfwear, aloha shirts, and jewelry made of opihi and Niihau shells. Everything here is Hawaiian, most of it made or designed by the Neffs. Luana's pikake oil is the best we've found, true to the last pheromone.

Mauna Kea Galleries. 276 Keawe St. ☎ **808/969-1184**.

Mark Blackburn, who wrote *Hawaiiana: The Best of Hawaiian Design,* has made this his showcase for the treasures he loves to collect. He and his wife, Carolyn, amass vintage Hawaiiana in mint condition from estate sales and collectors all over the country, then respectfully display it in their two-story Hilo gallery. Much is hidden here, but what is visible is riveting: large selections of monarchy and Ming jewelry; mint-condition Santa Anita and Don Blanding dinnerware, including very rare pieces; adz-hewn, not lathed, koa- and kou-wood bowls; and vintage photography and menus, all individually stored in plastic sleeves ($10 to $300). Rare books and prints, including hand-colored 1870s lithographs; old koa furniture; original Hawaiian fish prints from the early 1900s; and limited-edition, vintage, black-and-white, museum-quality reproductions of hula-girl photos from the 1890s are also among the limitless finds.

The Most Irresistible Shop in Hilo. 256 Kamehameha Hwy. ☎ **808/ 935-9644**.

It's not really the most irresistible shop in Hilo, but the selection is varied: T-shirts, greeting cards, Tahitian and Balinese pareus, jewelry, glass and ceramic ware, koa cutting boards, plumeria hand lotion, and gift items aplenty.

Plantation Memories. 179 Kilauea St. ☎ **808/935-7100.**

The owner, Billy Perreira, has a particular fondness for plantation memorabilia. In his shop of plantation memories, everything has a story, and he's likely to know most of them. You might find the one-of-a-kind handmade wooden wheelbarrow, made by a man for his young son; the handpainted wooden signs from the neighboring sugar communities of Honomu, Hakalau, and Hilo; plus vintage Hawaiian clothing, toys, china, furniture, lamps, baskets, textiles, and countless other collectibles from the turn of the century through the 1950s.

✪ **Sig Zane Designs.** 122 Kamehameha Ave. ☎ **808/935-7077.**

My favorite stop in Hilo, Sig Zane Designs, evokes such loyalty that people make special trips from the outer islands for this inspired line of authentic Hawaiian wear. The spirit of this place complements the high esthetic standards; everyone involved is completely immersed in Hawaiian culture and dance. The partnership of Zane and his wife, the revered hula master Nalani Kanaka'ole, is stunningly creative. One step in the door and you'll see: The shop is awash in gleaming woods, lauhala mats, and clothing and accessories—from handmade house slippers to aloha shirts, pareus, muumuus, dresses, T-shirts, note cards, bags, and high-quality, made-in-Hawaii crafts. New designs appear constantly, yet the classics remain fresh and compelling: ti, koa, kukui, taro, the lehua blossoms of the ohia tree. The Sig Zane bedcovers, cushions, and custom-ordered upholstery bring the forest into your room. To add to the delight, Sig and his staff take time to "talk story" and explain the significance of the images, or simply chat about Hilo, hula, and Hawaiian culture. Fabrics, including upholstery fabrics, are sold by the yard.

A SPECIAL ARTS CENTER & GALLERY

East Hawaii Cultural Center. 141 Kalakaua St. (across from Kalakaua Park). ☎ **808/961-5711.**

Part gallery, part retail store, and part consortium of the arts, this cultural center is run by volunteers in the visual and performing arts. Keep it in mind for gifts of Hawaii, or if you have any questions regarding the **Hawaii Concert Society, Hilo Community Players, Big Island Dance Council,** and **Big Island Art Guild.** The art gallery and gift shop exhibit locally made cards, jewelry, handmade books, sculptures, and wood objects, including museum-quality works.

EDIBLES

Abundant Life Natural Foods. 292 Kamehameha Ave. ☎ **808/935-7411.**

Stock up here on healthy snacks, fresh organic produce, vitamins and supplements, bulk grains, baked goods, and the latest in health foods. There's a sound selection of natural remedies and herbal body, face, and hair products. The takeout deli makes fresh fruit smoothies and sprout- and nutrient-rich sandwiches and salads. Senior citizens get a 10% discount.

✪ **Big Island Candies.** 585 Hinano St. ☎ **808/935-8890** or 800/935-5510 (toll-free mail order).

A recent move to a 5,300-square-foot location has expanded this landmark Hilo business. Owner Alan Ikawa has turned cookie-making into an art and spectator sport: large viewing windows allow us to watch the hand-dipping from huge vats of chocolate while the aroma of butter fills the room. Abandon all restraint as you pull in—the smell of butter mixing with chocolate is as thick as honey, and chocolate-dipped shortbread and macadamia nuts, macadamia nut rocky road, and dozens of other dangers will make it very hard to be sensible. Ikawa uses eggs straight from a nearby farm, pure butter, Hawaiian cane sugar, no preservatives, and premium chocolate. Giftboxes are available, and they're carted interisland in staggering volumes. The Hawaiian Da Kine line is irrepressibly local: mochi crunch, fortune cookies, animal crackers, and other crunchy morsels—all dipped in chocolate. By far the best are the shortbread cookies, dipped in chocolate, peanut butter, and white chocolate. Big Island Candies ships all over the country and has a thriving mail order business.

✪ **Hilo Farmers Market.** Kamehameha Ave. at Mamo. ☎ **808/969-9114.**

This has grown into the state's best farmers market, embodying what we love most in Hawaii: local color, good soil and weather, the mixing of cultures, and new adventures in taste. More than 60 vendors from around the island bring their flowers, produce, and baked goods to this teeming corner of Hilo every Wednesday and Saturday from sunrise to 4pm. Because many of the vendors sell out early, go as early as you can. Expect to find a stunning assortment: fresh, homegrown oyster mushrooms from Kona—three or four different colors and sizes—for about $5 a pound; the creamy, sweet, queenly Indonesian fruit called mangosteen; moist, warm breads, from focaccia to walnut; an array of flowers; fresh aquacultured seaweed; corn from Pahoa; Waimea strawberries; taro and taro products; foot-long, miso-flavored, and traditional Hawaiian laulau;

made-from-scratch tamales; and fabulous ethnic vegetables with un-pronounceable names. The selection changes by the week, but it's always reasonable, fresh, and appealing, and a good cross-section of the island's specialties.

O'Keefe & Sons. In the S. Hata Building, 308 Kamehameha Ave. ☎ **808/935-0215.**

You can enjoy O'Keefe's breads throughout the island, served in the best delis, coffee shops, and restaurants. But come to the source, this friendly Hilo bakery, for the full selection hot from the oven: Hilo nori bread, black-pepper/cilantro bread, focaccia in many flavors, cracked rye, challah, three types of sourdough, carrot-herb bread, and the classic French country loaf.

Paradise Gourmet. 308 Kamehameha Ave. ☎ **808/969-9146.**

Hilo is the crunchy-snack capital of the world, and the snack center of Hilo is Paradise Gourmet, where fish jerky, beef jerky, Maui on-ion jelly, taro-chip popcorn, and a sublime macadamia-nut shortbread will clamor for your taste buds. Ohelo-berry jam, from berries said to be the favorite food of the volcano goddess, is one of the big sellers, but our favorites are the silky hot guava sauce, the Maui onion sauce, and the buttery corn-flake cookies. Pure Kona coffee and a variety of tropical teas, from mango to passion fruit to an apple-litchi blend, are also sold here. There's another Paradise Gourmet in Prince Kuhio Plaza, 111 E. Puainako (☎ **808/959-2339**).

HAWAII VOLCANOES NATIONAL PARK & VOLCANO VILLAGE

Kilauea Kreations. Old Volcano Rd. ☎ **808/967-8090.**

This is the quilting center of Volcano, a co-op made up of local Volcano artists and crafters who make quilts, jewelry, feather leis, ceramics, baskets, and fiber arts. Gift items made by Volcano artists are also sold here, but it's the quilts and quilting materials that dis-tinguish the shop, a boutique the size of a small living room. Visi-tors interested in quilting are usually happy to discover that starter kits are available to initiate the needleworthy into this Hawaiian and American craft. A few choice Hawaiian crafts also appeal; we espe-cially like the Hawaiian seed leis and items made of lauhala.

✪ Volcano Art Center. Hawaii Volcanoes National Park. ☎ **808/967-8222.**

The Volcano Island's frontier spirit and raw, primal energy have spawned a close-knit community of artists. Although their works appear in galleries and gift shops throughout the island, the Volcano

Art Center (VAC) is the hub of the island's arts activity. Housed in the original 1877 Volcano House, VAC is a not-for-profit art-education center that offers exhibits and shows that change monthly, as well as workshops and retail space. Marian Berger's watercolors of endangered birds, Dietrich Varez oils and block prints, Avi Kiriaty oils, Kelly Dunn and Jack Straka woods, Brad Lewis photography, and Mike Riley furnishings are among the works you'll see. Of the 300 artists represented, 90% come from the Big Island. The fine crafts here include baskets, jewelry, mixed-media pieces, stone and wood carvings, and the journals and wood diaries of Jesus Sanchez, a third-generation Vatican bookbinder who has turned his skills to the island woods.

Volcano Store. At Huanani and Old Volcano Hwy. ☎ **808/967-7210.**

Walk up the wooden steps into a wonderland of flowers and local specialties. Tangy lilikoi butter (transportable, and worth a special trip) and flamboyant sprays of cymbidiums, tuberoses, dendrobiums, anthuriums, hanging plants, mixed bouquets, and calla lilies (splendid when grown in Volcano), make a breathtaking assemblage in the enclosed front porch. Volcano residents are lucky to have these blooms at such prices. The flowers can also be shipped (orders are taken by phone); Marie and Ronald Onouye and their staff pack them meticulously. If mainland weather is too humid or frosty for reliable shipping, they'll let you know. Produce, stone cookies (as in hard-as-stone) from Mountain View, Hilo taro chips, cookies, bottled water (a necessity in Volcano), and other food and paper products round out the selection.

✪ STUDIO VISITS

Adding to the vitality of the art environment are the studio visits offered by the **Volcano Village Artists' Hui,** several respected artists in various media who open their studios to the public by appointment. The airy, geometric studio/showroom of **Chiu Leong** (☎ **808/967-7637**) is a mountain idyll and splendid backdrop for his raku, pitfire, and porcelain works. His Japanese-style house and studio include a large, 25-foot-high performance room with a glass ceiling, where guest artists dance, play music, and present dramatic performances to widespread community support. Leong and his wife, dancer Eva Lee, built their redwood home from scratch, and it is a marvel, large enough to house his award-winning large-format (5 feet high), black-and-white photographs as well as his ceramic pots. All this occurs in an atmosphere of peaceful hospitality. Other artists in the hui, who form the artistic core of the Volcano community: **Ira Ono** (☎ **808/967-7261**), who makes masks, water containers, fountains, paste-paper journals, garden vessels, and goddesses out of clay and found objects; **Pam Barton** (☎ **808/967-7247**), who transforms vines, leaves, roots, bark, and tree sheddings into stunning fiber sculptures and vessels, from baskets to handmade paper and books; photographer **Mary Walsh** (☎ **808/985-8520**); and **Randy Takaki** ☎ 808/985-8756, who works in wood, metal, and ceramics. These artists are tops in their fields and have their work displayed in fine galleries throughout the islands.

3 The Big Island After Dark

by Jocelyn Fujii

Jokes abound about neighbor-island nightlife being an oxymoron, but there are a few pockets of entertainment here, largely in the Kailua-Kona and Kohala Coast resorts. Your best bet is to check the local newspapers—**Honolulu Advertiser, West Hawaii Today**— for special shows, such as fund-raisers, that are occasionally held at venues like Kona Surf. Other than that, regular entertainment in the local clubs usually consists of mellow Hawaiian music at sunset, small hula groups, or jazz trios.

Some of the island's best events are held at **Kahilu Theatre** in Waimea (☎ **808/885-6017**), so be on the lookout for any mention of it during your stay. Hula, the top Hawaiian music groups from all over Hawaii, drama, and all aspects of the performing arts use Kahilu as a venue.

IN & AROUND KAILUA-KONA

The only oceanfront luau in Kailua-Kona is the **Royal Kona Resort**'s **Drums of Polynesia** in the hotel's coconut grove area on Friday, Saturday, and Monday. At the other end of the bay, **King Kamehameha's Kona Beach Hotel** (☎ **808/329-2911**) holds a **luau and Polynesian revue** on the beach, next to the Ahuena Heiau, on Tuesday, Wednesday, Thursday, and Sunday. The hotel also offers Hawaiian and contemporary music at its **Billfish Bar** Tuesday through Sunday nights.

Elsewhere in Kailua-Kona, the activity seems to have moved down an octave since our last edition. At the Kona Surf, the **Polynesian Paradise Revue** (☎ **808/322-3411**) is a 20-year tradition, offered Tuesday and Friday from 5:30 to 7pm on the Nalu

Terrace, a large room on the cliffs above Keauhou Bay; it's free to the public and very popular.

LUAU!

Kona Village Luau. Kona Village Resort. ☎ **808/325-5555.** Part of the Full American Plan for Kona Village guests; for nonguests, $69.75. AE, MC, V. Fridays at 5pm. Reservations required.

The longest continuously running luau on the island is still the best—a combination of an authentic Polynesian venue with a menu that works, impressive entertainment, and the spirit of old Hawaii. The feast begins with a ceremony in a sandy kiawe grove, where the pig is unearthed after a full day of cooking in a rock-heated underground oven. In the open-air dining room, next to prehistoric lagoons and tropical gardens, you'll sample a Polynesian buffet: poisson cru, poi, laulau (butterfish, seasoned pork, and taro leaves cooked in ti leaves), lomi salmon, squid luau (cooked taro leaves with steamed octopus and coconut milk), ahi poke, *opihi* (fresh limpets), coconut pudding, taro chips, sweet potatoes, chicken long rice, steamed breadfruit, and the shredded kalua pig. The generosity is striking. The Polynesian revue, a fast-moving, mesmerizing tour of South Pacific cultures, manages, miraculously, to avoid being clichéd or corny.

THE KOHALA COAST RESORTS

Evening entertainment here usually takes the form of a luau or indistinctive lounge music at scenic terrace bars with scintillating sunset views. The **Kona Village Resort's Friday luau** (see above) is the best choice. Otherwise, the resort roundup includes the Hilton Waikoloa Village's **Legends of the Pacific** dinner show (☎ **808/885-1234**) on Fridays, and the **Mauna Kea Beach Hotel's luau** (☎ **808/882-7222**) on Tuesdays.

Our favorite night spot on the Kohala Coast is the ✪ **Mauna Lani Bay's Honu Bar** (☎ **808/885-6622**), a sleek, chic place for light supper, live light jazz with dancing, gourmet desserts, fine wines, and after-dinner drinks in an intimate, convivial atmosphere. There's nothing like being able to order toothsome pastas and light suppers with fine wines by the glass when most other restaurants are closing.

If you get a chance to see the **Lim Family,** don't miss them. Immensely talented in hula and song, members of the family perform in the intimate setting of **the Atrium Bar at Mauna Lani Bay Resort** (☎ **808/885-6622**) and at the **Hapuna Beach Prince**

Hotel (☎ **808/880-1111**), where their celestial voices fill the open-air Reef Lounge as the sun sets on Hapuna Beach below.

HILO

Hilo's most notable events are special or annual occasions such as the **✪ Merrie Monarch Hula Festival,** the state's largest, which continues for a week after Easter Sunday. The festivities include hula competitions from all over the world, demonstrations, and craft fairs. A staggering spirit of pageantry takes over the entire town. Tickets are always hard to come by; call ☎ **808/935-9168** well ahead of time, and see "The Big Island Calendar of Events" in chapter 1 for further information.

Special concerts are also held at the **Hawaii Naniloa Hotel's Crown Room** (☎ **808/969-3333**), the Hilo venue for name performers from Oahu and the outer islands. You can always count on a great act here, whether it's the Brothers Cazimero or Willie K. For dancing and live music on weekends, head for **Fiascos** at Waiakea Square (☎ **808/935-7666**). On Friday and Saturday nights, dancing and live contemporary and Hawaiian music take over the second floor; on Thursday nights, it's line dancing and country music.

Index

See also separate Accommodations and Restaurant index.
Page numbers in *italics* refer to maps.